# THE RIPPER'S HAUNTS

## WAX EFFIGIES AND HIS SEARCH FOR THE ELIXIR OF LIFE

### Michael L. Hawley

With a Foreword by Stewart P. Evans

SUNBURY
P R E S S

Mechanicsburg, PA USA

Published by Sunbury Press, Inc.
105 South Market Street
Mechanicsburg, Pennsylvania 17055

**www.sunburypress.com**

For information about special discounts for bulk purchases, please contact Sunbury Press Orders Dept. at (855) 338-8359 or orders@sunburypress.com.

To request one of our authors for speaking engagements or book signings, please contact Sunbury Press Publicity Dept. at publicity@sunburypress.com.

ISBN: 978-1-62006-724-6 (Trade paperback)
ISBN: 978-1-62006-731-4 (Mobipocket)

Library of Congress Control Number: 2016937687

FIRST SUNBURY PRESS EDITION: April 2016

*Product of the United States of America*
0 1 1 2 3 5 8 13 21 34 55

Set in Bookman Old Style
Designed by Crystal Devine
Cover by Amber Rendon
Edited by Jennifer Cappello

***Continue the Enlightenment!***

# CONTENTS

# FOREWORD

It is not easy to write a worthwhile factual book about the Whitechapel murders of 1888 and 'Jack the Ripper'. It is a contentious subject and, it seems, both publishers and readers much prefer a volume that offers an interesting suspect and a satisfying conclusion rather than a book that deals more with recorded facts and the historical record. Having written several books on the subject I have tried to adhere to the rule of thumb that unless a book provides new and valid information on the story then it really cannot be justified. However, because virtually any book with 'Jack the Ripper' in the title has a guaranteed sales level we have seen many published which offer little or nothing new factually but provide a profusion of speculation and opinion, usually with a preferred suspect in mind. The books that set out to make a case against one suspect person or another are generally classed as 'suspect' books. They may make for entertaining reading, depending on the writing talent of the author, but they inevitably fall short of actually proving the case they try to make and are never as satisfying as a true final solution would actually be. It is here that I should state, with complete confidence, that the identity of the unknown murderer, or, indeed, murderers of that long-past and terrifying autumn of 1888, will never be proven. Therefore you may forget all the claims of 'final solution', 'case solved', 'final word', call it what you will, as there never will be a final answer in this enduring and amazingly popular historical mystery.

Having had a real interest in this case for the past fifty-five years or so I have devoured every book, article or reference to the case that I have been able to find. I photographed the murder sites in the City and East End of London back in 1967 and read my first book on the case years earlier. Despite this great interest in the mystery, and the longevity of that interest, I never thought I could write a book on the subject that would offer anything new or useful on the vexed question of the identity of the unknown 'Whitechapel fiend'. That was until 1993. For it was in February of that year that I purchased a letter that was to change my whole outlook on the case and which, I knew, meant that I *had* to write a book about 'Jack the Ripper'. Until then I felt that everything there was available on the case had been published; the official records had, after all, been released years earlier. Any suspects to whom the police attached any real interest, or whom they had named, had already been looked at, assessed and had been written about. We lived in a criminological world where viable suspects had been pared down to a mere two—a suicidal barrister/teacher and a poor Polish Jew. Other contenders, such as a royal physician and a Russian doctor were gradually being discarded along with the Masonic conspiracy and Russian secret service stories that went with them. Another problem was that much fantasy, myth and downright error had also attached to the story making it very difficult to separate the facts from the fantastic accretion that obscured them. The Royal/Masonic conspiracy of the seventies was a favourite with the public and the media and even resulted in films based on it. But rays of light were first cast in the sixties with the excellent work of authors such as Tom Cullen and Robin Odell. The seventies gave us even more hope with the more informed and objective work of real life policeman Donald Rumbelow. Around the centenary year, 1997-8, we saw the appearance of the well researched works of Martin Fido, Keith Skinner and Paul Begg. In 1991 a definite watershed was reached with the publication of *The Jack the Ripper A To Z* by Messrs Fido, Skinner and Begg. Now authors presuming to write on the subject would really have to do their research thoroughly and properly.

I had always, I hoped, kept an open mind as to the possible identity of the Ripper but, as many others have found, I was greatly influenced by various books that I read about the murders. In the early days, swayed by the case put by Cullen, I favoured Druitt as the most likely culprit. I enjoyed reading the royal conspiracy books of the seventies and Donald Rumbelow's more sober but nonetheless entertaining overview of Ripper case history. At the time of the centenary arguments for a poor Polish Jew suspect, epitomised by Aaron Kosminski with the formidable if somewhat circumstantial support of ex-Superintendent Swanson's notes in his copy of Sir Robert Anderson's *The Lighter Side of my Official Life*, steered me away from Druitt and towards the Polish Jew as the more likely explanation. I still didn't for one moment consider writing anything on the case myself. But my interest in the case had been increased in the late 1980s by meeting and getting to know Keith Skinner, Martin Fido and Paul Begg.

As a long standing bibliophile and collector of crime ephemera I moved in the circles of antiquarian dealers and fellow collectors and I had built up a useful collection of such material. It was in February 1993 that I purchased some 'Jack the Ripper' associated letters from Richmond-based antiquarian book dealer Eric Barton. One of the letters, I knew immediately, meant that I had to write a new book on the subject. If I didn't I knew that someone else would pick up on the material and write the book themselves. So it was that I found myself preparing to write on a 'new' suspect who was genuinely described as such, 'a very likely suspect', by none other than ex-Chief Inspector John George Littlechild, head of Scotland Yard's Special Branch from 1883 to 1893 and an established part of the Yard hierarchy in 1888. By this time I knew most of the Ripper authors including Don Rumbelow, a fellow ex-police officer who became a close friend. I also received great help and valuable advice from another connoisseur of true crime, my close friend Richard Whittington-Egan. As I researched and prepared my first book, I met and was encouraged by another new and influential Ripper author, Philip Sugden, whose own history of the Whitechapel murders was to result in an instant best-seller. The late Melvin Harris also gave me much help and encouragement. Finally, in 1995, my book, co-authored by a work colleague, Paul Gainey, was published and the name of Francis Tumblety, a quack American doctor and police suspect was introduced to the world. I knew that we couldn't actually prove he was the Ripper, but he looked to me the best suspect I had yet seen and, with the endorsement of Littlechild, a genuine and very likely one.

As the years passed the influence of the Internet grew, digital searching of newspapers became a reality, and the popularity of the subject did not wane. I wrote further books that were intended as research tools and were, I hoped, objective and non-suspect based. I wished to maintain objectivity and after the revised edition of my book was published in 1996 I did no real further research on Tumblety. I hoped that an American writer and researcher might take up where I left off, flesh-out Tumblety and reveal more on this fascinating character. There were various capable writers and researchers interested in the USA and I was pleased to see many, such as Joe Chetcuti, Roger Palmer and Timothy B. Riordan, take up the challenge. Then along came the author of the present volume, gifted academic Mike Hawley. I immediately saw Mike's genuine intense interest in his subject, and his energy and persistence. At last I felt that a capable person was further researching the suspect I had discovered back in 1993; I knew that I was going to learn much more about Francis Tumblety late of Rochester, New York. I can only let his work speak for itself. I have not been disappointed.

Stewart P. Evans

# PREFACE

Crime scene and documentary evidence on the unsolved 1888 Jack the Ripper murder mystery is limited, yet the subject involves an incredible amount of historical detail—from the backgrounds on the suspects, police, victims, and eyewitnesses, to the politics of the day and socioeconomic pressures on the leaders, press, and citizens, and even the events surrounding each murder. Much of the evidence has been lost through time and even destroyed by war, some may have been misinterpreted or unavailable to corroborate, and still some has purposely been blocked from the prying eyes of researchers. Because of incomplete and suspect evidence, unintended bias has likely crept into conclusions made by experts, causing conflicting theories.

In terms of logic, selected evidence can convincingly lead straight to a particular conclusion making an argument *valid*, but it still might not be *sound*. Limited evidence can give an argument the illusion of truth. For an argument to be both valid and sound, thus revealing the truth, all of the evidence must be presented. Of course, this is impossible, especially in the century-plus old Jack the Ripper case, so when reliable evidence is discovered, it is prudent to reevaluate old conclusions. A discovery of this magnitude occurred in February 1993. Retired Suffolk Constabulary police officer and crime historian Stewart Evans discovered an important piece of evidence that was hidden for decades. Amongst other letters, Evans acquired a private letter from a book dealer written by the chief inspector of Scotland Yard's Special Branch Division at the time of the murders. The letter was dated 1913 and was addressed to a well-known British journalist, who had previously written a letter to the retired chief inspector asking about the twenty-five-year-old murder case. Not only did the chief inspector name the journalist who likely coined the killer's nickname of Jack the Ripper, but he also gave the name of a suspect that he—a man who was inside Scotland Yard's inner circle—considered as "a very likely one." Evans, along with Keith Skinner and Paul Gainey, then discovered additional facts supporting the chief inspector's suspicions.

Since Evans' and Gainey's publication of this discovery in 1995, more evidence on this newly-discovered suspect was published by numerous researchers, most casting doubt upon the chief inspector's comments and his suspect's status with Scotland Yard. Established opinions and conclusions prior to Evans' discovery again seemed to be back in favor. I will be presenting a volume of further discoveries on this particular suspect and the overall murder case, demonstrating that the chief inspector was right all along. At the very least, these discoveries will add to a healthy new debate.

While researching the Jack the Ripper murders and the subsequent Scotland Yard investigation, I read countless contemporary newspaper articles from both sides of the Atlantic and official documents such as court calendars and coroner's reports. As I studied these articles and reports, I was struck by how vibrant and alive they were. These newspaper correspondents and officials were reporting as the terror was unfolding. Although it is our past, this was their present: experiencing the anxieties of knowing a vicious maniac was still on the loose but not knowing what the future held. In an attempt to have the reader also experience this, many of the actual reports are incorporated within the chapters.

# AUTHOR'S NOTE

Because this book relies heavily on original source material, every effort has been made to preserve the integrity of the original language—including spelling and grammar. While the author and publisher are aware that some of these dated and unusual conventions may appear to be errors on the part of the author, they have been checked against original source material and have been left untouched and unmarked to retain the historical accuracy and flavor of the primary source. Since marking every single "error" would have been tedious and distracting to the reader, this note serves as the disclaimer that those "mistakes" knowingly exist in the manuscript. In addition to this note, there are still several prominent instances of mistakes in quoted source material, which have been marked (using "[*sic*]") throughout the following pages, as determined by editorial discretion.

To clarify, the use of brackets in quoted material throughout this book refers to interjections by the author; the use of parentheses in quoted material refers to either notes and asides found in the original source or this author's citation of said material.

Additionally, since much of the scholarship and primary and secondary source material in this genre comes from British authors, the UK spellings (and some punctuation) have been left unedited. While these conventions may seem unusual to an American reading audience, they are indicative of traditional British spelling and grammar practices and are not errors.

All efforts in these areas have been made to ensure quality scholarship practices and to help clarify the origins of source material for readers and other researchers in the field.

# ACKNOWLEDGMENTS

My sincere gratitude goes out to those who have given their assistance in creating such a quality read. Thank you Joe Chetcuti and Jonathan Hainsworth for your continuous efforts and outstanding advice. Thank you Stewart Evans for not only your much needed expert comments and advice but also for bringing to the Whitechapel murders mystery incredible scholarship. Much appreciation also goes out to Roger Palmer, Neil Storey, Jeff Bloomfield, Don Souden, Chris George, Chris Phillips, Adam Went, Moody Frogg, Jonathan Menges, Howard Brown, David Barratt, and the community of enthusiasts and experts.

I certainly appreciate the support from my wife, Anita, and my kids, Bree, Zack, Jake, Braden, Max, and Tanner. Thank you Nick & Jenn Rastelli, Marty Rastelli, David & Judy Grundy, and Gouv Cadwalader for your patience and help.

I am so grateful to my editors. Thank you Jennifer Cappello, Barbara DeWitt, and Scott Benson. Thank you Tom DeWitt for your expert marketing advice. Lastly, thank you Sunbury Press for all of your support.

# 1

# MYSTERIOUS MURDERS BEGIN, THE FORMATIVE STAGE OF THE RIPPER INVESTIGATION

## Backdrop

Have you ever heard of Jack the Ripper? Chances are you have, and it is highly likely that most people you know have heard of this late nineteenth century London serial killer. If you encounter someone at a Halloween event wearing a black suit, a long black cape, a top hat, and holding onto a cane, he is probably disguised as Jack the Ripper. Other than this, details about the "Whitechapel fiend" are far less known. The case remains unsolved to this day, thus, we have no idea what he actually wore as he prowled the London streets in 1888, and his name was most likely not Jack.

Between the months of August and November 1888, a handful of prostitutes, referred to at the time as unfortunates, were murdered and mutilated within a square mile of each other in London's poor East End District of Whitechapel and neighboring Spitalfields. They were attacked in the dark side streets along two main business thoroughfares that crossed each other: Whitechapel High Street, which blended into Whitechapel Road, and Commercial Street. These two busy streets were packed with small businesses, slaughterhouses, cheap entertainment, public houses (or pubs), and gin palaces. The gin palaces, sometimes called gin mills, were unsavory drinking establishments that sold spirits, while the pubs not only sold spirits but they also offered cheap rooms and meals. With the busy streets dimly illuminated by the burning naphtha lamps at night, along with the constant smell of fish in the air, it would have felt like being at a large, noisy fair. Off-duty military servicemen and visiting sailors on liberty mixed into the crowds for a night's entertainment. It should come as no surprise that these streets were a hotbed for prostitution.

Popular conspiracy theories about Jack the Ripper performing a Masonic or Satanic ritual by creating a pentagram with the geographic locations of the murder sites ignore the much simpler explanation that these harlots were merely murdered just off the two main thoroughfares where they solicited their male customers, known as "punters." On the evening or early morning of their untimely deaths, the unfortunates were solicited by Jack the Ripper. They then escorted the killer to a secluded location in order to avoid being caught in the act by a police constable walking his beat. Or, what may have occurred was that the unfortunate was solicited by a different man, and as she escorted him, Jack the Ripper hid in the shadows as he followed the two, then seized the moment once the other man finished and left her alone. Regardless, once the killer felt assured he could complete his ruthless agenda, he attacked and worked fast in the dark, knowing full well a constable would soon walk by. In effect, these women selected their own murder sites.

Victorian England was the most powerful and wealthy country in the world with London as its centerpiece, yet its East End was incredibly impoverished; a forgotten place. Crime, violence, and untimely deaths were commonplace in these slums. The following are comments made by a contemporary British newspaper correspondent explaining daily life in "these squalid parts" of the Whitechapel District:

*The Day's News, Whitechapel Terror*
*This neighbourhood is described as a very rough one, and respectable people are accustomed to avoid it. It is inhabited by dock labourers, market porters, the tenants of common lodging-houses, and a certain number of cabinet-makers, who supply the furniture establishments of Curtain-road. Leather aprons and knives are, therefore, by no means uncommonly to be seen in the district. In these squalid parts of the Metropolis aggravated assaults, attended by flesh wounds from knives are frequently met with, and men and women become accustomed to scenes of violence. The people do not appear, however, to interfere with each other's affairs, unless provoked. Late at night there are many scenes of degradation and immorality, and with these the man now sought by the police was evidently familiar.*
[*Echo*, September 10, 1888]

Immorality or not, many of these women were just trying to survive. The term "unfortunate" was very appropriate; destitute women earning just enough money to eat, rent a night's bed, and in most cases, maintain a drunken stupor on cheap gin. The only other alternative for many of these women in such a male-dominated society was to endure the turmoil of living with an all-too-often abusive man.

Even though this tough area knew violence on a daily basis, the series of murders associated with Jack the Ripper exhibited an altogether different kind of brutality. Murder was not the means to an end; it was the end. In other words, these killings were not the usual violent domestic dispute or mugging for financial gain, but they had the appearance of murder for murder's sake. Authorities were convinced a sadistic bloodthirsty maniac was on the loose.

The Whitechapel murders quickly became an international sensation, even before the killer was nicknamed Jack the Ripper. A contributing factor to this abrupt popularity was advancement in communications technology. Ten years before the murders, timely news transmitted by telegraph only occurred across continents, so even though San Francisco picked up news from New York within minutes, news from Europe was still weeks old. News across the Atlantic was received through transatlantic shipping.

In 1882, Western Union signed a major contract with the owner of a newly-laid transatlantic cable system, the American Telegraph and Cable Company. This agreement allowed for a greater volume of news cable transmission, and by 1888, US households were reading timely international news. A possibility as to why the Whitechapel murders caught the attention of North American and European readers so passionately, where earlier, equally horrific murder sprees did not, was that they were now experiencing the fears of East London residents along with them, in real time, as the elusive fiend was stalking his prey. Reader interest prompted daily newspapers to continue reporting the story, quickly pushing it to the front page, which further propagated its fame.

The headquarters for the Metropolitan Police Service, known as Scotland Yard, was responsible for the law enforcement for all of London, with the exception of the inner square mile: the City of London. The police force in the inner city was called the City of London Police. Although the Metropolitan Police Force, or Met, began in 1829, its detective division began in 1842, and in 1878, it expanded into the Criminal Investigation Department, or CID. All of the Ripper crime scenes, with the exception of one, fell within Scotland Yard's jurisdiction. The Catherine Eddowes' homicide actually fell within the jurisdiction of the City of London Police, and because of this, they initiated their own Whitechapel murder investigation. Sadly, the German bombings of London in World War II destroyed the city's records.

When comparing investigative procedures at the time of the Ripper murders with today, detectives then had a severe disadvantage. They could not rely upon modern techniques in crime scene investigation such as the analysis of latent fingerprints, DNA, fibers, blood type, and other types of trace evidence. In this case, eyewitness testimony was also questionable since no one reported seeing any of the murders. Realizing this, the Metropolitan Police commissioner believed the Whitechapel fiend would most likely not be apprehended by the ongoing CID investigation but by a street-walking police constable stumbling upon the killer in action, which justified his assigning extra police officers to the Whitechapel District.

Another major issue the British government and Scotland Yard had at the time of the murders was the ongoing violence against the government brought about by the Irish Independent Movement. John George Littlechild, chief inspector of Scotland Yard's secretive Special Branch in the CID, explained in his later memoirs about the larger, more enduring issue involving the violent activities in the Irish movement. He stated:

> It fell to my duty to arrest many dynamiters and to be brought into contact with men whose names stand out prominently in the history of the 'physical force' policy, adopted by the extreme wing of the Irish party, and which began in this country with a mild, though unfortunately fatal, explosion at Salford Barracks on January 14, 1881, and ended, practically, as far as London was concerned, with the breaking up of the dynamite conspiracies in the Jubilee year, 1887.

While the failure of Scotland Yard to quickly solve the Whitechapel murder case was an international embarrassment for the British government, the Irish Independence/self-rule matter was considered a much bigger, more enduring problem.

Special Branch formed in 1883 under Scotland Yard's CID for the specific purpose of combating the Irish physical force problem, and was appropriately titled Special Irish Branch. In 1887, its name was changed to Special Branch, taking on an expanded role in all matters of national security, similar to today's Central Intelligence Agency (CIA) in the United States. On certain occasions, Special Branch involved itself in the Whitechapel murder investigation since numerous Ripper suspects had a history outside of London.

One of the most intriguing and coincidental events that took place in the London area during the Whitechapel murders was the showing of the play the *Strange Case of Dr. Jekyll and Mr. Hyde* at a number of theaters, most notably, the famous Lyceum Theatre in London's wealthy West End. The Lyceum Theatre was run by the famous British actor Sir Henry Irving, and his business manager was none other than Bram Stoker, author of *Dracula*. On August 6, 1888, the British newspaper, *The Daily News*, published the following. The correspondent explains Mansfield's transformed Mr. Hyde in vivid detail:

### THE THEATRE
### MR. RICHARD MANSFIELD AT THE LYCEUM

*Mr. Mansfield's first entrance on the stage on Saturday caused some surprise, and, we are bound to add, some shade of disappointment. The spectators were not prepared to find the grave and stately Jekyll transformed into a young gentleman of slight stature and of somewhat insignificant appearance.*

*. . . But a moment had passed since Jekyll had left the terrace by the drawing room windows when this strange creature reappeared, bent and twisted of form, with odd contortions of the hands and stealthy, tiger like movements, hissing out words of scorn and defiance. . . . As much as to anything else, the chill of terror felt by the spectator was attributable to the fierce, raucous tones of the monster as he shouted with devilish glee, clawing at his victim's breast and trampling him under foot 'with apelike fury' as the story says. The subsequent changes from Jekyll to Hyde were still more impressive, and were for the most part effected on a half darkened stage in full view of the spectator. Whenever Mr. Mansfield becomes Hyde, his savage chuckles, his devilish gloating over evil, his malignant sarcasms, his fierce energy of hate and reveling in all sinful impulses awaken strange sensations in the spectator; and the unearthly*

*restless figure of this variation upon Frankenstein's fatal handiwork takes a powerful hold on the imagination.*

Once officials realized the Whitechapel murderer was taking organs from his victims, as if he had anatomical knowledge, parallels between Jack the Ripper and *Dr. Jekyll and Mr. Hyde* sprang up immediately. Could Jack the Ripper be an upstanding physician by day and a medical maniac by night? Mansfield's transformation was so real that on October 5, 1888, the City of London police received a letter signed "M.P."; the author "felt at once that he was the man wanted."

Another popular attraction operating in London during the murders may also have had a direct influence upon Jack the Ripper. In London's more affluent West End was Madame Tussauds Wax Museum, which portrayed wax effigies of famous personalities. Pertinent to the Ripper story was the sideshow exhibition of the "Chamber of Horrors," a series of wax displays of executions of well-known criminals of the day. The very same *Daily News* article published the following:

### MADAME TUSSAUD'S EXHIBITION

*Madame Tussaud and Sons are putting forth an extensive programme for the Bank Holiday, when they usually receive many hundreds of excursionists. A portrait of the present Emperor of Germany will be shown in the Great Hall, near to the imposing group portraying the lying in state of the late Emperor William. It should be mentioned that this group also contains artists' models of the ever remembered Emperor Frederick and of the great Chancellor. The Chamber of Horrors also is interesting, as containing the model of the notorious Jackson and of the many criminals who have marked the year. During the holiday week the orchestra will be greatly strengthened.*

Hidden from history for over a century, a very popular East End, Tussaud-like chamber of horrors wax museum—albeit a less reputable version—operated in Whitechapel only a few hundred yards away from arguably the very first Jack the Ripper murder site. Of particular note, the main attraction in the fall and winter of 1888 was a basement presentment displaying wax effigies of the Ripper victims, each added soon after their murder! In effect, the museum may have acted as the hunter's trophy case, his prizes displayed for all who dared to tread into his hunting grounds to gaze upon.

### The Murders Begin

All told, there were well over a dozen suspected Jack the Ripper victims in East End London, beginning with Emma Smith on April 3, 1888, but the crime scene characteristics of five, both in *modus operandi* and offender signature, were so similar that most researchers agree they were from the hands of one killer. Because of this, these victims, beginning with Mary Ann (Polly) Nichols on August 31, 1888, have since been dubbed "the canonical five," quite possibly the only murders at the hands of Jack the Ripper. Even so, two unfortunates were murdered earlier in 1888, and within one square mile of the Nichols murder site. Ironically, when the first of the canonical five victims was murdered, authorities already began to consider they had what would later be called a serial killer on their hands due to these two earlier murders. In view of this, the story begins with the pre-canonical murder of Emma Smith.

### Emma Smith, April 3, 1888, Easter

The unfortunate Emma Smith was walking the streets looking for business on Bank Holiday night, Easter Monday. Late in the night she returned to her lodgings, beaten and bloodied, prompting the lodging house deputy and another lodger to bring her to the London Hospital. She claimed she was attacked by three or four youths, who beat, stabbed, and raped her. Four days later, she died from her injuries. Since gangs frequented the neighborhood, this attack did not seem out of the ordinary. Note the article in London's *Lloyd's Weekly News*, Sunday, April 8, 1888:

> *HORRIBLE MURDER IN WHITECHAPEL*
> *Mr. Wynne Baxter held an inquiry yesterday morning at the London Hospital into the terrible circumstances attending the death of an unfortunate, named Emma E. Smith, who was assaulted in the most brutal manner early on Tuesday morning last in the neighbourhood of Osborn-street, Whitechapel, by several men. The first witness, Mary Russell, the deputy-keeper of a lodging-house in George-street, Spitalfields, deposed to the statement made by the deceased on the way to the London Hospital, to which she was taken between four and five o'clock on Tuesday morning. The deceased told her she had been shockingly maltreated by a*

*number of men and robbed of all the money she had. Her*
*face was bleeding, and her ear was cut. She did not describe*
*the men, but said one was a young man of about 19 . . .*

It was not entirely unusual for a prostitute to be murdered in
the rough slums of Whitechapel, so the idea of a ruthless maniac
on a killing spree was not yet considered. Today most researchers
believe Smith was the victim of a "high rip" gang known to prowl
the area. These gangs would extort money from prostitutes,
promising them protection.

Fast-forward five months . . .

### Martha Tabram, August 7, 1888

On the very next evening after the publication of the
aforementioned August 6, 1888, *Daily News* article on Mansfield's
*Strange Case of Dr. Jekyll and Mr. Hyde*, and just three days after
its opening, the next prostitute was murdered in the Whitechapel
District. The body of unfortunate Martha Tabram was found with
39 stab wounds around her breasts, stomach, and groin. Note the
following August 8, 1888, *Daily News* article reporting the event:

*SUPPOSED MURDER IN WHITECHAPEL*
*About ten minutes to five o'clock yesterday morning, John*
*Reeves, who lives at 37 George yard buildings, Whitechapel,*
*was coming downstairs to go to work, when he discovered*
*the body of a woman lying in a pool of blood on the first*
*floor landing. Reeves at once called Constable Barrett, 26 H,*
*who was on his beat in the vicinity of George yard, and Dr.*
*Keeling, of Brick lane, was communicated with and*
*promptly arrived. He made an examination of the woman,*
*and pronounced life extinct. Giving it as his opinion that she*
*had been murdered, there being knife wounds on her breast*
*and abdomen . . .*

Martha Tabram was thirty-nine years old, about five feet and
three inches in height, her complexion and hair were dark, and on
the night of her murder she wore a dark green skirt, a brown
petticoat, a long black jacket, and a black bonnet. She was
unknown to the occupants who lived near the murder site
because she did not reside in the area, only using it for
prostitution.

In late nineteenth-century England, utilizing a detective force
for investigating a death was relatively new, and they continued to

rely upon a medieval form of inquiry called a coroner's inquest. An inquest was judicial in nature and was designed to determine the cause of death, while Scotland Yard ran a concurrent investigation in order to solve the crime, if one was committed. The inquest for the Tabram murder was held by the local coroner, Mr. George Collier, who held it at the Working Lads' Institute in Whitechapel, even though George Yard was in the adjacent Spitalfields District. The coroner stated that Tabram received 39 wounds with a long sharp implement, such as a bayonet. The jury returned a verdict of "Willful murder against some person or persons unknown." The inquest's reference to a bayonet indicates suspicions of a military member as the perpetrator, and Scotland Yard agreed with these suspicions. Soldiers assigned to the Tower of London frequented this area often while off duty. Note a report in the *Daily News* on August 15, 1888:

> *It is stated that on the night preceding the murder the deceased and a woman named Connolly were in company with two soldiers, and that something was said as to the deceased accompanying one of the men to George yard. Police Constable Barrett was on duty in the neighbourhood of George yard at about two o'clock on the morning of the tragedy. He noticed a soldier loitering, and remarked that it was quite time he was in barracks, when the soldier replied that he was waiting for a comrade who had accompanied a woman to one of the buildings close at hand. At a parade of soldiers which took place at the Tower, Barrett identified the man whom he had accosted, but the soldier refused to give any account of himself. A parade will take place at Wellington Barracks probably today, and Barrett will then be accompanied by the woman Connolly . . .*

Other than it being an unusual and mysterious murder, neither Scotland Yard nor the British press considered the attack to be the beginnings of a murder spree. There was, though, one connection between the murders that made the papers: both murders occurred on a bank holiday.

*Daily News, August 24, 1888*
*. . . The murder was committed on the night of last bank Holiday, and it is remarkable that a similar murder was committed near the same spot on the night of the previous Bank Holiday. . . . The Coroner, in summing up, said that*

9

*the crime was one of the most brutal that had occurred for some years. For a poor defenseless woman to be outraged and stabbed in the manner in which this woman had been was almost beyond belief.*

Interestingly, Colonel Francis Hughes-Hallett, active member of parliament for Rochester, Kent, and formerly of the Royal Artillery, took it upon himself (he claims) to don a disguise and investigate the Tabram murder. The following is part of his interview reproduced in the *Atlantic Constitution* on October 7, 1888:

### COLONEL HUGHES-HALLETT ON THE WHITECHAPEL FIEND

*New York, October 6. (Special)*
*Said Colonel Hallett:*
*'You may remember that the second of the mutilated bodies discovered in Whitechapel was that of Martha Turner [Tabram], a hawker, which was found on the second floor landing of the George Yard buildings in Commercial Street, Spitalfields. The similarity of the mutilation, the identity of the district and of the woman's occupation with those of the first victim, convinced me that I had to deal with a case of homicidal mania. I chose a bright, moonlight night for my expedition to Whitechapel, just the kind of night that the thug whom I wanted to trail had a predilection for. I had already a theory of my own about the kind of man the assassin would turn out to be. I had more upon my mind, and I have seen since no reason to change it, that the perpetrator of these atrocities is a West End man, a gentleman, a person of wealth and culture perhaps, but certainly of intellectual qualities, finesse and keen discrimination.*

*'. . . So short is the distance from Club Land to the dens of the East End, that I had not been out on my expedition more than three quarters of an hour now, and I was already at the door of the house where the latest disemboweled and murdered woman had been found. There was not a soul in sight save a policeman a block away, watching the doorway as if he expected to see the fiend come out, hoofs, horns and all. I crossed the street to him, and after a great deal of persuasion he described the appearance of the latest victim, where she was found a few hours before, bleeding like an*

10

*abattoir, and sliced to suit the murderer's purpose with anatomical accuracy . . .'*

At the time of Hughes-Hallett's interview on October 7, 1888, everyone was convinced a single ruthless killer was on the loose murdering harlots on the East End, but not when he visited the Whitechapel District in disguise in early August. Hughes-Hallett, though, claims the similarity of the Smith and Tabram murders convinced him enough to conduct his own private investigation. The fact that few even considered the possibility of a single killer in early August raises doubts. Researcher Joe Chetcuti suggests the real reason he engaged in a clandestine investigation—even unknown to Scotland Yard—was because of the possibility that a member of the military may have brutally attacked Martha Tabram.

### Mary Ann (Polly) Nichols, August 31, 1888

Serious concern by Scotland Yard that they had a murder spree on their hands began with the mutilation of the next unfortunate on August 31, 1888, three weeks after the "willful murder" of Martha Tabram. The unfortunate was Mary Ann (Polly) Nichols, the first of the canonical five victims. Although this attack differed from the Smith and Tabram attacks, the fact that all three were prostitutes, the murder sites were near each other, and all were murdered in the same year, gave Scotland Yard reason for concern. A single ruthless killer on the loose, waiting for an opportunity to strike again was big news, and the story finally went international, albeit page two news. The *New York Times* London correspondent, Harold Frederick, who was based in the West End of London, picked up the story and quickly cabled it across the Atlantic to their home office. The following report was published in the *New York Times* on September 1, 1888:

*LONDON CRIME AND GOSSIP*
*'A Terribly Brutal Murder in Whitechapel'*
*from our own correspondent.*
*London, Aug. 31 — A strangely horrible murder took place at Whitechapel this morning. The victim was a woman who, at 3 o'clock, was knocked down by some man unknown and attacked with a knife. She attempted to escape and ran a hundred yards, her cries for help being heard by several persons in adjacent houses. No attention was paid to her cries, however, and when found at daybreak she was lying*

*dead in another street, several hundred yards from the scene of the attack. Her head was nearly severed from her body, which was literally cut to pieces, one gash reaching from the pelvis to the breastbone. The strangest part of the affair is that this is the third murder of the kind which has been done lately. In the last one, two weeks ago, the victim was stabbed 39 times. In the case before it, some months ago, the victim was stabbed with a stick, which was forced through the body. All three victims have been women of the lowest class; all three murders have taken place in the same district, at about the same hour, and have been characterized by the same inhuman and ghoul-like brutality. The police have concluded that the same man did all three murders and that the most dangerous kind of a lunatic is at large. The excitement is intense over the matter, and the women in Whitechapel are afraid to stir out of their doors unprotected after dark.*

At about 3:40 a.m. on Friday a horse-cart driver named Charles Cross was walking westerly to work along a dark, narrow back road called Buck's Row in Whitechapel. Although poorly lit, he noticed the body of Nichols lying on the south side of the street in front of a stable entrance. As he approached, another horse-cart driver, Robert Paul, was walking by. Cross pointed Paul's attention to the woman's body. In the dark, Cross felt her cold hand and believed she was dead, but Paul thought he saw her breathing. Both Cross and Paul left the scene and located Police Constable (PC) Jonas Mizen and reported it. In the meantime, PC John Neil happened upon the body from an easterly direction. Using his lamp, Neil spotted blood flowing from her deep neck wound. PC Thain approached and assisted. Buck's Row was PC Neil's beat, and he claimed he had passed through this location thirty minutes earlier at 3:15 a.m. convinced there was no body.

At the mortuary, it was discovered that not only did Nichols' body have a deep neck wound down to the spine but it also had a deep abdominal wound along the left side up to the sternum. No organs were taken.

The last person reported to have seen Polly Nichols that night was an acquaintance, Emily Holland, who stated she saw her at 2:30 a.m. in a state of drunkenness. She claimed Polly left her to make some money in order to pay for a bed for the evening. Polly said to Emily, "I've had my doss money three times today and spent it. It won't be long before I'm back." No one came forward and stated they spotted Polly with anyone just prior to her death. Scotland Yard suspected employees of a slaughterhouse because of her abdominal wound and since there were many slaughterhouses in the location. They also considered sailors since the district was frequented by sailors on liberty who commonly solicited prostitutes.

Recall that Charles Cross was the first person to spot the body. Although Scotland Yard did not take seriously Cross being the possible killer, some modern researchers are suggesting this possibility.

According to Chief Inspector Walter Dew's later memoirs—he being a young detective constable assigned to the Whitechapel District at the time of the murders—three experienced first class inspectors were immediately assigned to the case by Scotland Yard: Inspectors Frederick Abberline, Walter Andrews, and Henry Moore. Dew explained that the three were extremely competent detectives. Soon after the Nichols murder, Abberline quickly ruled out any connection between it and the Smith and Tabram murders because of the clear differences. Scotland Yard was unconvinced they were in the throes of a murder spree. This all changed one week later with the murder of the next victim, Annie Chapman.

# 2

# A SINGLE KILLER,
# JACK THE RIPPER

## Annie Chapman, September 8, 1888

Annie Chapman, a.k.a., Dark Annie, was brutally murdered on September 8, 1888, and just like Polly Nichols, her body exhibited abdominal mutilation and her throat was cut to the spine. Chapman was forty-seven years old, five feet tall, stout, and had blue eyes and dark brown wavy hair. This murder, just a week after the Nichols murder, caused much more concern. In addition to throat and abdominal mutilation, this time the offender harvested the uterus and surrounding appendages. He also collected her rings.

The last person reported to have seen Annie Chapman alive was Timothy Donovan, a lodging house deputy, at 2 a.m. He stated she was drunk and left the lodging house in order to earn enough money for a bed. At around 5:30 a.m., during daylight, Elizabeth Long saw a man approach a woman—identified later by her as Annie Chapman—and stand and talk with her near the murder site at 29 Hanbury Street. She claimed the man asked the woman, "Will you?" and the woman replied, "Yes." She stated she only saw the back of the man and would not be able to recognize him. According to her recollection, he was over forty years of age, a little taller than the woman, wearing a brown deerstalker hat, a dark coat, and he looked like a foreigner. Chapman's body was discovered at 6:00 a.m. by a resident of 29 Hanbury Street, John Davis. Interestingly, Dr. Bagster Phillips, police surgeon, arrived at the scene at 6:30 a.m. and gave the opinion that the death had occurred two or three hours earlier, conflicting with Long's eyewitness account. Coroner Baxter accepted Elizabeth Long's eyewitness account over the doctor's opinion of the time of death, since Dr. Phillips admitted the coldness of the morning and the victim's loss of blood may have caused him to miscalculate the time of death.

When the American Airlines commercial airliner crashed into the North Tower of the World Trade Center on September 11, 2001, public response was surprise, confusion, and suspicion, but when the United Airlines commercial airliner crashed into the South Tower seventeen minutes later, everyone had no doubt that the crashes were related and deliberate. A shock wave of anxiety spread across America, everyone fully aware the country was under attack by an unknown foe meaning to do harm. A similar public awareness of relatedness and shock occurred after the Chapman homicide. The brutal attack on her was nearly identical to the attack on Nichols one week earlier, convincing everyone—including all of Scotland Yard—they had a single killer on their hands, likely to kill again. Note what the *New York Times* London correspondent, Harold Frederick, wrote in his follow-up report dated September 9, 1888:

### OLD WORLD NEWS BY CABLE
#### 'Whitechapel Startled by a Fourth Murder'
##### from our own correspondent.

*London, Sept. 8.— Not even during the riots and fog of February, 1886, have I seen London so thoroughly excited as it is to-night. The Whitechapel fiend murdered his fourth victim this morning and still continues undetected, unseen, and unknown. There is a panic in Whitechapel which will instantly extend to other districts should he change his locality, as the four murders are in everybody's mouth. The papers are full of them, and nothing else is talked of. The latest murder is exactly like its predecessor. The victim was a woman street walker of the lowest class. She had no money, having been refused lodgings shortly before because she lacked 8d. Her throat was cut so completely that everything but the spine was severed, and the body was ripped up, all the viscera being scattered about . . .*

*All day long Whitechapel has been wild with excitement. The four murders have been committed within a gunshot of each other, but the detectives have no clue. The London police and detective force is probably the stupidest in the world. . . . The assassin, however, is as cunning as he is daring. Both in this and in the last murder he took but a few minutes to murder his victim in a spot which had been examined but a quarter of an hour before. Both the character of the deed and the cool cunning alike exhibit the qualities of a monomaniac.*

*Such a series of murders has not been known in London for a hundred years. There is a bare possibility that it may turn out to be something like a case of Jekyll and Hyde, as Joseph Taylor, a perfectly reliable man, who saw the suspected person this morning in a shabby dress, swears that he has seen the same man coming out of a lodging house in Wilton-street very differently dressed. However that may be, the murders are certainly the most ghastly and mysterious known to English police history. What adds to the weird effect they exert on the London mind is the fact that they occur while everybody is talking about Mansfield's 'Jekyll and Hyde' at the Lyceum.*

In modern terms, most experts today agree that Jack the Ripper was a serial killer. Late nineteenth-century medical experts had little understanding of this rare kind of killer and classified him as a "monomaniac." The term monomaniac reveals their inexperience in dealing with serial offenders, the term suggesting that anyone capable of this kind of bloodthirsty brutality must be insane. Today, experts do not consider most serial offenders criminally insane—i.e., not knowing right from wrong—but categorize them as either psychopathic or sociopathic. According to Dr. Scot Bonn, PhD, professor of sociology and criminology at Drew University, psychopathy and sociopathy are considered personality disorders in which subjects are aware of right from wrong and are characterized by a complete lack of empathy or remorse. While a psychopath (a product of genetics) is generally intelligent, cunning, emotionless, and manipulative, as well as capable of holding a good job, a sociopath (a product of childhood emotional trauma) is emotional, exhibiting fits of rage and living on the fringes of society. For many criminologists, the extensive wounds inflicted upon the Ripper victims suggest that Jack the Ripper was a sociopathic serial killer. This literal overkill suggests hatred and extreme rage.

Scotland Yard was also convinced that Jack the Ripper had to have been sadistic with a lust—even a sexual lust—for blood. Note the comments of Chief Inspector John G. Littlechild, head of the Special Branch division at the time of the murders. Littlechild was corresponding about a particular suspect, and as he did, he explained how convinced he was that Jack the Ripper was sadistic:

"Although a 'Sycopathia Sexualis' subject he was not known as a 'Sadist' (which the murderer unquestionably was) but his feelings toward women were remarkable and bitter in the extreme, a fact on record."

Forensic pathologist Dr. William Eckert, MD, and forensic scientist and criminal profiler Brent Turvey both interpret Jack the Ripper's behavior as non-sadistic. They explain that the mutilations show a lack of sexual assault and clearly exhibit anger-retaliatory and reassurance-oriented behaviors. Turvey states, "There is a lot of passive anger evidenced in these crimes and other behaviors speak to a lot of inadequacy on the part of the offender."

Incidentally, the term serial killer evolved as the understanding of serial offenders improved. Grierson Dickson, in his 1958 book *Murder by Numbers*, referred to these kinds of murders as "series murders," since the murders occurred in a temporal series. In 1966, John Brody published *The Meaning of Murder*, in which he used the term "serial murder." Lastly, in 1970, the FBI hired expert Robert Ressler to research serial homicides, and he coined the phrase "serial killer." When he used this term publicly in the mid-1970s during the Ted Bundy case, it soon came into common use.

If Nichols was indeed the first victim of Jack the Ripper, then how intriguing that there were suspicions of a killing spree when it had not yet begun. This should have given Scotland Yard a head start in routing out Jack the Ripper, but their misunderstanding of the mind of serial offenders likely impeded the investigation.

Dr. George Bagster Phillips stated at the later Chapman inquest that the victim's uterus was taken. To Phillips, the perpetrator seemed to take care in avoiding damage to the uterus and other sections of the abdomen, convincing him that the killer possessed anatomical knowledge but not necessarily surgical skill.

The leading suspect after the Chapman murder was John Pizer, a Polish Jew nicknamed "Leather Apron," and members of the press strongly suspected him of being the killer. The British press was particularly aggressive and even wrote slanderous stories about Pizer. Scotland Yard quickly confirmed his alibi and eliminated him from the suspect list. Pizer reportedly sued the press and received some level of compensation.

As evidenced by reporter Harold Frederick's reference to Mansfield's *Jekyll and Hyde* in his *Times* article in connection with the Ripper case, both Scotland Yard and the press were perfectly aware of the similarities this popular play shared with the murders and the suspicious timing of its showing. Not only were the mysterious murders coldblooded and Hyde-like, the case now shared the similarity of it being a murder spree. By the end of September, Mansfield discontinued the show but still performed at the Lyceum Theatre in a different play, *A Parisian Romance*.

On September 26, 1888, day five of the Chapman inquest, Coroner Wynne E. Baxter stated that a sub-curator of a pathological museum was asked by an American medical professional months prior to acquire a number of uterus specimens, the same organ that was missing from Chapman's body. Baxter proposed a theory that the killer, having knowledge of a demand for uterus specimens, was attempting to possess these organs by murdering unfortunates. This theory was generally dismissed by the London medical establishment because any medical professional could acquire these specimens at a relatively low price in America.

One day later, on September 27, 1888, the Central News Agency received a possible letter from the killer, now known as the "Dear Boss letter." [Note: The underlining of selected words was in the original handwritten letter. Spelling and grammar inconsistencies left intact.]

*Dear Boss,*

*I keep on hearing the police have caught me but they wont fix me just yet. I have laughed when they look so clever and talk about being on the <u>right</u> track. That joke about Leather Apron gave me real fits. I am down on whores and I shant quit ripping them till I do get buckled. Grand work the last job was. I gave the lady no time to squeal. How can they catch me now. I love my work and want to start again. You will soon hear of me with my funny little games. I saved some of the proper <u>red</u> stuff in a ginger beer bottle over the last job to write with but it went thick like glue and I cant use it. Red ink is fit enough I hope <u>ha. ha.</u> The next job I do I shall clip the ladys ears off and send to the police officers just for jolly wouldn't you. Keep this letter back till I do a bit more work, then give it out straight. My knife's so nice and sharp I want to get to work right away if I get a chance. Good Luck.*

*Yours truly*

*Jack the Ripper*
*Dont mind me giving the trade name*

*PS Wasnt good enough to post this before I got all the red ink off my hands curse it No luck yet. They say I'm a doctor now. ha ha*

When Scotland Yard became aware of this letter, they initially considered it a hoax, but then came the "Double Event" murders on the night of Saturday September 30, which seemed to show he made good on his threat of clipping the ears.

### Elizabeth Stride & Catherine Eddowes, September 30, 1888

On September 30, 1888, not one but two murders occurred, those of Elizabeth Stride and Catherine Eddowes. The evening tragedy is now known as the Double Event. At around 1:00 a.m., a jewelry salesman named Louis Deismschutz drove his cart and pony into the pitch black Dutfield's Yard, which was adjacent to the International Working Men's Educational Club, in Berner Street, off Commercial Road, and upon entering, the pony abruptly stopped and refused to continue. Elizabeth Stride's lifeless body was discovered just in front of the pony. Her throat was cut just like the Nichols and Chapman bodies, but there was no signature abdominal mutilation. Evidence suggested to the coroner that Deismschutz and his cart and pony interrupted the offender before he could accomplish his vile agenda. First, the pony exhibited unusual behavior, more in line with being surprised by a living, threatening figure as opposed to just a lifeless body. The coroner also noted that the body was warm to the touch for a significant amount of time after the discovery, suggesting the attack on Stride must have been at the time of the surprise encounter. Also, there were no abdominal mutilations—a signature trait of Jack the Ripper. If Jack the Ripper was indeed interested in harvesting internal organs, then the fact that his next victim, murdered just forty minutes later, had her left kidney and uterus removed, supports this assertion. The fiend was bound and determined to collect internal organs on that night. Knowing full well that Scotland Yard and the Whitechapel citizens would be on full alert within the hour, he apparently decided to accomplish his task quickly, and he did.

Although there were no witnesses to any of the murders, in this particular case, there was a possible witness to the events only minutes before Stride was killed. An immigrant Hungarian Jew named Israel Schwartz claimed to see Elizabeth Stride attacked at the murder scene at 12:45 a.m., just fifteen minutes before Deismschutz drove his cart and pony into Dutfield's Yard. The claim was taken seriously enough to have Schwartz closely interviewed by Inspector Abberline. Schwartz told the police he saw a man stop and speak to a woman standing in front of Dutfield's Yard. The man attempted to pull the woman away from the yard and throw her onto the footway. She screamed three times. Schwartz attempted to avoid the scene, so he crossed the street, encountering a second man lighting a pipe. The man attacking the woman yelled, "Lipski." Schwartz assumed he was yelling at the man with the pipe. He claimed to the police that the man with the pipe apparently began to follow him, but he eventually got away. He did admit he was not sure the two men were with each other, since the "Lipski" comment may have been directed toward him. Schwartz described the man with the pipe as thirty-five years old, five feet and eleven inches tall, having a fresh complexion and light brown hair. He claimed the man with the woman was about thirty years of age, shorter but stoutly built, and wearing a brown moustache. He was dressed in dark clothes and wearing a felt hat.

Interestingly, the London newspaper, *Star*, claimed that "the Leman-street police have reason to doubt the truth of the [Schwartz] story." In fact, Schwartz was not called at the official Stride inquest. Clutched in the hands of the deceased Elizabeth Stride was a packet of cachous—nineteenth-century breath mints —as if Stride was surprised from an attack and quickly murdered. If Stride was thrown to the ground—away from Dutfield's Yard—then hauled back into Dutfield's Yard where her body was found, she probably would not have been holding onto cachous.

Catherine Eddowes was the second victim that evening. Her body was discovered no more than a half mile away and less than an hour later, around 1:40 a.m. The short amount of time between the murders suggests to some researchers that there were two killers that night, but if Jack the Ripper was determined to harvest organs as fast as possible, the location of the second murder site was ideal: private, but just off the main thoroughfare and populated with unfortunates. Once the Ripper left the first murder site, all he had to do was rush off in a westerly direction to the intersection of the two busy streets, spot an unfortunate—in this case Eddowes—and either solicit her or more likely just follow her as she escorted a customer to a secluded location. The murder site was at a place known as Mitre Square. Since Mitre Square was just outside of the Whitechapel District and within the city limits of London, the London City police had jurisdiction over the case, not Scotland Yard, so they were now involved in the overall Whitechapel murder investigation.

The following is the *NY Times* London correspondent Harold Frederick's account, published in the *New York Times* on October 1, 1888:

*DISMAY IN WHITECHAPEL*
*'Two More Murdered Women Found'*
*from our own correspondent.*

*London, Sept. 30.— The Whitechapel fiend has again set that district and all London in a state of terror. He murdered not one woman but two last night, and seems bent on beating all previous records in his unheard-of crimes. His last night's victims were both murdered within an hour, and the second was disemboweled like her predecessors, a portion of her abdomen being missing as in the last case. He contented himself with cutting the throat of the other, doubtless because of interruption. Both women were street walkers of the lowest class, as before.*

*These crimes are all of the most daring character. The first woman was killed in the open roadway within a few feet of the main street, and though many people were within a few feet distance, no cry was heard. This was at midnight; before 1 o'clock the second victim was found, and she was so warm that the murder must have taken place but a few minutes before. This was in Mitre-square, which is but a few blocks distant from the Bank of England, in the very heart of the business quarter. The square is deserted at night, but is patrolled every half hour at least by the police.*

The mutilation of Eddowes' abdomen was very similar to Chapman's three weeks earlier. This time, the Ripper attacked the face as well. London police surgeon Dr. Frederick Gordon Brown was called, and he agreed with the opinion of the coroners of the other victims that the offender had to have a significant amount of medical knowledge to position unwanted organs in the abdominal cavity in order to collect both the left kidney and uterus. This was accomplished in the dark and in an extremely short amount of time.

In the Eddowes case, one witness may have seen the killer, stating he saw a man with a woman near the location of the crime scene. The eyewitness was Joseph Lawende, sometimes called Lavender, and if his estimate of the time was correct, he saw them

21

just ten minutes before Eddowes' mutilated body was discovered. Lawende explained that he left a local Jewish club with two other men at 1:35 a.m. and noticed the couple standing at a street corner, which was along the path to the crime scene. He admits he did not get a good look at the woman and only identified her as Eddowes by matching the clothes he'd seen on the woman in the couple and those of the victim. The City of London Police Department and the Metropolitan Police Department took his eyewitness account seriously. Lawende gave his account at the Eddowes inquest eleven days later. His description of the man varies, depending upon the source, but the first publication in the *Times* on October 2, 1888, stated the man was "of shabby appearance, about 30 years of age and 5ft. 9in. in height, of fair complexion, having a small fair moustache, wearing a red neckerchief and a cap with a peak."

There are problems with his eyewitness account. Lawende admitted he "only had a short look at him," they were in a dark location, and it was a rainy evening, yet he claimed he could see that his neckerchief was red. Also, he did not actually see the couple leave toward the crime scene. To have this couple observed in a conversation at a corner—not yet at the location of the murder—and in ten short minutes have her body discovered completely disemboweled is stretching the limits of credulity. The better explanation is this was a case of mistaken identity. Keep in mind, Jack the Ripper just attacked and killed Stride with a knife—in darkness—only thirty-five minutes before. Would he have attempted to solicit another unfortunate, chancing her spotting blood on him, or might he have merely encountered her alone at Mitre Square, making the quick decision to accomplish his evening's bloodthirsty agenda?

Interestingly, the Double Event had a number of Jewish connections, almost as if Jack the Ripper was taunting the police with the recent popularity of the Jewish Leather Apron. Elizabeth Stride, the first of the Double Event murders, was killed in a Jewish populated area. The second, Catherine Eddowes, was murdered in an area less populated by Jewish residents, but part of her apron was torn off and discovered a few blocks away in a highly populated Jewish area. One version of the story states that above the piece of torn evidence, written in chalk, was a note that said, "The Juwes are the men that will not be blamed for nothing." It may only have been a coincidence that the apron was discovered below this message, since a note referencing "Juwes" within a Jewish population would not be surprising.

On October 1, a postcard was received by the Central News Agency, which was likely from the same author as the September 27 Dear Boss letter:

*I was not codding dear old Boss when I gave you the tip, you'll hear about Saucy Jacky's work tomorrow double event this time number one squealed a bit couldn't finish straight off. ha not the time to get ears for police. thanks for keeping last letter back till I got to work again.*
   *Jack the Ripper*

After the double murder event, Scotland Yard took the Dear Boss letter and subsequent postcard seriously, most likely because one of the victims had a portion of her ear cut off; very similar to a threat made in the letter. They decided to reproduce the letter in the daily newspapers in hopes that someone might recognize the handwriting. Once published on October 5, 1888, it received the attention of a wide audience, and an unintentional consequence resulted: the Dear Boss letter had been signed, "Jack the Ripper," and the name stuck.

Another result of the Dear Boss letter was Scotland Yard took seriously the possibility that the Whitechapel fiend may be American. They quickly realized that the letter possessed numerous "Americanisms," or phrases spoken by Americans, as opposed to Englishmen. Many in the British public realized these Americanisms in the Dear Boss letter, as well. Note the following editorial in London's *Evening News* on the very same day they published the Dear Boss letter:

*Evening News*
*London, U.K.*
*5 October 1888*

### THE EDITOR'S DRAWER.
### THE WHITECHAPEL MURDERS.
### TO THE EDITOR OF 'THE EVENING NEWS.'

*Sir—Having resided for nearly ten years in America, and having carefully examined the facsimile letters you published this afternoon from 'Jack the Ripper,' I have not the slightest hesitation in saying they are written by an American, or by a person who had resided many years in the States. They are full of Americanisms from beginning to the end, such as boss, fix me, right track, real fits, shan't quit, squeal, fit enough, give it out straight, right away.*

*Many of these expressions are in constant use by all classes of Americans, but never by Englishmen. This fact might become important in tracing the assassin.*

Reinforcing Scotland Yard's suspicions about an American killer was Coroner Baxter's recent theory involving an American medical professional attempting to acquire uterus specimens. The London correspondent for the *New York World* reported on the American connection:

*The Evening World, October 2, 1888.*
*Horror-Stricken.*
*(Special Cable to the Evening World)*
*London, Oct. 2 – The London police are still working at random in the Whitechapel cases. No arrests have yet been made this morning, though it is not at all unlikely that a half a dozen suspicious characters may be taken into custody before night, as was done yesterday. . . . And the late seizure of the mysterious gentleman with the 'American hat' are proceedings which have only gone to strengthen the discredit with which the populace regards the police efficiency in this emergency.*

*The curious disposition to connect the crimes with an American has been carried to an absurd extreme. 'An American hat,' 'an American medical student,' an American what not! An English friend, who has travelled enough across seas to become imbued with a just idea of things, whispers half reluctantly in my ear that if, instead of giving such a direction to their suspicions, the London detectives would give an American directness and simplicity to their researches and investigations, they might hope sooner to strike a trail which would lead them to the desired accomplishment . . .*

Since the Dear Boss letter was not yet published, the London correspondent had no idea about the Americanisms in the letter, so he believed Scotland Yard's American suspicion was evidence of their incompetence. The reporter was referring to an American arrest that occurred just after midnight on October 1, 1888. The British papers reported the suspect as a tall American wearing an "American slouch hat" (a soft felt, creased, wide-brimmed hat turned down the middle) with a dark beard. It was reported that he was traced from the locality of the latest murder and then was later seen at Albert Chambers on Union Street in the Borough of South London. This borough is located across the river from Whitechapel. When he was arrested he was reportedly unable to give an account of himself on the night of the double murders. The report then stated, "the police were investigating his antecedents and movements, of which he refuses to give any information."

Scotland Yard's suspicions about an American suspect did not wane in the coming months, as evidenced by the following October 29, 1888, article in the *Echo* reporting an arrest of a man in an American hat:

*Echo, London, 29 October 1888*
### *EAST-END ATTROCITIES*
### *POLICE ACTIVE—STILL NO CLUE*
*The various districts are being patrolled by extra constables, and their zeal has lead them into several excesses, notably, an arrest of three young men made on Thursday night in Berner-street. The police, according to a morning contemporary, have so much in mind the vague stories of an American perpetrator of the dastardly crimes that any person in a wide-a-wake or soft felt becomes an object of suspicion.*

The month of October 1888 saw no Ripper murders. Why? Perhaps it was just not in the Ripper's plans, or maybe he was an opportunist and one did not present itself, especially with the increased number of constables assigned to the area and patrolling the streets. Many have attempted to find a temporal pattern to the murders. Assuming Tabram and the canonical five were all victims of Jack the Ripper, Tabram to Nichols spanned 24 days; Nichols to Chapman was about 8 days; and Chapman to the Double Event murders spanned about 21 days. Breaking down the Double Event, the time between Stride and Eddowes was less than an hour. An argument can be made that Stride was unfinished business, thus, he killed Eddowes on the same night in order to complete his evening's agenda. This may also have been the case with Nichols if part of his agenda was harvesting a uterus. The Whitechapel fiend then murdered Chapman just a week later for the uterus. Regardless, a rough pattern seems to be successive murders in less than a month.

A meteorological event plagued much of the month of October, which may have caused the Whitechapel fiend's hiatus. In

October 1888, London was in the grips of its notorious London fogs. These fogs were not the usual fogs produced by the condensation of water vapor in muggy air above cold ground, but were the product of water vapor condensing upon high volumes of soot in the air caused by the use of cheap coal by the poor to heat their homes. These fogs produced a stinging in the eyes and a hacking cough, ultimately causing poor health and even death. It was not until the Clean Air Act in the 1950s that the London fogs discontinued. Note a number of references to the October London fog in many British newspapers:

*The Star*
*LONDON. WEDNESDAY, 17 OCTOBER, 1888.*
*. . . London is clothed in a pea-soup colored fog to-day. It had been gathering all night, and when sub-editors and market porters came out this morning it lay thick in the suburbs. Every hour it grows blacker, and the lights of London show through the opaque atmosphere with Whistlerian dimness.*

*The Daily Telegraph*
*FRIDAY, NOVEMBER 2, 1888*
*. . . A LONDON FOG. — Yesterday morning, about nine o'clock, a dense fog suddenly enveloped the City and West-end, necessitating the use of artificial light in places of business. Traffic on the Thames was stopped, and the road service was carried on with difficulty by the drivers of cabs, omnibuses, & c., who were obliged to use their lamps as at nighttime.*

The month of October saw the Whitechapel murders investigation and police procedures in full swing, which is another reason why Jack the Ripper did not attempt an attack. Multiple leads and theories were being thoroughly investigated by CID. The *Evening News* of October 18, 1888, commented on a force of police dressed in plain clothes searching house to house throughout a dozen East End neighborhoods and the distribution of thousands of handbills in every room in boarding houses. The number of police constables assigned to the East End was doubled and they were given much more aggressive directives, such as hauling in any suspicious lone males, and using a very liberal definition of "suspicious." They would quickly discover the suspect's identity and residence, release him, then go back to their beat collecting the next suspicious character. Two realities support this forceful police approach as being a reason for the October lull. First, the next murder occurred during the popular annual Lord Mayor's Day celebration when the police were reassigned for the event. Second, Jack the Ripper murdered his next victim inside and not on the streets where there was a greater chance of being caught in the act.

### Mary Jane Kelly, November 9, 1888

The last of the canonical five Ripper murders occurred on November 9, 1888, and this time it was indoors in the victim's room, allowing the killer hours of uninterrupted time with the body. The victim was Mary Jane Kelly. The offender signature was very similar to what was observed with the Chapman and Eddowes murders: mutilation of the abdominal region and reproductive parts, followed by a collection of at least one organ. Unsurprisingly, the level of bodily mutilation was even more extreme. In this case, the heart was taken. The following is Harold Frederick's account, published in the *New York Times* on November 10, 1888:

*EXCITING LONDON EVENTS*

*London, Nov.9.— At 11 o'clock this morning the body of a woman cut into pieces was discovered in a house on Dorset-street, Spitalfields. The police are endeavoring to track the murderer with the aid of bloodhounds. The appearance of the body was frightful, and the mutilation was even greater than in the previous cases. The head had been severed and placed beneath one of the arms. The ears and nose had been cut off. The body had been disemboweled and the flesh was torn from the thighs. Some of the organs were missing. The skin had been torn off the forehead and cheeks. One hand had been pushed into the stomach.*

*The victim, like all the others, was disreputable. She was married and her husband was a porter. They had lived together at spasmodic intervals. Her name is believed to have been Lizzie Fisher, but to most of the habitues of the haunts she visited she was known as Mary Jane. She had a room in the house where she was murdered. She carried a latch key and no one knows at what hour she entered the house last night, and probably no one saw the man who accompanied her. Therefore it is hardly likely that he will ever be identified. He might easily have left the house at any time between 1 and 6 o'clock this morning without attracting attention. The doctors who have examined the body refuse to make any statement until the inquest is held. Three bloodhounds belonging to private citizens were taken to the place and put on the scent of the murderer, but they were unable to keep it for any great distance and all hope of running the assassin down with their assistance will have to be abandoned.*

An unfortunate named Mary Ann Cox claimed to have seen Mary Jane Kelly at 1:00 a.m. walking with a stout man around the age of thirty-five or thirty-six, five feet and five inches tall, shabbily dressed in a long overcoat and a billycock hat. He had a blotchy face with small side whiskers and a carroty mustache. He was carrying a pail of beer. Cox claimed she followed them to Miller's Court, the location of the murder site.

Witness George Hutchinson claimed to have seen Kelly back on the streets at 2:00 a.m. Both were acquainted with each other. She asked him for money, and when he said he did not have any, she replied, "Good morning. I must go and find some money." He then observed a man strike up a conversation with her. He was carrying a small parcel in his left hand. Hutchinson claimed the man was dressed affluently, wearing a long dark coat with collar and cuffs trimmed with astrakhan and a dark felt hat turned down in the middle. He had button boots and gaiters with white buttons. The man wore a thick gold chain, white linen collar, and a black tie with a horseshoe pin. He had a pale complexion, a moustache that curled up at the end, dark eyes, bushy eyebrows, and was about five feet and six or seven inches tall. Hutchinson stated he "looked Jewish."

He claimed the couple walked by him and the man "hung his head with his hat over his eyes" in an attempt to hide his face from Hutchinson, so he bent over in an attempt to look at his face. As the couple walked down a dark side street, Hutchinson followed and noticed the man hand Kelly a red handkerchief. They both then entered Miller's Court. He went to the court but he lost sight of them. He then waited for 45 minutes "to see if they came out." When they did not, he left. Witnesses claimed to have heard a female voice in the vicinity of Kelly's room yell, "murder" around 4:00 a.m., an hour and fifteen minutes later.

Inspector Abberline considered Hutchinson a significant witness immediately after he interviewed him, but controversy does surround him. First, Hutchinson strangely waited a full three days to inform the police of his experience, yet he was suspicious enough of the guy that he waited 45 minutes at the entrance of the darkened residential court. Second, he recollected the color of the handkerchief in a location that was not well lit. Third, when wealthy men were "slumming" on the East End at night by themselves, in a place filled with gangs of ruffians looking to mug anyone, the habit was to be inconspicuous, not blatantly showing off a gold watch. Fourth, if Kelly asked Hutchinson for some money, it was likely for a drink, as opposed to the night's rent money. Kelly already owed multiple days' rent, yet the landlord gave her latitude. Why would Kelly ask for drink money when she just made enough from the man with the blotchy face less than an hour ago? Of course, she may have just been greedy, but the pattern of behavior of East End unfortunates was to make just enough money to either get drunk or pay for a night's bed. Lastly, when many of the Scotland Yard officials discussed the case in their later years, Hutchinson's account was rarely used in their discussion.

Assuming Hutchinson was telling the truth, notice that Kelly was already on the street prostituting after her interlude in her room with blotchy-faced man in less than one hour, between 1:00 a.m. and 2:00 a.m. Recall the time a witness heard a female voice in the vicinity of Kelly's room scream, "Murder," around 4:00 a.m. She may have given the Jewish-looking man extra time, but this does leave the possibility that they had finished their business around 3:00 a.m. and Kelly had already hit the streets again, soliciting a third customer—Jack the Ripper.

### Post-Kelly Murders

The monthly murder spree stopped after the Kelly homicide, the last of the canonical five victims. A few months later, in early 1889, Scotland Yard even reassigned Inspector Abberline, the detective they directed to head the investigation. There were two more murders of unfortunates with similar offender signatures, which convinced many in Scotland Yard that Jack the Ripper was still killing. Alice Mackenzie was murdered on July 17, 1889. The coroner, Dr. Thomas Bond, believed that "the murder was performed by the same person who committed the former series of Whitechapel murders." Metropolitan Police Commissioner James Monro was also convinced, and he even deployed an extra two sergeants and 39 constables to the Whitechapel District. Because of the knife wounds being dissimilar to the wounds found on the canonical five victims, few now consider Mackenzie a Ripper victim. On February 13, 1891, unfortunate Frances Coles was murdered. Her throat was cut, but she did not have any abdominal wounds. A number of officials believed that Coles was a Ripper victim, but the fact that there were no abdominal wounds and so much time separation from the canonical five murders, few now embrace this view.

# 3

# WHITECHAPEL'S WAX CHAMBER OF HORRORS, 1888

On the morning of Monday, September 10, 1888, just two days after the gruesome murder of Annie Chapman, East Middlesex Coroner Wynne E. Baxter held the first of a series of inquests; a standard practice in Victorian England after a death. Scotland Yard's detective division, or CID, was also tasked to investigate the Chapman case. CID was a relatively new, nineteenth-century creation designed to better investigate all crime, while the coroner's inquest had been in place since medieval times. They too investigated, but with a slightly different goal. The coroner's responsibility was limited to determining the identity of the deceased and the details of the death. The coroner's inquest was, and still is, a court of law, and the coroner had the authority to sequester juries, summon witnesses, subpoena, and even order arrest.

This particular inquest was held in the Alexandra Room at the Working Lad's Institute at 285 Whitechapel Road. Just three years earlier, the princess of Wales, accompanied by the prince, officially opened the institute. In her honor, the coroner's seat faced a large painting of the princess.

The inquest lasted all day; they took a trip to view the body, returned to the institute, and ended late. Upon release, the jurors and witnesses, disgusted by the site of the poor victim, left the inquest, walked onto Whitechapel Road, and encountered a large crowd of approximately 200 people gathered in front of a neighboring chamber of horrors featuring a wax museum and live entertainment shows. In front of the crowd and museum entrance was a boisterous showman standing next to a wax model of a police constable and pointing to a canvas painting of three mutilated women. He proclaimed that for the admission price of one penny, anyone could enter the museum and behold a wax display of the three victims of Jack the Ripper. The resulting confrontation made the British papers:

*Echo, September 10, 1888*
*. . . The excitement has, as we say, been intense. The terror is extreme. The house and the mortuary were besieged by people, and it is said that during part of Saturday people flocked in in great numbers to see the blood-stained spot in the yard, paying a penny each. In the Whitechapel-road, 'Lines on the Terrible Tragedy' were being sold, and men with the verses round their hats, were singing them to the tune of 'My Village Home.' A wretched wax-work show had some horrible picture out in front, and people were paying their pence to see representations of the murdered woman within. The result of all this sort of thing working up the excitement natural to the shocking tragedy is startlingly illustrated by the experience of the divisional surgeon of police. Mr. Phillips says that he and his assistant were out of their beds nearly all Saturday night in attendance on cases of assault, some of them of the most serious character, arising directly or indirectly out of the intense excitement occasioned by the discussion of this affair. Unless Mr. Phillips' experience is different from that of other medical men in the locality, this certainly shows that even so dreadful a murder as that which has just taken place is only a part of the mischief such an occurrence originates.*
*SCENE AT THE WAX-WORKS.*
*There is, as we have stated, a wax-work show, to which admission can be obtained for one penny, in the Whitechapel-road, near the Working Lads' Institute. During the past few days a highly-coloured representation of the George-yard and Buck's-row murders—painted on canvas—have been hung in front of the building in addition to which there were placards notifying that life-size wax models of the murdered woman could be seen within. These pictures have caused large crowds to assemble on the pavement in front of the shop. This morning, however, another picture was added to the rest. It was a representation of the murder in Hanbury-street. The prominent feature of the pictures was they were plentifully besmeared with red paint; this, of course, representing wounds and blood. Notices were also posted up that a life-*

*size wax-work figure of 'Annie Sivens' could be seen within. After the inquest at the Working Lads' Institute had been adjourned, a large crowd assembled outside the 'show.' Much indignation was expressed at the exhibition of these revolting pictures. The result was that some of the crowd seized them and tore them down.*

*. . . CONSIDERABLE CONFUSION FOLLOWED,*

*and order was only restored by the appearance of an inspector of police and two constables. A man attired in workman's clothes, and who appeared to be somewhat the worse for drink, then addressed the crowd. He said, 'I suppose you are all English men and women here—(cries of "Yes, yes")—then do you think it right that that picture (continued the orator, pointing to the one representing the murder in Hanbury-street) should be exhibited in the public streets before the poor woman's body is hardly cold.'*

*Cries of 'No, no; we do not,' greeted this remark, and another scene of excitement followed. The crowd however was quickly dispelled by the police before the showman's property was further damaged.*

By February 1889, three months after the last of the canonical five homicides, this museum displayed a total of six images of the murdered women, beginning with the unfortunate Martha Tabram, who had met her death on 7 August 1888. In his 1892 memoirs, Worship Street Police Court Magistrate Montague Williams recalled his walk-through of this chamber of horrors in early September 1888, just prior to Chapman's murder:

There lay a horrible presentment in wax of Matilda Turner [Martha Tabram], the first victim, as well as one of Mary Ann Nichols, whose body was found in Buck's Row. The heads were represented as being nearly severed from the bodies, and in each case there were shown, in red paint, three terrible gashes reaching from the abdomen to the ribs.

Not only did the proprietor of the waxwork museum operate a chamber of horrors, but he also offered nightly live entertainment in the adjacent building. Ever cognizant of the moneymaking formula consisting of, first, satisfying the public's desire for vice—in this case violence against women—and, secondly, adding a pinch of sex, the proprietor had as the main attraction of the show a tough young lady named Miss Juanita. Dressed only in "fleshings," a close fitting skin-colored garment intended to give the appearance of nudity, Miss Juanita engaged in daily boxing bouts with any man weighing less than ten stone. Williams stated that, "pugilism was high in favour with the management, for the audience was." As a result, an additional boxing match ensued between Daniel the Dutchman and the Welshman.

In *The True History of the Elephant Man: The Definitive Account of the Tragic and Extraordinary Life of Joseph Carey Merrick* (2010), Peter Ford and Michael Howell remarked:

> A waxworks museum certainly flourished opposite the London Hospital, for in September 1888, in the midst of the Whitechapel murders committed by 'Jack the Ripper,' a correspondent called John Law was writing in the columns of the Pall Mall Gazette: 'There is at present almost opposite the London Hospital a ghastly display of the unfortunate women murdered. . . . An old man exhibits these things . . .'

The reason why Ford and Howell wrote about the waxworks museum is because they believed it occupied the same building at 123 Whitechapel Road (259 Whitechapel Road since 1910) where the Elephant Man—the subject of their research—was put on display for three weeks in 1884 by his manager, Tom Norman. Ford and Howell quoted Norman:

> The premises used for the exhibition of Meyrick [sic] had for several years previously been a waxworks museum, owned by a man named Cotton. I came to London and rented it from him, and removed Meyrick thereto . . .

But Ford and Howell had mistaken Cotton's pre-1884 wax museum for the museum that exhibited waxen images of the Ripper victims in 1888.

An article titled "A Penny Show" in the *Era* of 9 February 1889 reported on the waxwork museum displaying the Ripper victims and the adjoining live entertainment shows: "There was a waxworks inside, and boxing and other performances went on." The article added that the penny show occupied two buildings at 106 and 107 Whitechapel Road (now 223 & 225 Whitechapel Road at the corner of Thomas Street). It even named the proprietor: Thomas Barry. It underlined that 106 Whitechapel

Road was the wax museum, which even had pictures of the Ripper victim exhibit in the front window, and added that: "One picture showed six women lying down injured and covered in blood, and with their clothes disturbed."

In an editorial in the *Echo* of 11 September 1888, the pseudonymous "East-Ender" discussed the show, which he considered as an evil business:

> I refer to several low penny shows at the corner of Thomas's-street, Whitechapel-road, nearly facing the London Hospital. These sinks of iniquity are at the present time doing a roaring trade by exhibiting horrible pictures representing the poor victims who have been so brutally murdered of late.

Thomas Barry's solicitors, Abbott, Earle, and Ogle of 11 Worship Street, wrote an editorial published in the *Echo* on 13 September 1888, stating:

> There are only two houses (operated by Thomas Barry and his daughter) at the corner of Thomas Street, Whitechapel, and they are next door to one another. . . . There are wax figures of celebrated persons, a chamber of horrors, an exhibition . . .

The *Times* of 6 February 1889 went into further detail:

> At the corner of Thomas-street was No. 106, Whitechapel-road, and next door was 107. Up till November, 1887, shows were carried on at the two houses, pictures and placards being exhibited. . . . In the autumn of last year waxwork effigies of the women who were murdered in Whitechapel were included in the show, and a picture on the subject was exhibited. This picture was, however, considered by the public to be too strong, and the people threatened to tear it down. (Thomas Barry) took the picture away. A wax effigy of 'Jack the Ripper' was added to the exhibition.

An editorial in *Lloyd's Weekly Newspaper*, 10 February 1889, not only commented on the proprietor operating out of two locations but it also described the public's reaction to the Ripper display:

(Thomas Barry) was the occupier of two houses in the Whitechapel-road . . . finding his ordinary attractions had entirely failed to arouse public interest he took advantage of the excitement which had been caused by the murders in Whitechapel to exhibit ghastly and disgusting representations of the victims. It was stated that the public exhibited disgust at this feature of the exhibition, and that it was modified to some extent, but the horrible crimes that had taken place in the neighbourhood were still sought to be made objects of attraction to the public.

Thomas Barry's solicitors referred to the wax museum as a chamber of horrors in their 13 September 1888 editorial in the *Echo*. Why did they so describe it? There are actually two answers to this question. The first is, simply because of its contents.

A reporter from the *Daily Telegraph,* William Beatty-Kingston, visited the museum in November 1888. In the 29 November 1888 edition of the newspaper, he noted that the museum was filled with all the most notorious homicides of the day:

*Another establishment, bearing some distant relation to one of the plastic arts, is situated at a street corner nearly opposite the democratic picture-shop, within a vigorous stone's-throw of the London Hospital. It is no exaggeration to say that the most remarkable waxworks of this or any other age are now on view in a western section of the Whitechapel-road. This amazing exhibition occupies the ground floor and cellarage of a frowsy two-storeyed house, the upper floor of which appears to be unoccupied. And no wonder, for who would willingly live under the same roof with the ghastly dolls that tenant the lower part of this sordid messuage? A penny is the fee for admission to the display, the attractions of which are incessantly proclaimed urbi et orbi by the stentorian voices of two curiously ill-favoured male attendants, while a slatternly, unkempt girl, as grimy as the most approved Old Master, sits at the receipt of custom hard by the entrance. When we visited them, the showrooms were thronged with blowzy, bonnetless women and unshaven, unwashed men, affording to more than one of the senses conclusive evidence that they had recently been somewhat assiduously engaged in 'sampling' the wares of the neighbouring gin shop. Squeezed in here and there among these miscellaneous adults, and eagerly striving to catch a glimpse of the hideous effigies lining either wall of the long, low room, dimly lighted by slender and tremlous jets of gas, were a few pallid, precocious children, whose language was no less 'painful and frequent and free' than that of their elders. The show itself, however, despite its many repulsive characteristics, could not possibly lower their moral tone; and yet it is unquestionably a 'penny dreadful' of the most blood-curdling description, mainly consisting of long rows of vilely executed waxen figures and plaster busts, propped up, some upright, some askew, against either wall of the showroom, rigged out in the refuse of a Petticoat-lane old clothes shop, and professing (according to the halfpenny catalogue) to be striking likenesses of all the most notorious homicides of modern times. From Palmer to Pranzini the collection claims to be complete, and its serried ranks, whatever their artistic shortcomings may be—and in this respect we believe them to be unrivalled—unquestionably teem with the strangest of surprises, a few of which are ineffably comical. For instance, there is a deeply-pitted, broken-nosed, plaster-of-paris head, surmounted by a faded green hat and issuing from a threadbare double-breasted jacket. It looks like a slovenly cast of some mutilated classical bust dressed up in modern 'slops' by way of a mild joke, the contrast between its lifeless whiteness and shabby-genteel 'get-up' being wildly ludicrous. In the catalogue, however, this outrageous anachronism is set down as the correct effigy of Eliza Webster, who, as an artless critic in our immediate vicinity suggested, while contemplating her astounding lineaments, 'must a' been a rum 'un to look at' when alive, if she ever bore the least resemblance to her 'portrait-model.'*

Beatty-Kingston then commented upon the Ripper victim display:

*The chief attraction of the show, as might have been expected, considering its locality, is a blood-boltered display of revolting figures, purporting to represent the victims of the Whitechapel murders, laid out on the floor, side by side, at the farther end of a darksome cellar, connected with the ground-floor room by a rickety corkscrew staircase. These horrible objects are like nothing that ever lived or died. They can only be compared to the visionary offspring of an uncommonly severe nightmare—unearthly combinations of hideous waxen masks and shapeless bundles of rags. One of them is tightly swathed in a cerement of bright blue glazed calico, scored and blotched with dabs of red ocre [sic], indicative of the unknown assassin's butcherly handiwork. The others are somewhat less grotesquely arrayed in dark wrappers profusely stained with mimic gore . . .*

The second reason for the Whitechapel Road wax museum being called a chamber of horrors seems to have been of a legal nature. In 1857, the Obscene Publications Act had been passed in Britain. The act was, in part, a response to public anatomical museums which, under the guise of medical professional education, displayed graphic and sexually explicit models and sold supporting pamphlets and literature to the public. One of the most popular wax displays in these anatomical museums was the Florentine "Anatomical" Venus, a lifelike image of an attractive woman lying down in a seductive position. Both her sexual and her internal organs were fully exposed.

In 1873, Dr. Joseph Kahn's Anatomical and Pathological Museum was successfully prosecuted under the Obscene Publications Act, which set a precedent for the bringing of lawsuits against other anatomical museums and led many of them to close their doors. In his article "Dr Kahn's Museum: Obscene Anatomy in Victorian London," Dr. A.W. Bates of the Department of Histopathology at the Royal Free Hospital, London, stated:

The prosecution of Kahn's museum in 1873 effectively ended public anatomy museums as an arena for medical education in England. The Jordans [a family of museum operators] shipped Kahn's collection to America, where it competed with increasingly sensational dime museums in the Bowery.

The Liverpool Anatomy Museum, successor of the Manchester Museum, closed and specimens were sold to Louis Tussaud's waxwork show ('true-to-life representations of prominent people').

Interestingly, Kahn's museum was closed at the same time that three other New York anatomical museums were closed in January 1888, the very year of the Ripper murders. The police acted in cooperation with Anthony Comstock, a United States postal inspector and crusader against gambling, prostitution, and obscenity. An article in the *New York Sun* of 10 January 1888 titled "Raiding the Museums" read:

> Kahn's Museum, the most pretentious of those raided. . . .
> Its manager threatens to make it warm for Comstock, who
> in turn threatens to make it too warm for their waxworks.

One London wax museum avoided this prosecution: Madame Tussauds. According to Pamela Pilbeam of the University of London, not only did Tussauds cater to a higher-end audience but it also focused upon wax representations of well-known historical personalities, especially contemporary figures, and eschewed the less savory popular anatomical museum approach. In her dissertation, *Madame Tussaud and the Business of Wax: Marketing to the Middle Classes*, Pilbeam states:

> Much of the Tussauds' wax fare was similar to that in
> other shows, the royals, assorted witches, and aspects of
> history, but her models were better made and far more
> luxuriously dressed and housed than in the average
> waxworks. . . . There was never a risk that Tussaud would
> fall foul of the Obscene Publications Act of 1857. They were
> careful to avoid anatomical models, some of which were
> sexually explicit, without having any real scientific or
> medical rationale.

Even though Tussauds shied away from sexually explicit models, it did realize that much of its business came from its waxworks of celebrated villains and murderers and decided to separate these into a side gallery, or chamber, in order to detach them from the waxen representations of prominent figures in history. This allowed Tussauds to boast that its main emphasis was still on respectable waxworks.

Tussauds' primary galleries exhibited exquisite effigies of Queen Victoria and Prince Albert, Czar Alexander II of Russia, Louis XVI and Marie Antoinette, Maximilian, Emperor of Mexico, Garibaldi, Bismarck, and Presidents Lincoln and Johnson. They also had historical and literary figures, such as other kings and queens of England, Voltaire, Lord Byron and Sir Walter Scott, and even King Louis-Philippe of France. There were many others. By separating waxworks into galleries, Tussauds could also name them, and named officially its villain and murderer gallery the "Chamber of Horrors."

The stage was now set for penny show waxwork museums, such as the Whitechapel Road wax museum, to offer a gory and brutally explicit chamber of horrors show without fear of legal repercussions from the Obscene Publications Act of 1857. Note how Thomas Barry's solicitors' editorial in the *Echo* on 13 September 1888 compared his establishment to Tussauds. They were responding to a previous editorial in the 11 September edition, which complained about how disgraceful Barry's low penny shows were, especially the Ripper murder victim display and its pictures:

*Sir, Referring to your letter under the above heading in your last night's issue, we beg to be permitted to place the real facts before you. There are only two houses at the corner of Thomas street, Whitechapel, and they are next door to one another. The one belongs to Mr. Barry, who holds a lease of the premises, and this has for seven years been carried on by him as a waxwork show. The other premises are leased to his daughter, Mrs. Roberts, and here she has, in conjunction with her husband, carried on a similar show to that of Mr. Barry for the last twelve months. These places, we are informed by the proprietors, so far from being 'sinks of iniquity,' as alleged by your Correspondent, simply serve at the East, at the cheap rate of one penny for admission, the highly useful purpose that the deservedly well patronized exhibition of Madam Tussaud serves at the west. There are wax figures of celebrated persons, a chamber of horrors, and exhibition of ghosts (according to the plan of Professor Pepper). As regards the pictures at which your Correspondent is so horrified, we are informed there are only two, the one single and the other double in the events depicted, and that their character has been greatly exaggerated. Trusting you will find space for this explanation in the next issue of your valuable paper. We are, Sir, yours faithfully,*

*Abbott, Earle, and Ogle, Solicitors for Mr. Barry and Mrs. Roberts. 11 Worship street, Sept. 12.*

Thomas Barry was finally convicted in central criminal court. His crime had not been violating the Obscene Publications Act but being a nuisance to neighboring businesses in Whitechapel Road.

The live entertainment had spread onto the street, and tradesmen and the administrators of the London Hospital finally got together and successfully prosecuted Barry. The *Era* of 9 February 1889 reported:

> Thomas Barry, a showman, was indicted at the Central Criminal Court, on Tuesday, before the Recorder, upon the charge of creating a nuisance and exhibiting figures illustrating a show, and thereby causing idle people to assemble and remain in the Queen's highway. . . . After a long consideration, the jury returned a verdict of guilty. . . . The only object of the prosecution was to stop a nuisance (to the satisfaction of the inhabitants of the locality). The Recorder adopted this course and the defendants were discharged on entering into their own recognisances in the sum of £100 each to come up for judgment if called upon.

Did Jack the Ripper ever haunt the Whitechapel chamber of horrors wax museum during his three month murderous agenda and gaze upon the wax display of his mutilated victims? The museum's shocking models of the Ripper victims—and a display of Jack the Ripper himself—just yards away from the murder site of Polly Nichols, the first of the canonical five, certainly heightens the intrigue of the Whitechapel murder mystery. This presents the possibility that the fiend may have received inspiration from the museum's presentments and possibly incited further violence.

The chamber of horrors was in operation for at least one year before Jack the Ripper began his murder spree, and it is not a stretch of the imagination to see a psychopath prone to murder being drawn to such a morbid place, connecting with famous murderers; in effect, he could have been romanticizing their murderous exploits. Further, seeing his murderous handiwork immortalized in wax would have allowed him to relive his bloodthirsty deeds and even experience a feeling of power and control over the horrified onlookers. Beatty-Kingston certainly thought of the influencing possibility when he wrote about the chamber of horrors:

> To what extent it may influence the East-enders deleteriously, by fostering a morbid interest in crime and criminals, can of course only be a matter of conjecture; but it seems a pity that such a debasing exhibition should

constitute one of the principal amusements available to the population of a poverty-stricken neighbourhood.

A serial killer receiving inspiration by visiting a graphic wax museum and viewing morbid displays is not unique. Peter Sutcliffe, the Yorkshire Ripper, who was convicted of murdering thirteen prostitutes between 1975 and 1980, would visit a local wax museum in Morecambe, Lancashire, as a young man. Crime historian and author Elisabeth Wetsch wrote:

> The roots of Sutcliffe's homicidal rage are difficult to trace. His family appears to have been torn by dark suspicions, on his father's part, of infidelity by Peter's mother, and the boy's opinion of all women may have suffered in an atmosphere of brooding doubt. As a young man, he found employment with a local mortuary, and was prone to 'borrow' jewelry from the corpses; in his comments, easily dismissed as 'jokes' by his co-workers at the time, there is a hint of budding necrophilia, more disturbing than the strain of larceny. A favorite outing for the would-be ripper was a local wax museum, where he lingered by the hour over torsos that depicted the results of gross venereal disease.

As a teenager, Sutcliffe worked in a mortuary and coworkers were concerned he may have had a touch of necrophilia. Keppel and Birnes, authors of *The Psychology of Serial Killer Investigations* (2003), stated that Sutcliffe was even employed as a grave digger and was known to have a "macabre" sense of humor.

### The Triple Murderer, Henri Pranzini, 1887

Beatty-Kingston mentioned a display in the chamber of horrors hall of the execution of Henri Pranzini, the "Rue Montaigne assassin." Pranzini's execution was by decapitation with the guillotine, which clearly made for an entertaining and gory display. He had been convicted of a triple homicide in Paris. A woman named Marie Regnault, her maid Annette, and the maid's daughter, Marie, were found in March 1887 with their throats cut. Regnault's body exhibited abdominal mutilation. An article in the *New York Times* of 31 August 1887 reported:

> The triple murder in the Rue Montaigne, for the commission of which Henri Pranzini has just surrendered

his head to the guillotine, was one of the most sensational tragedies which even Paris has furnished to the criminal records of the world. . . . Marie Regnault, who was also known as Madame de Montille, was found on the floor of her chamber dead, her throat cut and her body terribly mutilated. Lying near the door leading from the chamber to the drawing room was the dead body of Annette, whose throat had also been cut, and in her bed in another apartment was little Marie Gremeret, her head almost severed from her body by the murderer's knife.

Henri Pranzini was born to Italian parents in Alexandria, Egypt, in 1856. He was handsome, charismatic, and fluent in many languages. After being fired from the Egyptian post office for theft at a young age, he began a lucrative career as an interpreter. He was hired in this capacity by the English army in the Sudan, and had worked in countries such as Burma and Afghanistan. Pranzini was also hired by the Russian army during the Russo-Turkish war. Curiously, during Pranzini's short service with the Russians a few years prior to the Paris murders, he was employed by General Skobeleff. Soon afterward, the general's mother was robbed of her money and brutally murdered. Pranzini mysteriously left the service of the Russian army just after the crime, and the case went unsolved.

By 1886, he made his way to Paris, jobless and in need of money. In order to satisfy his affluent lifestyle, he began to exploit wealthy single women, such as Madame Regnault, by charming them, gaining their trust, and then spending their money. It was later discovered that just prior to the murder of Regnault, Pranzini was in correspondence with another wealthy woman who lived in the United States. Apparently Pranzini had murdered the three women at Regnault's home in order to steal her jewelery so as to finance his journey to the United States.

The details of Pranzini's preferred method of murder certainly do sound eerily familiar; the Ripper victims were also murdered with their throats cut deeply and their bodies mutilated. Compounded with the murders being "immortalized" in the museum at the same time the unfortunates were being killed, this certainly makes for an intriguing theory that the Pranzini murders had an influencing effect upon Jack the Ripper.

A further note about the Pranzini/Jack the Ripper connection: the very first of the Ripper's canonical victims, Mary Ann Nichols, whose body was found less than one hundred meters from the wax effigy of Pranzini's execution, was murdered on 31 August 1888, the first anniversary of Pranzini's execution. If intentional, it would explain why the Nichols murder was so far east of the other Ripper victims but only yards from the museum. This suggests the possibility that the Ripper was retaliating against the female gender for causing the ruination of men, specifically Henri Pranzini, and honoring him by killing them in a similar fashion. It also means that the signature Jack the Ripper murders may have been copycat Pranzini murders.

Lastly, Pranzini's wax effigy was not only displayed in the Whitechapel chamber of horrors; it was also exhibited at the famous Madame Tussauds Chamber of Horrors on the West End. The *Otago Witness* of 18 November 1887 stated:

> The murderer Pranzini has been added to Madame Tussaud's Chamber of Horrors. The artist has obtained a realistic effect by placing his model murderer near the guillotine, an exact facsimile of the one used in the Place de la Roquette on the morning of Pranzini's execution.

The Pranzini display at Tussauds was seen by multitudes of people even in the spring of 1888. In *Jack the Ripper and the London Press,* L. Perry Curtis comments:

> The popularity of Madame Tussaud's museum may be gauged by the fact that on a single day in the spring of 1888 some twenty-eight thousand visitors passed through the turnstiles to see royal personages and political heroes on display as well as such 'foreign-born' murderers as Lipski and the Parisian triple-murderer Pranzini.

With a popular chamber of horrors waxworks museum displaying Jack the Ripper's murderous handiwork on a nightly basis during his entire reign of terror, it is difficult to imagine that the fiend was not aware of it or never visited it. This is especially true given the fact that all of his victims were murdered within a square mile of each other. Interestingly, there were similar haunts in the Whitechapel District.

# 4

# ANATOMICAL AND PATHOLOGICAL MUSEUMS

The Whitechapel chamber of horrors waxworks museum was not the only museum containing effigies of the female anatomy that was a stone's throw away from the Nichols murder site:

*The Daily Telegraph*
*FRIDAY, SEPTEMBER 28, 1888*
*WHITECHAPEL MURDERS*
*Inquiry at the London Hospital, Whitechapel-road, the nearest institution to the scene of the murder, elicited the fact that no applications [for uterus specimens] of the kind indicated have recently been made to the warden or curator of the pathological museum. An opinion was express [sic] that an American pathologist would scarcely endeavour to obtain his specimens from London, when the less stringent laws prevailing on the Continent would render his task comparatively easy there. It was stated, however, that a considerable number of Americans, holding medical degrees of more or less value, were in the habit of studying at London pathological museums. . . . The circumstances that two murders had been perpetrated in the streets of Whitechapel within a short period without causing much comment would have led, it is supposed, the miscreant to assume that the police protection in the neighbourhood was so insufficient that he might commit a third murder with impunity. Upon the body of Mary Anne Nicholls, the Buck's-row victim, there were indications that the murderer had entertained, but not fully carried out his project, and had had to hurry away to evade discovery. In the case of Annie Chapman, the opportunity was more favourable and the object was attained. Both women had had their throats cut by a left-handed assailant. Although many hospital*

*authorities do not attach very great importance to the story, the police have given due attention to the matter. In their view, however, it does not provide a clue which will facilitate the identification of the murderer.*

If Jack the Ripper was stimulated by anatomical female models, as the Yorkshire Ripper was, then the London Hospital's museum may have been his inspiration. It is true that only medical professionals—foreigners included—were allowed access, but once the coroner suggested the Whitechapel fiend may have anatomical knowledge, medical professionals were now on Scotland Yard's radar, especially Americans. Just as the article stated, if an American held a questionable degree, they would still have been allowed to study the anatomical specimens.

Eighteenth- and early nineteenth-century private anatomy schools, colleges, and teaching hospitals were using dissected cadavers with a limited shelf life almost exclusively, and the demand and competition for cadavers was intense—which created an illegal grave robbing business. These body snatchers selling their products to medical institutions eventually acquired the name "resurrectionists." The financial rewards for cadavers became so great that some even resorted to murdering, as in the case with the most notorious resurrectionists of all, William Burke and William Hare. Throughout 1828, Burke and Hare committed sixteen murders in Edinburgh, Scotland, and sold their corpses to a Dr. Robert Knox for his anatomy lectures.

Although authorities were well aware of the growing problem of body snatching, these murders prompted the passage of the Anatomy Act of 1832, in an attempt to reduce the incentive for such acts. After that, only authorized persons could supply cadavers to medical institutions.

Interestingly, a number of the Ripper victims had internal organs taken, and the killer seemed to know how to eviscerate the organs, which suggests that Burke and Hare may have been an inspiration for the killer. This was not unnoticed. On day five of the Chapman inquest, on September 26, 1888, Coroner Wynne E. Baxter stated this:

*It has been suggested that the criminal is a lunatic with morbid feelings. This may or may not be the case; but the object of the murderer appears palpably shown by the facts, and it is not necessary to assume lunacy, for it is clear that there is a market for the object of the murder. . . . I received a communication from an officer of one of our great medical schools, that they had information which might or might not have a distinct bearing on our inquiry. I attended at the first opportunity, and was told by the sub-curator of the Pathological Museum that some months ago an American had called on him, and asked him to procure a number of specimens of the organ that was missing in the deceased. He stated his willingness to give 20 pounds for each, and explained that his object was to issue an actual specimen with each copy of a publication on which he was then engaged. Although he was told that his wish was impossible to be complied with, he still urged his request. He desired them preserved, not in spirits of wine, the usual medium, but in glycerine, in order to preserve them in a flaccid condition, and he wished them sent to America direct. It is known that this request was repeated to another institution of a similar character. Now, is it not possible that the knowledge of this demand may have incited some abandoned wretch to possess himself of a specimen? It seems beyond belief that such inhuman wickedness could enter into the mind of any man, but unfortunately our criminal annals prove that every crime is possible. I need hardly say that I at once communicated my information to the Detective Department at Scotland- yard. Of course I do not know what use has been made of it, but I believe that publicity may possibly further elucidate this fact, and, therefore, I have not withheld from you my knowledge. By means of the press some further explanation may be forthcoming from America if not from here. I have endeavoured to suggest to you the object with which this offence was committed, and the class of person who must have perpetrated it. The greatest deterrent from crime is the conviction that detection and punishment will follow with rapidity and certainty, and it may be that the impunity with which Mary Ann Smith and Anne Tabram were murdered suggested the possibility of such horrid crimes as those which you and another jury have been recently considering. It is, therefore, a great misfortune that nearly three weeks have elapsed without the chief actor in this awful tragedy having been discovered. Surely, it is not too much even yet to hope that the ingenuity of our detective force will succeed in unearthing this monster. It is not as if there were no clue to the character of the criminal or the cause of his crime. His object is clearly divulged. His anatomical skill carries him out of the category of a common criminal, for his knowledge could only have been obtained by assisting at post-mortems, or by frequenting the post-mortem room.*

By the next day, the press reported the coroner's report and highlighted his theory that the motive behind the Ripper murders was the harvesting of anatomical specimens:

*Times (London), September 27, 1888,*
*The Whitechapel Murder*
 *The lucid statement by the CORONER, which yesterday preceded the verdict of the jury in the inquest held upon the death of the woman CHAPMAN, throws an altogether different light upon the recent murders in Whitechapel, and attributes an appalling motive to what must be in any event a terrible crime. . . . Upon the nature of the communication made to the CORONER from the Pathological Museum of one of the great medical schools we shall not dwell in detail. It is enough to say that, taken in connection with the actual nature of the mutilation, it points strongly to the probability that the murder of CHAPMAN belongs to an unspeakable class of crimes which are committed in order to secure the premium offered by certain anatomists and pathologists for the possession of human bodies and human organs.*

The very same September 27, 1888, *London Times* article connected the coroner's theory to Burke and Hare:

*Atrocious and infamous, indeed, is such a crime, and yet, to the disgrace of humanity, it is not without precedent. Sixty years ago the BURKE and HARE murders showed that, for the sake of the few pounds which careless anatomists would give for a body, two creatures in the guise of humanity could commit 14 murders one after the other. Two or three years after BURKE was executed, another monster named BISHOP was convicted of a similar offence. In the time of BURKE and HARE and BISHOP the price current for a human body was from £7 to £10, which, even allowing for the depreciation in the value of money, is less than the reward referred to in the CORONER's statement as having been offered by an American. Hardly different in principle are the murders, which are now becoming so frequent, of children for the sake of the sums for which they are insured in burial clubs. But it would be idle to deny that this murder—or this series of murders, for it is impossible to dissociate one from the others—has elements of atrocity which distinguish it from all previous efforts in crime. Society must perforce stand breathless and expectant while this latest phase of criminality is being hunted down and stamped out. The whole civilized world is concerned in bringing the murderer to justice, and it cannot afford to be beaten in the attempt. The police will be expected to follow up with the keenest vigilance the valuable clue elicited through the CORONER's inquest, and, since the lines of their investigation are plainly chalked out by information which they themselves failed to collect, it will be a signal disgrace if they do not succeed.*

The British medical community pounced upon the coroner's theory as ridiculous, since specimens could easily be acquired cheaply in the United States. Additionally, it was discovered that the museums were not approached by an American medical student but an established gynecologist from Philadelphia. Note one report from the *Chicago Tribune*, October 7, 1888:

*SPECIAL CABLE DISPATCH TO THE TRIBUNE.*
*(Copyright, 1888, by the Press Pub. Co., N. Y. World.)*
*LONDON, Oct. 6.—*
*. . . that the mysterious American who was here a few months ago offering money for specimens of the parts taken from the bodies of the victims has been discovered. He is a reputable physician in Philadelphia with a large practice, who was over here preparing a medical work on specific diseases. He went to King's College and Middlesex Hospitals and asked for specimens, and merely said he was willing to pay well if he could not get them otherwise. The statement that he offered £20 each . . .*

Once the report of the Philadelphia gynecologist became known, modern theorists immediately ignored it, but interestingly, many in Scotland Yard at the time did not. Years later in 1907, famed journalist George Sims—a man with Scotland Yard connections—stated in the *Sunday Referee*:

*The other theory in support of which I have some curious information, puts the crime down to a young American medical student who was in London during the whole time of the murders, and who, according to statements of certain highly respectable people who knew him, made on two occasions an endeavour to obtain a certain internal organ, which for his purpose had to be removed from, as he put it, 'the almost living body.'*

*Dr. Wynne Baxter, the coroner, in his summing up to the jury in the case of Annie Chapman, pointed out the significance of the fact that this internal organ had been removed. But against this theory put forward by those who uphold it with remarkable details and some startling evidence in support of their contention, there is one great fact. The American was alive and well and leading the life of an ordinary citizen long after the Ripper murders came to an end . . .*

Regardless, the coroner was not necessarily suggesting that the American offering twenty pounds was Jack the Ripper, as many researchers have misinterpreted; he was suggesting someone harvesting in order to sell these specimens, similar to Burke and Hare. Coroner Baxter stated at the inquest, "Now, is it not possible that the knowledge of this demand may have incited some abandoned wretch to possess himself of a specimen."

If Burke and Hare were an inspiration to Jack the Ripper, he did not have to go too far to see a wax display of them—they were represented in Whitechapel's wax chamber of horrors. In his article, British reporter Beatty-Kingston not only mentioned specific murderers in the Whitechapel chamber of horrors hall—Henri Pranzini, William Palmer, and Eliza Webster—but he also gave a hint as to who else was in the "serried ranks" on display:

From Palmer to Pranzini the collection claims to be complete, and its serried ranks, whatever their artistic shortcomings may be—and in this respect we believe them to be unrivalled—unquestionably teem with the strangest of surprises, a few of which are ineffably comical.

Beatty-Kingston agreed with the Whitechapel wax museum proprietor's claim that it was complete, and at the time, the most famous chamber of horrors wax museum was Tussauds on the West End. Being a resident of the West End, Beatty-Kingston would have had firsthand knowledge of Tussauds, which might very well have been what he was comparing the Whitechapel museum to. The three murderers Beatty-Kingston mentioned in the Whitechapel chamber of horrors—Henri Pranzini, William Palmer, and Eliza Webster—were also displayed in Tussauds, confirming the suggestion that the Whitechapel chamber of horrors was mimicking Tussauds. Because of this we could infer the contents of the Whitechapel chamber of horrors if we knew the contents of the more famous Tussauds in 1888; and we do. According to Tussauds' 1887 guidebook, its Chamber of Horrors contained dozens of murderers, both men and women. Of note were James Carey, the 1882 Phoenix Park murderer; the burglar and murderer Charles Peace; railway train murderer Percy Lefroy Mapleton; Walter Miller; mass murderer Jean-Baptiste Troppmann; Luigi Buranelli; Emanuel Barthelemy; William Godfrey Youngman; murderer Henry Wainwright, who dismembered his lover; William Sheward, who dismembered his wife; vampiric serial killer Martin Dumollard and his wife; Daniel Good, who dismembered Jane Jones; and George Pavey, who murdered a ten-year-old girl.

The Burke and Hare theory eventually fell out of favor for reasons explained in the following news cable dispatch, which was picked up by the *Te Aroha News* on November 17, 1888:

> *The Burke and Hare theory for accounting for the murders, advanced by the Coroner at the inquest on Anne Chapman, falls partially to the ground in view of the statement (made by Sir James Risden Bennett and backed by other medical authorities) that a scientific specialist could obtain as many uteri as he wanted for dissection or examination at any of the medical schools for the asking. As for any man offering £10 apiece for such things, that (they say) is absurd on the face of it. Why, a whole pickled pauper could be obtained for from £3 5s to £3 10s (according to his condition), whilst pickled human legs, arms and bits of the breast (I mean thoraxes) cost only 15s apiece. Supposing, however, persist a few obstinate people, this American doctor who made such a quaint mistake as to offer £10 for what he could her [sic] gratis required the uterus to be as nearly living as possible. Would the authorities permit him in the cause of science to cut up the corpse of a dead pauper whilst it was still warm?*
>
> *'Certainly not; to get a uterus in that state would be practically impossible, and even a bribe of £10 might fail to produce one.'* [Sir James Risden Bennett]
>
> *The Burke theory is therefore not absolutely tenable.*

The ancestor to the professional anatomical and pathological museum, such as in the London Hospital's museum, and the nineteenth-century chamber of horrors waxworks museum, was the eighteenth-century anatomy museum. These museums spawned even a third type of anatomy museum.

According to Dr. A.W. Bates, PhD, MD, of the histopathology department at Royal Free Hospital, London, the modern medical profession in England was in its infancy in the nineteenth century and set anatomy courses for medical students were a thing of the future. Expensive and exclusive colleges and professional medical schools were effectively closed to the general populous, so affordable private anatomy schools sprang up, which gave less-privileged future doctors and surgeons much needed practice. Anatomical waxwork exhibitions began to spring up in London in the early eighteenth century, which gave an alternative to working at anatomy schools with cadavers, and it only cost one shilling to enter. These museums were composed mostly of bones and preserved dried and wet specimens. For many, it was preferable to work on models as opposed to cadavers, thus, not experiencing the horror of seeing real corpses.

The Anatomy Act of 1832 was passed in an attempt to eliminate the demand for cadavers by regulating a legal trade only to professional medical installations. It had a positive effect on deterring the theft of cadavers from cemeteries, but private anatomy schools were directly impacted and they soon closed their doors for business. This spawned a demand for medical training at anatomy museums, and the number of museums increased in England by thirty-nine between 1739 and 1800. Not only did they increase in numbers but their collections expanded in volume and quality, specifically, of anatomical waxworks. One was noted to have a "figured moulding from a woman dissected for the muscles." The *London Daily Post,* dated January 3, 1747, stated:

> The FIGURE of ANATOMY, contriv'd by Mr ABRAHAM CHOVET, Surgeon, which represents a Woman eight Months gone with Child; wherein the Circulation of the Blood is made visible through Glass Veins and Arteries, by a red Liquor, in Imitation of Blood, being convey'd through them; At the same Time the Action . . . Knowledge of Anatomy, may, at one View, be acquainted with the Circulation of the Blood, and in what Manner it is perform'd in our living Bodies. Note, Due Attendance to

shew the Figure, and other curious Anatomical Preparations. A proper Person to attend the Ladies.—Price One Shilling.

As popular interest turned toward models and museums, so did the colleges and teaching hospitals. According to Michael Sappol, curator-historian at the National Library of Medicine, Bethesda, Maryland, the professional anatomical museum in the United States was an integral part of the nineteenth-century medical profession from students in medical school to even seasoned practices of established physicians. He states:

> In the nineteenth century, any medical college worth its salt had an anatomical museum and pathological cabinet. There was a pedagogical circle of life: medical students and colleagues were expected to study specimens and also to produce them. Membership in the profession was consolidated by a common culture of collectorship. In formal medical discourse the specimen was accounted as an educational aid or as a record of a typical or unusual anatomical feature or pathological condition. . . . The professional anatomical museum was a repository of medical souvenirs. In other words: stuff in jars, skeletons, dried preparations, casts and models in wax, plaster, paper mâché, and wood.

Dr. A.W. Bates affirms this point and explains it was the same in mid-Victorian England. He states:

> Anatomy teachers assembled their own collections or 'museums' of material with which to illustrate lectures. . . . Ownership of a museum indicated that a teacher was likely to be financially solvent and, in the 1820s, possession of a museum worth more than 500 pounds was suggested as a prerequisite for an anatomy teacher to be recognized by the College of Surgeons.

The London Hospital Pathological Museum, referred to in the *Daily Telegraph* Whitechapel murder article of September 28, 1888, fit into the professional anatomical museum category. Note that the visiting Americans studying at the museum, albeit some possessing questionable medical credentials, were observed to have medical degrees. This demonstrates that these particular anatomical museums were not open to the general public.

Specific to the individual doctor, professional anatomical collections were a visible testimony of their medical expertise and legitimacy. Sappol states,

> Doctors were known to keep a few specimens or a cabinet of material on display in their offices as trophies and, more broadly, as objects that advertised a medical vocation (as did diplomas, weight medical tomes, medicines, and instruments). The specimens served as a credential, proof that the doctor had dissected and had special knowledge of the interior of the body.

Just as medical diplomas and credentials placed on the wall of a doctor's office advertise their medical credibility, a private collection of anatomical specimens in the nineteenth century—presented to a carefully chosen audience—had a similar effect. A non-expert would generally not be in possession of such a cache, since it requires a significant amount of medical knowledge and expertise to create the models.

The anatomical specimen practice even produced competition among medical professionals. The following was advertised to medical professionals in *The Homoeopathic Sun, Volume 1– Missouri Homoeopathic Medical College* publicizing prizes given at a nineteenth-century medical symposium:

> The prizes were awarded as follows:
> Dr. J.R. Reed, Pittsburgh, for the best anatomical specimen, a set of surgical instruments, given by Professor Franklin.

Knowledge of the human anatomy was one way for trained medical professionals to separate themselves from *soi disant* doctors, or quack doctors practicing without medical credentials, since it required time and appropriate training to receive this knowledge and experience.

Public interest spawned a second type of anatomical museum. Sappol calls these "popular anatomical museums." By the mid-nineteenth century, these museums evolved into a combination of a freak show and a medical show designed to exploit sexual desires and human curiosity of the grotesque and morbid. Sappol states,

The popular anatomical museum was a museum among dime museums. It inhabited the Bowery and other plebeian entertainment districts, places where novelty acts and freak shows proliferated alongside houses of prostitution, gambling, and all kinds of petty and not so petty crimes. . . . Its province, in other words, was pathology and grotesquery, sex and impulsive desire, savagery and murder, death and decay. The anatomy museum—a mix of real specimens and models—blurred those categories, and staged them as a theater of the body.

Antonio Sarti opened London's first public anatomical museum in March 1839, and in order to keep patrons entering the front door and paying one shilling, he began to import intricate and sexy models from Italy, France, and Germany. The centerpiece in Sarti's anatomical museum was a Florentine "Anatomical Venus," a model of a beautiful woman in a revealing nightgown lying on a bed with her internal anatomy exposed. Since it was common knowledge in England that continental European countries allowed promiscuity, museum owners like Sarti intentionally described these models as French or Parisian. In order to combat the growing complaint of obscenity, Sarti promoted his museum as an "opportunity for the humble artisan to learn the laws of health and as an unanswerable argument against atheism."

A self-proclaimed German medical doctor named Joseph Kahn became the most successful owner of the popular anatomical museums. He established a museum in London in 1851. Bates states:

His London museum comprised some 40 specimens including 'natural' preparations 'preserved in spirits' and anatomical models 'in wax and leather, copied form nature with the utmost fidelity,' among which were an 'Anatomical Venus,' human fetuses from two weeks to full term, and waxworks showing 'obstetrical operations,' syphilis, and the 'dreadful result of tight lacing.' Admission cost one shilling and included 'popular lectures by a medical gentleman every hour.'

Up until 1855, the daily newspapers and the medical press were favorable to Kahn and his popular anatomical museum, since he had set a room apart for members of the medical profession. The popular anatomical museum was claimed by the owners to be an extension of the medical field, especially surgery. Sappol states,

> The museum was a clinic of a peculiar sort, catering entirely to men. Its proprietor typically described himself as a physician (but was suspiciously silent as to where he obtained his medical degree). The museum also featured a resident 'lecturer' who transfixed customers with a pitch on the medico-moral-sexual maladies man was heir to. This was a long list that included syphilis, gonorrhea, chancre, impotence, incontinence (a category that included bedwetting, premature ejaculation, and nocturnal emissions), horniness, or a lack of libido. The lecturer's litany of woes . . . was designed to produce a state of anxiety in the clientele . . . the marks could then be easily persuaded to buy a book or patent medicine, or even better have a consultation with the doctor.

Sappol explains that professional and popular museums were very similar to each other, in that they contained similar items. The difference was in proportion: where professional museums displayed a higher percentage of anatomical specimens in jars, popular museums displayed more sex- and crime-related material. While the popular museum catered to the "gentlemen only" working class, the professional museum "was generally open only to doctors and medical students, although respectable members of the laity were sometimes granted access."

Once Kahn aligned himself with the Jordans (Perry and Company), his relationship with the professional medical community soured. The Jordans were considered by the medical profession as quacks, since they sold cures for venereal diseases.

Recall the passage of the Obscene Publications Act in Britain in 1857 that made it illegal for museums to display graphic and sexually explicit models and distributing similar literature. These museums ignored the act until Joseph Kahn's anatomical museum was successfully prosecuted in 1873. Even though the public anatomical museums closed up in England, in the United States, the practice continued up until the early twentieth century. According to Michael Sappol, the nineteenth-century anatomical museum was a well-known and very popular attraction in the larger US cities, and he explains none exist today. In his dissertation, *"Morbid curiosity": The Decline and Fall of the Popular Anatomical Museum*, Sappol states,

> Yet the [anatomical] museum was a part of American urban life for almost a hundred years. The nation's first popular anatomical museum appeared in the 1840s; the last closed its doors around 1930.

Interestingly, these public anatomical museums incorporated elements of the wax chamber of horrors, begun by London's Tussauds. These museums displayed "gruesome crimes and gruesome punishments." For example, the late nineteenth-century New York Museum of Anatomy was owned by one of the four infamous and shady Jordan brothers known for participating in the practice of claiming medical certifications, providing services for abortions, and even selling sexually explicit medical pamphlets. In the museum was displayed the gory execution of murderer Anton Probst, perpetrator of the Philadelphia Massacre of 1866 where Probst casually mutilated a family of six plus two nonmembers of the family.

Coincidentally, three of the four popular New York anatomical museums were destroyed by law enforcement officials in the same year of the Whitechapel murders. The *New York Sun* reported this on January 22, 1888:

> *Bowery Museum Wax Works Smashed.*
> *The wax works recently seized in the three 'anatomical museums' in the Bowery were destroyed yesterday at Police Headquarters in the presence of the Police Commissioners and Superintendent Murray. The trash was smashed and piled up in the store shed in the yard ready for the furnace by noon. There were more than two hundred figures or parts of figures, all of them nude and more or less repulsive. The aggregate value of the trash was put by the owners at over thirty-seven thousand dollars.*

### Anatomical Venus and Jack the Ripper Victim Mary Jane Kelly

The possibility of Jack the Ripper being inspired by exhibits of female organs displayed at an anatomical museum, such as the London Hospital, is intriguing, combined with the fact that he may have been motivated to continue his murder spree by gazing at displays of his handiwork in the Whitechapel chamber of horrors basement including six victims and even a model of Jack the Ripper, himself. Henri Pranzini, a main attraction at the chamber of horrors, may also have inspired him because Pranzini also murdered women with a deep throat cut and abdominal mutilation just a year earlier. Lastly, Burke and Hare were also displayed in the chamber of horrors, having murdered to acquire cadavers, which was strangely similar to a theory of the Whitechapel murderer's motive.

All of these facts make one take seriously the possibility that Jack the Ripper had some connection with anatomical exhibits, but the last fact is even more surprising: Mary Jane Kelly was displayed almost exactly like an Anatomical Venus, the main attraction at a popular anatomical museum. Mary Jane Kelly is considered by most experts as the last of the canonical five victims, exhibiting the same offender signature—i.e., throat cut to the spine, abdominal mutilation and evisceration, and the taking of an internal organ. It is quite apparent that the mutilation of Kelly's body was the most extreme, but then again, Jack the Ripper had hours with her body while hidden inside her room. The others were victimized outdoors, where the fiend had only minutes to work.

In view of this, the Kelly homicide may have resulted in the only victim on whom Jack the Ripper completed his agenda: recreating the Anatomical Venus. In Kelly's case, it seemed her body was displayed lying on the bed; her eviscerated organs set carefully around her body, such as her breasts being removed and set next to her body. This is exactly how the Anatomical Venus was displayed. The Venus was generally lying on her back, either completely nude or in some level of undress, staring seductively back at the viewer. Sections of the Venus' skin were removed, exposing her internal organs; specifically, the abdominal region. One or both of the breasts were commonly removed and displayed.

The origins of this reclined erotic pose can be found in art galleries all around Europe and the world. As early as 79 AD a reclining Venus was depicted in the Ancient Roman fresco of Venus—Aphrodite in Greek mythology—riding on a seashell across the sea (which was excavated from Pompeii in 1960). Jack the Ripper would not have known about this fresco, but he certainly may have viewed the original painting of the Italian Renaissance artist Titian called the *Venus of Urbino* (1538) at the Uffizi Gallery Museum in Florence, Italy. The *Venus of Urbino* not only portrays a beautiful nude Venus staring back at the viewer, in the background are allegories of marriage between a man and woman. Other famous paintings of the reclining Venus fill the art museums of Europe from artists such as Girolamo da Treviso (1520), Bordone (1540), Annibale Carracci (1602), Artemisia Gentileschi (1625), Reni (1639), Valazquez (1650), Goya (1792), Cabanel, 1863, and Manet (1683).

Probably most significant to the Whitechapel case is the reclining Venus in the National Gallery in London called the *Rokeby Venus*. The painting portrays a Venus lying in bed and staring at her beauty in a mirror being held by the roman god of physical love, her son, Cupid. It was painted by Diego Velazquez (1599 – 1660), and he completed it between 1647 and 1651.

The last of the British popular museums were closed down in 1873 under the authority of the Obscene Publications Act, which was fifteen years before the Ripper murders. This may suggest the killer would not have seen an Anatomical Venus, but two realities conflict with this. First, if the killer was at least in his thirties, he would have observed these museums during his formative teenage years. Also, if it is true that Jack the Ripper was an American, popular anatomical museums displaying the Anatomical Venus were still around in the United States in 1888. Note the following New York daily newspaper article:

> *The Sun, Jan 22, 1888*
> *BOWERY MUSEUM WAX WORKS SMASHED.*
> *. . . A letter was shown from Dr. Allan McLean Hamilton strongly condemning the museums. The Doctor wrote that weak-minded people had, without a doubt, been made lunatics by the horribly exaggerated sights they saw at them.*
> *Then Superintendent Murray knocked a subject of laparotomy on the head with an axe, and chopped in two a naked damsel, who was torn from her couch with such ruthless violence as to break one of her legs off. Inspector Steers thumped the wax bosom of Venus with a burglars' sledge hammer and ascertained that she had a muslin lining. Policemen did the rest. The stuff will be burned in the furnace.*

Considering an American Jack the Ripper, might the destruction of a favored waxworks museum portraying a lovely Anatomical Venus have incited rage in the Whitechapel fiend?

# 5

# THE SUSPECT

Officially, the Whitechapel murders case remains unsolved to this day. There is the possibility that the actual killer may have slipped through the cracks, unnoticed by everyone—even by today's researchers. Jack the Ripper had all the advantages over the Metropolitan Police Force and the City of London Police Department in Victorian England. In 1888, fingerprinting and fiber analysis were yet to become evidentiary tools in crime scene investigation. If the offender kept his bloodthirsty agenda to himself—as we now know many serial killers do—there would have been very little chance of the police being tipped off. The commissioner of the Metropolitan Police Force even stated publicly that success in the Whitechapel murder case would not be from the investigation by the detective division but from a lucky police constable walking his beat and happening upon the killer in action. This never happened.

Some dated opinions say the victims themselves hindered the investigation. Note the comments made by the famous British journalist George R. Sims in 1907 in the *Sunday Referee*:

> The public indignation over this series of unparalleled atrocities vented itself upon the police authorities, and the Home Secretary by declining to offer a reward came in for a considerable amount of fierce criticism. But when all has been said the fact has to be admitted that the best efforts of the police were foiled not so much by the cunning of the murderer as by the conduct of the victims themselves. Being of the unfortunate class, they willingly accompanied the man who was to murder them into dark and hidden places where, at the hour of night selected by the fiend as the most favourable for his purpose, there was little chance of attention being attracted.

Late nineteenth-century British political and social pressures also impeded the success of Whitechapel murder investigation. Those occupying the highest positions in Scotland Yard were not lifelong detectives or police officers, but appointees selected from within the upper crust of society. While some proved effective in their positions and listened to their expert subordinate chief inspectors, social and political issues generally took precedence over tried and tested investigative techniques when determining the direction of the murder case.

There were no witnesses to the actual murders; therefore, we have no definitive physical description of Jack the Ripper. If there were, this information could have been used to eliminate dozens of possible suspects. As mentioned earlier, there were witnesses to events near the time and location of the attacks, though. Researchers have taken seriously numerous eyewitnesses, but four have received the most attention: Elizabeth Long seeing victim Annie Chapman with a man one hour before her body was discovered; Israel Schwartz seeing victim Elizabeth Stride attacked just fifteen minutes before her body was discovered; Joseph Lawende seeing victim Catherine Eddowes with a man just ten minutes before her body was discovered; and George Hutchinson claiming to have observed victim Mary Kelly go into her bedroom with a man approximately one hour before someone heard the scream of "murder" from inside the very same bedroom.

A problem with each of these witnesses is conflicting evidence, which suggests their eyewitness accounts may be faulty. Long and Lawende may have misidentified the unfortunate; therefore, the accompanying male would not have been the killer. It was dark, and both Long and Lawende admitted they did not get a good look. Keep in mind, when the witnesses were observing these people, they were not in the mindset that they may be identifying Jack the Ripper. They did not realize the authorities were going to ask them to recall every moment in vivid detail.

In the cases with Israel Schwartz and George Hutchinson, they may not have observed the event that led to the unfortunate's murder. Schwartz spotted a man pulling who he believed to be Elizabeth Stride away from what would soon be the murder site, not toward it. Also, Stride was apparently thrown down by this man, but clutched in her death grip was a packet of cachous. Someone being thrown around would likely not still have cachous in her hand. Hutchinson's account also carries with it suspicions of falsehood. Hutchinson's account was over an hour before someone heard Kelly scream "murder," and she had completed her previous transaction in less than an hour. He waited three days before informing the police he may have seen Jack the Ripper with his friend an hour or so before she was mutilated. He then stated that the man was wealthy, walking with his gold watch chain exposed. Affluent people slumming in Whitechapel were not in the habit of flaunting their wealth, chancing them to become the target of the gangs of ruffians making their nightly rounds. Again, none of these eyewitness accounts were of the victims being mutilated, thus, any conclusions on the identity of Jack the Ripper that are based upon them must be considered fallible.

Recall, the Dear Boss letter of September 27, 1888, and the subsequent Saucy Jack letter of October 1, 1888, just after the Double Event murders, showed evidence of an American author, which prompted the police to take seriously American suspects. Note the October 1, 1888, *Central News* report in the *Evening Standard*; one of their reporters had investigated a rumor of an American suspect:

> *The Central News is informed that, shortly before midnight, a man, whose name has not yet transpired, was arrested in the Borough, on suspicion of being the perpetrator of the murders in the East-end. Yesterday morning a tall dark man, wearing an American hat, entered a lodging-house in Gravel-lane known as Albert Chambers. He stayed there throughout the day, and his peculiar manner riveted the attention of his fellow-lodgers. He displayed great willingness to converse with them, and certain observations he made regarding the topic of the day aroused their suspicion. Last night the mysterious individual attracted the notice of the deputy keeper of the lodging-house, whose suspicions became so strong that he sent for a policeman. On the arrival of the officer the stranger was questioned as to his recent wanderings, but he could give no intelligible account of them, though he said he had spent the previous night on Blackfriars Bridge. He was conveyed to Stone's-end Police-station, Blackman-street, Borough.*

These American suspicions did not wane especially after George Hutchinson gave his eyewitness account soon after the November 9 Kelly murder. Note the article published in the *Brooklyn Daily Eagle* on November 10, 1888, which discusses both Hutchinson and someone else in an American slouch hat, or "Yankee hat":

*Brooklyn Daily Eagle, New York, 10 November 1888*
*London's Reign of Terror*

The assassin of Whitechapel has claimed his ninth victim, having planned and executed his latest crime with all the deliberation and cunning that characterized his former exploits. . . . It has been said among other things that the assassin is an American, because he wears a slouch hat . . .

George Hutchinson watched Mary Jane Kelly with a suspicious man in Commercial St late Friday night, November 9, 1888. His description:

'. . . dress long, dark coat, collar and cuffs trimmed astracan [sic] and a dark jacket under, light waistcoat, dark trousers, dark felt hat turned down in the middle, button boots and gaiters with white buttons, wore a very thick gold chain, white linen collar, black tie with horse shoe pin, respectable appearance walked very sharp . . .'

Note the following excerpt in an article published in the *San Francisco Chronicle* on November 18, 1888:

*The San Francisco Chronicle, 18 November, 1888, GOSSIP OF LONDON.*
A Heavy Swell Arrested in Whitechapel. A Score of Prisoners, but No Clew.
*LONDON, November 17.*

That was the case with Sir George Arthur of the Price of Wales set. He put on an old shooting coat and a slouch hat and went to Whitechapel for a little fun. He got it. It occurred to two policemen that Sir George answered very much to the popular description of Jack the Ripper.

The following is a third case of the police arresting someone in a slouch hat reported in the *Eastern Daily Mail*, November 10, 1888:

Another respectably dressed man, wearing a slouch hat and carrying a black bag, was arrested and taken to Leman-street Station. The bag was examined, but its contents were perfectly harmless, and the man was at once released.

Even with all of the impediments, Scotland Yard was thorough in their investigation, as evidenced by their search for a suspect wearing an American slouch hat. In view of this, they may very well have identified Jack the Ripper, being one of the names on their suspect list. Since the CID Whitechapel case files are lost through time and the files in Special Branch on the case remain classified, a partial list can be gleaned from the available evidence. Requests have been made to make the Special Branch files public, but each request has been rejected. Over a dozen suspects have been identified, but the official Metropolitan Police website identifies only four, based upon the fact that they were the only suspects mentioned by contemporary Scotland Yard officials. Their website states:

*Suffice to say genuine suspects are far fewer than the prolific authors of the genre would have us believe. In fact, to reduce them to only those with a genuine claim having been nominated by contemporary police officers, we are left with a mere four. They are:*

**Kosminski**, *a poor Polish Jewish resident in Whitechapel;*

**Montague John Druitt**, *a 31 year old barrister and school teacher who committed suicide in December 1888;*

**Michael Ostrog**, *a Russian-born multi-pseudonymous thief and confidence trickster, believed to be 55 years old in 1888, and detained in asylums on several occasions;*

**Dr Francis J. Tumblety**, *56 Years old, an American 'quack' doctor, who was arrested in November 1888 for offences of gross indecency, and fled the country later the same month, having obtained bail at a very high price.*

*The first three of these suspects were nominated by Sir Melville Macnaghten, who joined the Metropolitan Police as Assistant Chief Constable, second in command of the Criminal Investigation Department (C.I.D.) at Scotland Yard in June 1889. They were named in a report dated 23 February 1894, although there is no evidence of contemporary police suspicion against the three at the time of the murders. Indeed, Macnaghten's report contains several odd factual errors.*

*Kosminski was certainly favoured by the head of the C.I.D. Dr. Robert Anderson, and the officer in charge of the case, Chief Inspector Donald Swanson. Druitt appears to have been Macnaghten's preferred candidate, whilst the fact that Ostrog was arrested and incarcerated before the report was compiled leaves the historian puzzling why he was included as a viable suspect in the first place.*

*The fourth suspect, Tumblety, was stated to have been 'amongst the suspects' at the time of the murders and 'to my mind a very likely one,' by the ex-head of the Special Branch at Scotland Yard in 1888, ex-Detective Chief Inspector John George Littlechild. He confided his thoughts in a letter dated 23 September, 1913, to the criminological journalist and author George R Sims.*

Many experts have attempted to match eyewitness descriptions with the list of suspects, and researchers have even produced a number of other valid candidates for the Whitechapel murderer, but this has produced absolutely no consensus. If Jack the Ripper did indeed haunt museums, such as the Whitechapel chamber of horrors wax museum and London's anatomical museum, maybe this new information can be used. Is there a Scotland Yard suspect who has a connection with anatomical museums? The answer is the same person who was named as a Whitechapel murder suspect by no less than three Scotland Yard officials, a man who admitted wearing an American slouch hat when he was arrested on suspicion: Dr. Francis Tumblety.

Francis Tumblety was a seasoned traveling Indian herb doctor since the mid-1850s, an occupation the nineteenth-century medical community considered as quack doctors. Regardless, he was very successful at it and quickly became wealthy. He was around 55 years old in 1888, stood over six feet, and was powerfully built. He had dark hair, a ruddy face, blue eyes, and had a clean-shaven chin and was known for his large mustache, which reached down in the shape of a beard. He waxed it black, likely to appear younger. At the time of the murders, he was semi-retired and claimed New York City and Brooklyn as his home, although he was in the habit of traveling to London biannually. By all accounts, he was considered a ubiquitous eccentric loner, preferring young males for sex partners, and even paying them to be his travel companions. He purposely hid his sexual orientation and desire for the company of very young men. Glimpses of this side have been reported in contemporary newspaper articles when he found himself on the wrong side of the law, and in most cases, he successfully sidestepped the charges:

In various cities the 'doctor' has been shadowed by the police. Detectives have followed him, watched his office, dogged his footsteps, noted his companions and tried in every way to find out the secret of his private life which he so jealously guarded, and not one of them had been successful. (*New York World*, Nov 27, 1888)

He began the year 1888 in Toronto, Canada, came back to New York, and by May or June he had traveled across the Atlantic and was living on the West End in London, England. One newspaper account claims he set up his herb doctor business near Whitechapel Road.

According to the contemporary newspaper reports, Francis Tumblety was originally arrested on suspicion for the Whitechapel crimes, and when they had insufficient evidence to prosecute, they released him. This arrest would likely have occurred on the streets of Whitechapel by a detective or police constable who then hauled him into a local police station, as they did with countless other lone males exhibiting suspicious behavior and matching certain physical descriptions. The loner Tumblety not only admitted to being in the Whitechapel District during the murders, he even admitted he was wearing an American slouch hat, a hat Scotland Yard regarded as what the killer might have been wearing. Notice his comments to a *New York World* reporter in their January 29, 1889 issue as he attempted to argue his innocence in the papers:

*'I happened to be there when these Whitechapel murders attracted the attention of the whole world, and, in the company with thousands of other people, I went down to the Whitechapel district. I was not dressed in a way to attract attention, I thought, though it afterwards turned out that I did. . . . My guilt was very plain to the English mind. Someone had said that Jack the Ripper was an American, and everybody believed that statement. Then it is the universal belief among the lower classes that all Americans wear slouch hats; therefore, Jack the Ripper, must wear a slouch hat. Now, I happened to have on a slouch hat, and this, together with the fact that I was an American, was enough for the police. It established my guilt beyond any question.*

Once the local police identified him as the New Yorker Dr. Francis Tumblety by "letters in his possession," they then followed procedure and quickly cabled Scotland Yard. Scotland Yard searched their records for a Francis Tumblety and they were in luck, finding he had been on the wrong side of the law in England on numerous occasions. In 1913, Special Branch Chief Inspector Littlechild replied to famous journalist George Sims in a private letter, commenting upon this incident. He stated there was, "a large dossier concerning him [Tumblety] at Scotland Yard." What they read in his file caused them concern specific to the Ripper case, and according to Littlechild, it highlighted his unusual hatred of women. He stated, ". . . his feelings toward women were remarkable and bitter in the extreme, a fact on record."

After being released, Tumblety was free to wander the streets, but unbeknownst to him, Scotland Yard began pursuing a misdemeanor case against him for gross indecency and indecent assault, based upon one particular incriminating correspondence they found on his person. This ultimately led to his arrest and remand hearing at Marlborough Police Court on November 7, 1888. The duration between the initial arrest on suspicion and the November 7 gross indecency arrest is unknown. It is only an assumption that the arrest on suspicion was that day, but the "slight investigation" may have been weeks long. Note the British newspaper report of this event in the *Evening Post,* February 16, 1889:

> A WHITECHAPEL SUSPECT.
> . . . *Dr. Francis Tumblety, who was arrested in London on suspicion in connection with the Whitechapel murders, but who was released immediately it was found there was no evidence to incriminate him. The World is probably not aware that Dr. Tumblety was afterwards taken into custody on another charge . . .*

Interestingly, there is an account of a tall American wandering the streets and matching the description of Francis Tumblety, wearing a "low" hat and exhibiting suspicious behavior in front of the London Hospital (and its pathological museum) and the wax chamber of horrors across the street. This person was even observed speaking to persons who looked to be unfortunates. The following is the account given in London's *Evening News*, October 19, 1888:

> A REMARKABLE STORY.
> *The City Police have under observation a man whose movements in Whitechapel, Mile End, and Bermondsey are*

attended with suspicion. A man, who is said to be an American, was arrested in Bermondsey at one o'clock yesterday morning, and taken to the police station. His conduct, demeanor, and appearance gave rise to great suspicion, and his apprehension and general particulars were wired to the City police. Following this a conference took place yesterday afternoon, between a young man named John Lardy, of Redman's-row, Mile End, and the head of the detective department at the Old Jewry, at which he stated as follows: 'At 10.30 last night I was with a friend and a young woman outside the Grave Maurice Tavern, opposite the London Hospital, when I noticed a man whom I had never seen before come across the road, look into each compartment of the tavern, and enter the house. He came out again directly, and carefully looked up and down the road, and then walked over the road to the front of the hospital, where two women were standing talking. They were, I believe, loose women. The man said something to them, but I did not hear his words. The women shook their heads and said "No."

IS HE THE MURDERER?

'I said to my friend, "What a funny-looking man! I wonder if he is the murderer." My friend replied, "Let us follow him." We said good-night to our friend and followed the man. When opposite the Pavilion Theatre he drew himself up in an instant, and looked carefully round. We believe that he saw us following him, and he disappeared into a doorway. We stopped for a moment or two, and he came out of his hiding-place and went into a newspaper shop next door. During the whole time we saw him his right hand was in his overcoat pocket, apparently clutching something. He bought a paper at the shop, and folded it up on his chest with his left hand, and then left the shop, looking up and down the road as he did so, and carefully reading the placards outside the shop window. He afterwards started off towards Aldgate, and we followed him.

HE NOTICES THAT HE IS PURSUED.

'When he got to the corner of Duke-street (the street leading to Mitre-square) he turned, and, seeing that we were following him, recrossed the road and walked back to Leman-street and went down it. When he reached Royal Mint-street he went into King-street, which is very narrow, and my friend and I ran round to the other end of the street, *hoping to see him come out there. Just as we got to the other end of King-street we heard a door close, and we waited to see if the man reopened it, for we felt sure that he was the man, although we had not seen him go into the house. We both waited for 25 minutes, when we saw the same man come out of the house. He came up the street, and we stepped back and allowed him to pass, and he went in the direction of the Whitechapel-road. He went away so quickly that we lost sight of him in the fog, which was then very thick. The time then was just after 12.*

*REAPPEARS DIFFERENTLY DRESSED.*

*'When he reappeared from the house we noticed that he was very differently dressed to what he was when we first saw him, the most noticeable being his overcoat. At first he was wearing a sort of short frock-coat, reaching his knees only, but when he came out of the house in King-street he had on a large overcoat which reached to within three inches of the ground. From what I could see he appeared to be between forty and forty-five years of age, and from 5ft. 11in. to 6ft. high.'* (A man 5ft. 11in. was placed before Lardy, who said, 'My man was a little taller than you.')

*LOOKED LIKE AN AMERICAN.*

*'He wore a low hat with a square crown, but I cannot describe either his trousers or boots. He had the appearance of an American. His cheek-bones were high and prominent, his face thin, cheeks sunken, and he had a moustache only, his cheeks and chin being clean shaven. The moustache was, I believe, a false one, for it was all awry, one end pointing upward, and the other towards the ground. His hair was dark, apparently black, and somewhat long.'*

This particular person may not have been Francis Tumblety, but the similarities in physical description and behavior are uncanny. Tumblety was tall, was an American, and his cheeks and chin were clean shaven. Tumblety was also known to own an extensive wardrobe, which likely included multiple coats. Lardy stated that this man crossed the road toward the tavern from the London Hospital. If this was Tumblety, not only does it show he was near both the hospital and the wax museum, but it also shows he had a room on the East End. Tumblety's residence was on London's West End, but he was also known for acquiring temporary quarters in numerous locations around New York and other US cities. Note that the police unit involved in this particular case was not the Metropolitan Police Department, but was the City of London Police. These two departments were not known to collaborate well, meaning Scotland Yard was likely not privy to this incident, other than reading it in the paper. If Tumblety was indeed arrested, it would not have been in Scotland Yard's files.

Tumblety's November 7, 1888, remand hearing at Marlborough Street Police Court was presided by Magistrate James L. Hannay, and was a hearing to determine if Tumblety should be remanded, i.e., placed into custody, at Holloway Prison until he had his committal hearing in front of the very same magistrate. A committal hearing allowed the magistrate to hear the evidence prepared by both sides of the case and determine if it warranted committal to the next judicial level, Central Criminal Court, presided by a full-fledged judge. In Tumblety's case, the committal hearing was scheduled one week later on November 14, 1888, and on that date, the magistrate did indeed execute a warrant of committal to Central Criminal Court once a grand jury reviewed the case. The date was scheduled for its next opening session on November 20, 1888. Tumblety was then remanded to Holloway Prison for "safe custody" until his trial, although the magistrate set bail at £300. By Victorian English law, the magistrate had discretionary powers to set bail at both the remand hearing and the committal hearing. Since Tumblety was allowed bail at the November 14 committal hearing, there is no reason to suggest he would have been declined bail at the earlier November 7 remand hearing.

The fact that three Scotland Yard officials considered Tumblety a murder suspect after Mary Kelly's murder on November 9, 1888, makes it a virtual certainty that Hannay executed his discretionary powers and released Tumblety on bail at the remand hearing—leaving him free to commit the last murder. A grand jury heard the case prior to November 20 and considered it a "true bill," i.e., the jury agreed that the evidence warranted a trial at Central Criminal Court.

According to the Certificate of Indictment written on December 20, 1888, Tumblety's case was postponed until December 10, 1888. Researcher David Barret discovered that it was not the prosecution who requested postponement, but Francis Tumblety.

As explained earlier, there were no witnesses to the murders. Most published research has focused on eyewitness accounts occurring just prior to the murders, with many making the assumption that one of these suspects was likely Jack the Ripper.

There is a lesser known eyewitness account of a suspicious person leaving the scene of the Mary Kelly murder who fits the description of Francis Tumblety:

> On Saturday afternoon a gentleman engaged in business in the vicinity of the murder gave what is the only approach to a possible clue that has yet been brought to light. He states that he was walking through Mitre square at about ten minutes past ten on Friday morning, when a tall, well-dressed man, carrying a parcel under his arm, and rushing along in a very excited manner, ran plump into him. The man's face was covered with blood splashes, and his collar and shirt were also bloodstained. The gentleman did not at the time know anything of the murder. (*Daily News* (U.K.), 12 November, 1888)

It is not known if Scotland Yard pursued this eyewitness account, but there is no reason to believe they foolishly ignored it. A Scotland Yard directive for all law enforcement officials was to not reveal any details of the Whitechapel investigation to reporters, so more may have been done than has been revealed.

### Background on Dr. Francis Tumblety, the Notorious Indian Herb Doctor

Francis Tumblety was a relatively well-known, even notorious figure in middle nineteenth-century North America. His chosen occupation, a newspaper-advertising traveling Indian herb doctor, ensured that his name was seen constantly in daily newspapers in every city he traveled to and practiced in. In any public setting where countless eyes were upon him, Tumblety displayed his flamboyant Liberace-type character. Although nearly all accounts describe him as peculiar, the fact that he was constantly called upon, earning hundreds of thousands of dollars, suggests his antics were, in part, smart business practices. For example, as he came upon a new city in the United States and Canada, he would enter circus-style, wearing a gaudy outfit and riding a beautiful horse, followed closely behind by a valet and two large dogs.

Tumblety had two personas. Publicly, he was this ubiquitous, eccentric, aristocratic medical professional, but privately he was a narcissistic loner, frequenting the slums of every city seeking encounters with young men. On countless occasions, Tumblety found himself in legal trouble, defending against various charges, even assault.

According to researcher Siobhan Pat Mulcahy, in her article, "Jack the Ripper's Cavan Origins," October 26, 2013, Francis Tumblety was the youngest of eleven children, born to James and Margaret Tumulty (correct spelling) in Killycollie (now known as Baileborough), Ireland, around 1830 to 1833. By 1847, the Irish Potato Famine forced the Tumblety family to emigrate, ending up in Rochester, New York. The mother, teenage Francis, and his sister, Ann, were the last to immigrate, traveling on the coffin ship, *Ashburton,* which arrived in New York on June 21, 1847.

Very soon after, Tumblety began working as a steward for a "Dr. W.C. Lispenard," self-proclaimed expert in the French cures of sexual diseases. In the early nineteenth century, it was believed the French, with their more promiscuous culture than Victorian England, were better able to handle sexual diseases, such as syphilis. Unsurprisingly, the name "Lispenard" was a French alias. He also went by the name of Ezra J. Reynolds. Part of this profession was the peddling of sexually explicit literature, and young Tumblety did so for Reynolds on the canal boats. In *American Publishers of Indecent Books, 1840-1890* (2005), Elizabeth Hawley discusses E.J. Reynolds, the practice of publishing this particular type of "medical information," and the legal crusade against it:

> *Rather than being a simple side story to Anthony Comstock's crusade against indecent publications . . . several types of books came to his attention, according to the New York Society for the Suppression of Vice arrest records. . . . Comstock pursued Ezra J. Reynolds, who published a version of W.C. Lispenard's Practical Private Medical Guide renamed as the Pocket Companion. . . . Only because of efforts by publishers to market such books as titillating rather than as medical information did American courts begin to rule them, in practice, to be obscene . . .*
> *(Published for the Author, 1854).*

Around 1853, Tumblety hooked up with an Indian herb doctor named Rudolf J. Lyons, who was making his way through Western New York, and he eventually left the city of Rochester with Lyons and learned the trade. Note the comments made in the *Rochester Union,* May 9, 1865:

> *As Tumblety resided in Rochester many years, and is well known here to almost all our citizens, we need not tell them*

*that the stories floating about in the newspapers are erroneous. His name is J.H. Tumblety, and Blackburn is an alias he has assumed somewhere. His mother resides here still, and he has other relatives, all respectable citizens. He is of Irish origin and no half breed, and has not Indian blood. He will be remembered by many some fifteen years or more since, as a peddler of books upon the cars, and subsequently in other avocations, not long in any one here in town. He once had an office in Smith's Block where he went by the name of Phillip Sternberg, and treated a certain class of disease. When on R.J. Lyons, an 'Indian Herb Doctor,' had an office over the Post Office, Tumblety used to be with him, and he probably picked up the information requisite to start him in his profession there.*

By 1855, Tumblety started on his own and was advertising in Detroit, Michigan, as a full-fledged Indian herb doctor, but with one difference. Tumblety continued with what he learned from Reynolds and sold "French" sexual disease curative literature, which he titled, "Private Medical Treatise." He also began signing his name with MD, claiming to have gone to medical school, which he never did.

Throughout the mid- to late-1850s, Tumblety moved his business into Canada, beginning in smaller towns to the west and south of Toronto and finally into Toronto, itself. His chosen herbal profession promoted botanical solutions to physical ailments, while the medical community opted for allopathic medicinal solutions, or chemicals. Allopathic medicine was still in its infancy and even inappropriately prescribed poisonous mercury as a treatment. Tumblety publicly exploited the evils of mercury, advertising in Toronto papers about the "iron grip of mercury." This eventually caused a direct confrontation between him and the Toronto physicians, who claimed he was practicing without a license—an accurate claim, since he had no official license. This, and other issues, ultimately forced him to shift his practice to Montreal and Quebec City in 1857, although, he did return to Toronto for a short time in 1858. By the summer of 1860, Tumblety found himself on the east coast of Canada in St. John, where he continued to compete with regular physicians. After a patient died in his care, he found himself arrested on the charge of manslaughter. Instead of challenging it in court, he sneaked across the border into the United States. Tumblety continued his profession and operated out of numerous east coast US cities, including Boston, but he eventually settled in New York and Brooklyn just before the Civil War broke out in 1861. Note the audacious method of promenading in the following account when President-elect Abraham Lincoln visited New York:

*The Charlestown Daily Courier, March 23, 1861*
*Correspondence of the Courier.*
*New York, March 20, 1861*

> *When President Lincoln arrived in this city and was escorted down Broadway in a barouche and four horses, amid the silence of hundreds of thousands of persons, there was a very military looking gentleman on a very warlike steed, riding immediately behind the carriage containing Old Abe. He attracted as much attention nearly as did Lincoln himself, and diverse were the conjectures as to his identity. All agreed that he must be a friend of the President elect, while a few suggested that it was no less a personage than 'Judd,' the immortal 'Judd' himself, old Abe's mentor besides his guide, philosopher and friend. The illustrious unknown has made his appearance in one of our Courts. Dr. Francis Tumblety has sued the Chemical Bank . . .*

> *I am afraid Dr. Tumblety is in a close place. He has been living at one our crack hotels, and doing the grandee in magnificent style. . . . I hope when President Lincoln has rid himself of the annoyances of Fort Sumter, the office seekers and Horace Greeley, that he will give an emphatic denial to the assertion that the military looking gentleman who rode behind him on the occasion of his reception was not an intimate or trusted friend. His character and position alike demanded it.*

The Civil War days were quite eventful for Francis Tumblety, from his "sojourn of over two years"—July 1861 to May 1863—to his arrest for complicity in the Lincoln assassination in 1865. His first experience in Washington DC at the beginning of the Civil War can be best understood by separating it into three periods: 1861, 1862, and 1863. The first period was from just after the First Battle of Bull Run when General McClellan took over command of the Army of the Potomac on July 21, 1861, to December 1861 when Tumblety traveled back to New York and stayed for well over a month. The second period was from March 1862 when he returned to the capital, then began his major full-column Washington DC advertising campaign from March to

August 1862, when the army left their camps for Manassas and fought in the Second Battle of Bull Run. The third period was when he returned from Fredericksburg, Maryland, in March 1863 up until he left for Philadelphia in May of 1863. In Tumblety's autobiographical pamphlets, *Dr. Francis Tumblety: A Sketch of the Life of the Gifted, Eccentric and World-Famed Physician Francis Tumblety New York, 1889*, he states:

> When General McClellan was appointed Commander of the Army of the Potomac I partially made up mind to tender my professional services as surgeon in one of the regiments. . . . At this period I was furnished by General McClellan with passes to go and come where and when I pleased. I mixed with the officers of his staff, was cordially received-trusted. . . . My sojourn in the city of Washington, which embraced a period of over two years . . .

Francis Tumblety certainly was deceptive in his writings, but his lies were mainly propping up his reputation as a successful Indian herb doctor and his interactions with prominent people. He was an incessant traveler, and the locations he claimed to have been to and their dates are quite accurate, including his time in the capital. We know Tumblety's "over two-year" sojourn ended with his departure in May 1863 to Philadelphia, because Tumblety ended the discussion by explaining how President Lincoln wrote a letter for him in June 1863:

> *About this period I experienced a decline of health, which induced me to seriously contemplate a trip to Europe. In the meantime my relations with the President were of the most gratifying character, and, as I informed him of my projected trip, he kindly furnished me with letters, one of which was an introduction to that distinguished English nobleman, Lord John Russell:*
> *PRESIDENT LINCOLN'S LETTER.*
> *WASHINGTON, June 12, 1863.*
> *Dear Sir—The bearer of this, Francis Tumblety, M. D., an esteemed friend of mine, is about to visit London for the first time, and will consequently be a stranger in your metropolis. Any attention which you may extend to him will be greatly appreciated by, Your friend and humble servant, A. LINCOLN.*

Tumblety's reference to a two year sojourn in Washington DC thus refers to the second half of 1861, March 1862 up to the Second Battle of Bull Run in August, and his two months in March to May of 1863. Note during this sojourn, Tumblety frequently left the capital on business, paying for a major New York City advertising campaign in the *Harper's Weekly*. This campaign actually went from July 13 to October 19, 1861, while Tumblety paid for a concurrent advertising campaign in the *Baltimore Sun* from September 14 to September 23, 1861. General McClellan standing up a major army at the capital was front page news, and it is logical to assume the ubiquitous Tumblety would exploit this business opportunity at the earliest moment.

Tumblety actually stated his sojourn was "a period of *over* two years" (italics mine). Interestingly, there is evidence of a *two-plus* year sojourn. Researcher Joe Chetcuti reported on the website Casebook.org in 2003 that, "Another researcher kindly shared a document with me which had Tumblety's attorney writing out a statement to a Board of Commissioners in DC. The statement declared that Tumblety's stay in Washington began on April 13, 1861 and ended May 15, 1863."

There is additional evidence that suggests Tumblety was indeed in Washington DC just after the First Battle of Bull Run at the end of July 1861. The following *St. Thomas Weekly Dispatch* article dated March 20, 1862, places Tumblety's arrival to the capital around August 1861:

### DR. TUMBLETY IN TROUBLE AGAIN

*Dr. Tumblety, who has been cutting large figures about Washington for the past six or eight months, and who was reported at one time to holding the position of Senior Surgeon on the staff of General McClellan—an idea that was probably created by the superb air of distinguished importance that the fellow knows how to wear—has come to grief, it appears, and is having his pretentious charlatanry exposed.*

In an interview with a *Chicago Daily Inter Ocean* newspaper reporter on November 20, 1888, William Pinkerton corroborated the report in the *Cleveland Morning Leader*, even his habit of galloping up and down Pennsylvania Avenue wearing a military-style uniform. In the *Chicago Daily Inter Ocean*, Pinkerton goes into detail:

*I'LL SHOW YOU, AND TRAIL HIM down, too, for you from that long ago, and then you can judge for yourself whether or not it is not the same man. I first knew that man—this Dr. Tumblety or Tumbledy or Twombly, (I think the last is it)—in Washington during the latter part of '61. . . . He wore a sort of military dress. He made himself as conspicuous by his dress as he did by his immense coal-black mustache. He wore a military cap, a black velvet coat, and lavender colored pants. . . . At that time my duties in Washington were connected with the secret service of the army, and my attention was naturally drawn to him a good deal by his military appearance. But had that not been the case I could not have failed to noticed him. . . . In passing up and down Pennsylvania avenue, he was the most conspicuous figure on the street . . .*

Out of character for Tumblety was not having a major newspaper advertising campaign concurrent with him making a public spectacle of himself in the 1861 period of his sojourn. He certainly did advertise in April 1862 when he came back to the capital. The answer lies in what every one of his newspaper ads were promoting—his Indian herb doctor practice. Just after the First Battle of Bull Run in July 1861, Tumblety was promoting himself as a candidate for a surgical position under General McClellan.

Tumblety began his major newspaper campaign months later in mid-March 1862 and ended it at the onset of the Second Battle of Bull Run in August 1862. This ad campaign was classic Dr. Tumblety, the Indian herb doctor, and had nothing to do with his surgical experience. Tumblety swamped the Washington DC newspapers with the full-column ads, which included multiple testimonies of prominent Washington DC residents claiming cures from being under his herbal care, beginning with a testimony from a US capital official John A. Laird sworn to Washington Mayor William T. Dove dated March 14, 1862. Laird is quoted, "I applied to Dr. Tumblety, the Indian Herb Doctor. My coughing, spitting blood, pain in chest, are all gone. . . . As I experienced so much benefit from the use of Dr. Tumblety's medicines, I feel as though I could not say enough in their favor."

Tumblety's large, full column ads in the Washington papers ended just before the second Battle of Bull Run, fought from August 28 to 30, 1862, suggesting he left when the army left. In September and October 1862, Tumblety did place mail order ads in the Washington papers. In early March 1863, Tumblety announced his return to DC from Frederick, Maryland, the opposite direction of the location of the major battle. This time, Tumblety only stayed in the capital for just over two months. Interestingly, on the night of March 30, 1863, Tumblety and his "colored servant" Rezin Alexander were robbed by two men. According to the *Evening Star*, April 1, 1863, the two men stole a ten and a five dollar treasury note and fifty cents postal currency from Alexander and a flute and a revolver from Tumblety. Both men were immediately apprehended and jailed.

In May, Tumblety left and set up an office in Philadelphia, but left in the cover of darkness to Buffalo, New York, after the mayor issued an arrest warrant on July 1, 1863. The charge was perjury, since he lied in court. He claimed a Joseph Aspinwall stole his $800 gold medal awarded to him by the citizens of Montreal. The Montreal authorities informed Philadelphia's police chief that they gave Tumblety no such award.

Numerous newspaper accounts reported that Tumblety frequented the theater and had even struck up a friendship with the actor John Wilkes Booth in Buffalo, New York. Booth was playing at Buffalo's Metropolitan Theater in July 1863, and according to extant Metropolitan programs, he began with *Richard III* on July 6, followed by *Lady of Lyons*, *The Apostate*, *Hamlet*, *Taming of the Shrew*, and lastly *Macbeth* on July 11. Note the following report in the May 31, 1914, issue of the *Buffalo Courier*, discovered by researcher Howard Brown:

*One particular week that will ever remain notable in local history was in July, 1863. The city was celebrating the recent northern victories (Civil War). . . . One day in the week in question a tremendous riot took place along the docks abutting Ohio street. . . . Among the people who were observed to study them (rebel trophies displayed in a large storefront window on Main Street) closely was J. Wilkes Booth, the actor, brother of Edwin Booth, and who was then playing at the Metropolitan theater . . . Booth opened Monday night with a performance of 'Richard III,' Allan Halford, the leading man, playing Richmond . . . Booth made a very singular acquaintance while in Buffalo. In fact quite an intimacy sprang up between him and a Dr. Tumblety—or Tumulty. He drove around selling cure-alls for everything, giving lectures with Thespian emphasis. He frequently located himself on the Terrace, where he would draw big*

*crowds by distributing bags of flour. He was particularly
susceptible to the allurements of the theatrical profession.
He sought Booth and they were seen together treating each
other with familiarity.*

In 1864, Tumblety was back in his Brooklyn, New York, office,
and even found himself in police court for kicking a patient,
Fenton Scully, down the stairs of his office after Scully demanded
his $14 back, since treatment for his asthma was a failure. The
*Brooklyn Eagle* reporter joked:

It was bad enough to have a patient who obstinately
refused to be cured; but to ask for his money back was
adding insult to injury. He ordered Scully to leave the
premises. Scully, like his asthma, was obstinate, and
wouldn't go. The Doctor then tried a course of physical
treatment on the refractory patient with the most signal
success. The prescription read: Patient taken vigorously by
the collar; well shaken after taken; sole leather promptly
applied to the base of the dorsal vertabrae; result, prompt
evacuation—of the premises by the patient. (*Brooklyn
Eagle*, May 6, 1864)

Tumblety brought his lawyer, Mr. Parmenter, to court and the
case was dismissed for lack of evidence. Interestingly, the May 6
article reported the rumor being spread on how Tumblety became
an Indian herb doctor, a less-than-truthful story perfectly suited
for gaining legitimacy:

It is given out that he was a great medicine man of the
Saltz-an-Sennah tribe, who, instead of placing himself in
the Museum of the L. I. Historical Society, as a curiosity,
concluded to make a living and bless his fellowmen by
practicing the healing art.

On April 15, 1865, President Lincoln was assassinated, and
his funeral was held at Springfield, Illinois, on May 4. Tumblety
attended the presidential funeral and afterward made his way to
St. Louis by the next day. He was promptly arrested by the
Provost Guard for impersonating a federal officer, coming about
because of his Prussian-style uniform he was so fond of wearing.
At the same time in Washington DC, it became known that David
Herold, an accomplice of John Wilkes Booth in the assassination

plot, worked work for Tumblety while in Brooklyn. After being jailed for two days in St. Louis, Tumblety was transferred to Washington DC for questioning. Not only was he implicated in the assassination plot, he was also implicated in a strange yellow fever plot to infect northern cities. He was jailed for three weeks but was released when there was not enough evidence to support either claim. It is interesting that he had a close relationship with both Booth and Herold within those two years. In 1867, Tumblety explained his experience in his an autobiographical pamphlet titled, *Narrative of Dr. Tumblety. How He Was Kidnapped During the American War. His Incarceration and Discharge:*

> *After a confinement of two days, during which I succeeded in discovering that, beside being charged as the identical Dr. Blackburn, of yellow-fever-plot notoriety, I was also accused of complicity in the assassination of the President. I was carried to Washington, where I was thrust into the Old Capitol Prison, and without the formality of an examination, or any effort on the part of Stanton or his underlings to establish my identity with the notorious person for whom I was arrested, I was detained there three weeks, after which I was turned loose in the same reckless manner that distinguished my arrest—no examination whatever having been made of the case—nor was I afforded the opportunity, the right of every free-born man, to meet face to face my accusers, if there were such.*

Tumblety's 1865 arrest was covered in most of the major US papers. Even though he enjoyed positive publicity—a boon for his business—he hated negative publicity such as this. His later pamphlets show the hallmarks of a man attempting to repair his reputation.

Tumblety continued his business practices in various US cities, but beginning in 1869, he began his European adventures, visiting Ireland and London before returning to the United States. He eventually opened up an office in Liverpool, England, in 1873, titling himself as, "The Great American Doctor." He continued to cruise the London streets for teenage boys; case in point, young Londoner, Henry Carr. In front of the police magistrate in 1873, Carr's father explained that Tumblety "decoyed" his son away to be his secretary in Liverpool. As alluded to later by William Pinkerton, Tumblety's intentions were to have young Carr be his homosexual companion.

In Liverpool, Tumblety began a short relationship with 24-year-old Thomas Henry Hall Caine, soon to gain fame and knighthood as a novelist and playwright. Hall Caine was working as a young journalist at the time, and having chronic ill-health, it is no surprise he met up with the newspaper advertising American doctor. Hall Caine was likely attracted to Tumblety's apparent higher social status and wealth, while Tumblety likely saw a great writer assisting him in his autobiographical booklets. The relationship lasted for just a few years but ended as did all of Tumblety's relationships. Personal letters from Tumblety were discovered in Hall Caine's private collection by historian and lecturer Neil R. Storey. In them, it was clear that Tumblety's ubiquitous and selfish nature added strain to their two-year relationship. In almost every letter, Tumblety discussed some issue Hall Caine was tasked to do for him, such as editing his autobiographical booklets. Tumblety even revealed his threatening temper in a letter dated August 6, 1875, beginning, "Dear Caine, Don't trifle with my patience any longer, send me two pounds & our friendly correspondence shall go on . . ."

In Liverpool, we see for the first time Tumblety's misogyny being revealed. In the February 2013 issue of *Whitechapel Society Journal,* Joe Chetcuti's *Ripping Diatribes* article revealed a series of newly discovered British newspaper articles, thanks to the assistance of Chris Phillips and Robert Linford. In the January 9, 1875, issue of the *Liverpool Leader,* an article was published warning readers of the Great American Doctor:

> There comes to us a tale of a decent woman from the Isle of Man who sought his advice respecting a bad leg. He told her it was due to the immorality of her parents, but would cure it for 3 pounds. This she declined, whereon he [Tumblety] ordered her to get out legs and all or else he would kick her out! Other women young and unmarried, have fled in alarm from his premises, and say his language and conduct suggested danger.

By the late 1870s and into the 1880s, Tumblety discontinued his aggressive newspaper advertising and went into semi-retirement. He maintained an office in Brooklyn, yet traveled incessantly, spending months at a time in London, but then returning to New York. There are numerous accounts of him returning to Canada and spending time in Toronto, apparently unconcerned about the possibility the Canadian authorities would arrest him for the unresolved manslaughter case twenty years earlier. He did find himself in trouble again with the Toronto authorities in 1880, for the usual reason of homosexual advances upon a fourteen-year-old boy. Note the *Toronto Globe* report in the October 15, 1880, issue:

*CITY NEWS.*

*AN UNNATURAL CRIME.—Francis Tumblety was arrested last night by Policeman Clark on a charge of having committed an indecent assault on a youth named Bulgar. He was detained at Court-street Station.*

Researcher Roger Palmer discovered an article in the *Toronto Mail*, November 20, 1888, explaining Tumblety being back in Toronto in November 1883:

*Sir,—We notice an article in the Mail of to-day headed 'The Same Tumblety,' in which is given the history and a description of a Dr. Tumblety recently arrested in connection with the Whitechapel murders. In November, 1883, a man of the same name ordered a coat and other things from us. He was in the store several times, and, being of striking appearance, excited our curiosity. He was over six feet in height, stout and dark. He was possessed of plenty of money and showed us several very valuable diamond rings which he carried in his pocket. At that time his arm was in a sling, but for what reason our utmost scrutiny and questions failed to discover. Shortly afterwards he vanished, and we have not seen him since, but from the description in this morning's paper, we have no doubt but that he is the same Dr. Tumblety as mentioned in the article you print from the New York Times. —Yours, etc., Geo. Harcourt*

Tumblety continued to visit Toronto right up to the year of the Whitechapel murders. Before he left for London in the spring of 1888, he spent time in Toronto, and according to the *Toronto Globe*, November 23, 1888, he made the trip from Toronto to London in May 1888:

Dr. Tumblety, who was recently acquitted of a charge of being concerned in the Whitechapel murders, was in Toronto last May and sailed for England shortly afterwards. His fellow- passengers became much interested in the doctor, who is a man of striking presence, pleasant manners and great conversational powers. He had traveled much and had practiced medicine in San Francisco, New York, Toronto, and Montreal . . .

Throughout Tumblety's adult life, anytime he stayed in one particular location for an extended amount of time, such as Liverpool, England, in the 1870s, he maintained an herb shop. There is no reason why he did not do the same for his extended London visits in the late 1880s. His residence was in the wealthy West End of London, but his herb shop would have been in a different location. One particular report in the *Bridgeport Morning News*, October 8, 1888, stated that a Scotland Yard detective interviewed an "American who used to live in New York, and who now keeps an herb shop in the Whitechapel district . . ." Was this Francis Tumblety? Note the report in the *Bucks County Gazette*, December 13, 1888:

His 'herb doctoring' finally became unprofitable in America; so he went to London, located near the Whitechapel road and for a while did a big business. His oddity of manner, dress and speech soon made him notorious as the 'American doctor'; but he enjoyed notoriety and turned it into money, till the Whitechapel horrors caused a general overhauling of suspicious characters.

# 6

# ESCAPE FROM ENGLAND

## Tumblety Implicated – The *New York World*'s Source

By all accounts, Francis Tumblety was a successful traveling Indian herb doctor, earning great wealth, and he accomplished this through exploiting the reaching power of the nineteenth-century daily city newspapers. He routinely paid for periodic advertising campaigns, but he was also known to get free advertising by making the papers. Case in point, on February 21, 1859, Tumblety published in daily newspapers in Buffalo, New York, that he would distribute twenty barrels of free flour to the poor at a traditional gathering spot on February 22. The *Buffalo Express* certainly did cover this event.

In view of his propensity for seeking the limelight, might Tumblety have made up the whole story about being arrested on suspicion for the Whitechapel murders? Was he the source for the New York papers reporting on his arrest? The murders were capturing the attention of the world and it certainly would have given him free front page advertising. This argument has been made by a few reputable researchers, claiming Tumblety lied to the New York press when they questioned him as he sat behind bars, either at the local London police station or in Holloway Prison awaiting trial for gross indecency and indecent assault case. Per the claim, Tumblety told the reporter that the real reason why the London police arrested him was because they suspected him of being Jack the Ripper. Attracted by the sensationalist story, the New York reporter telegraphed it, and the story then went viral in the United States and Canada. Not only would this have given Tumblety international attention, but it would also have created a smokescreen for the embarrassing gross indecency and indecent assault arrest.

In order to answer this appropriately, we need to begin with the initial newspaper article reporting on Tumblety's arrest on suspicion, then follow the trail to the original source. The very first newspaper article claiming that Tumblety was arrested on suspicion occurred in the United States on November 18, 1888, published concurrently in numerous US city daily newspapers:

*Chicago Daily Tribune Nov 18, 1888*
*GOSSIP SENT BY CABLE.*
*A BARONET GOES ON A LARK THAT GETS HIM IN TROUBLE.*
*SPECIAL CABLE DISPATCH TO THE TRIBUNE.*
*(Copyright, 1888, by the Press Pub. Co., N.Y. World.)*
*LONDON, Nov. 17.—Just think of it. One of the Prince of Wales' own exclusive set, a member of the Household Cavalry, and one of the best known of the many swells about town who glory in the glamor of the Guelphs, getting into custody on suspicion of being the Whitechapel murderer! . . . That was the case with Sir George Arthur of Prince Wales' set. He put on an old shooting coat and slouch hat and went to Whitechapel for a little fun. He got it. It occurred to two policemen that Sir George answered very much to the description of 'Jack the Ripper.' They watched him, and when they saw him talking with a woman they collared him. He protested, expostulated, and threatened them with the vengeance of the royal wrath, but in vain. Finally a chance was given him to send to a fashionable in the West End Club and prove his identity, and he was released with profuse apologies for the mistake. The affair was kept out of the newspapers, but the jolly young baronets at the Brooks Club consider the joke too good to keep quiet.*
***Another arrest was a man who gave the name 'Dr. Kumbletty of New York.' The police could not hold him on suspicion of the Whitechapel crimes, but he has been committed for trial in the Central Criminal Court under a special law passed soon after the modern Babylon exposures. The police say this is the man's right name, as proved by letters in his possession from New York, and that he has been in the habit of crossing the ocean twice a year for several years.***
*A score of men have been arrested by the police this week on suspicion of being the murderer, but the right man still roams at large and everybody is momentarily expecting to hear of another victim. The large sums offered in private rewards hundreds of amateur detectives to take a hand in the chase, but to no avail. Leon Rothschild has offered an*

*income of 2 pounds a week for life to the man who will give information that will lead to the arrest and conviction of the assassin.* [Author emphasis added.]

Notice that the "Kumbletty" story is a subordinate story imbedded in a larger article, which contained four or five other stories on the Jack the Ripper case. In short, the news cable dispatch was an update on the Whitechapel murder investigation one week after the murder of Mary Kelly. In 1888, the *San Francisco Chronicle*, the *Boston Globe*, *Chicago Daily Tribune*, and the *Ottawa Free Press* paid the *New York World* for their extensive cable news gathering network, which included its international news, and all four dailies, and along with the *New York World*, printed at least part of the November 17, 1888, dispatch. Only the *Chronicle*, *Globe*, and *Tribune* reported this particular arrest, spelling his name Kumblety, Kumbelty, and Kumbletty, respectively. On the following day, the *New York World* spelled his name Kumblety, which makes it probable that the original telegraph spelled his name this way. Regardless, all four began his name with the upper case letter of K. It was not until the next day in the New York dailies, the *Sun, Herald, Times,* and *World,* that Dr. Kumblety of New York was positively identified as the notorious Indian herb doctor Francis Tumblety. Interestingly, even though the *New York World* correctly identified Kumblety, they reported the spelling of Tumblety's last name as "Twomblety."

The origin line of the article is clear: the telegraph originated out of London, England, and with the copyright line stating it was owned by the *New York World*, the reporter who broke the story was their own London correspondent, or "special correspondent." In the same dispatch published by the *Ottawa Free Press*, they even stated, *"The World's London correspondent says . . ."* At the time of the murders, the *New York World's* chief London correspondent was E. (Edwin) Tracy Greaves. Greaves began as a London correspondent for the *New York World* in January 1888, and when T.C. Crawford, the chief London correspondent, left in August 1888, Greaves took the helm. Tracy Greaves was born in England in 1858, was educated in Hartford, Connecticut, but lived in New York City. In 1885, he worked for the *New York Times*, having already worked for the *New York Herald*. In 1886, he came to the *New York World* as a night editor of its *Evening World* paper, and in 1887 he was the managing editor until he left for London in January 1888. In London, he was a member of the Savage Club, a club all foreign correspondents joined. "Amongst the US foreign correspondents," the thirty-year-old Greaves was considered the hard-charger:

> GETTING LONDON NEWS, Yankee Correspondents at the World's Capital.
> LONDON, Sept. 7.—There is probably no post in journalism which American newspaper men desire so much as that of London correspondent. . . . By common consent the hardest working American newspaper man in London is Mr. E. Tracy Greaves, correspondent for the New York World. He has offices in Trafalgar Square, where you may have a reasonable chance of finding him at any hour of the day or night. (The Day: New London, Connecticut, Sep. 22, 1891)

In November 1888, Greaves was the sole journalist reporting European news for the *New York World*, with his old boss, T. C. Crawford, having left in August 1888 and James Tuohy not joining his office until early 1889. There is evidence that Tuohy gave Greaves assistance in late 1888. In addition to news out of London, Greaves was responsible for all European news, and efficient use of news sources was paramount.

When US foreign correspondents reported on events originating in London, like the Whitechapel murders, they took advantage of two time-saving yet credible news sources: the London daily newspapers and the police. Note two examples out of the *New York World*. In the first report, Greaves blamed these two news sources for misinformation sent over the wire by him and the other foreign correspondents, including the *Associated Press* reporter:

> Evening World, November 2, 1888.
> (SPECIAL CABLE TO THE EVENING WORLD.)
> LONDON. Nov. 2.—The excitement over the alleged tenth attempt. . . . The sensational London evening papers and the police themselves are responsible for the reports sent out from London to all parts of the world yesterday by special correspondents and the Associated Press . . .

> Evening World, November 10, 1888.
> (SPECIAL TO THE EVENING WORLD.)
> LONDON. Nov. 10.— . . . The papers are having enormous sales, though they contain little besides speculation and

*rumors. Beyond the broad facts of this ninth atrocity the police are endeavoring to keep everything secret . . .*

In the November 2 article, Greaves is blaming misinformation he telegraphed to his own New York paper on his two usual news sources: the London papers and the police. In the *Illustrated American*, December 22, 1894, a journalist who worked as US foreign correspondent out of London during the murders reported on how extensively American correspondents used the British press for European news:

> . . . like the NY World and the NY Herald, to the doing of 'Our Special Correspondent,' the fact remains . . . essential news . . . cabled to America not from Tokio, Shanghai or Corea but from London, where it has been filched from the great English dailies . . .
>
> In 1888, I was attached to the Herald's London bureau with Oakey Hall, and every morning at intervals between three and four o'clock, cabs from Fleet street would dash up to the office door bringing copies, still damp from the presses of the Post, Chronicle, News, Daily Telegraph and last of all, the Times, which we would rip open with the speed of experts, selecting in a few seconds what we wanted and then, with a dash of scissors, paste and blue pencil, hurrying it onto the wire in time to be printed in Paris or New York the same morning. Thus we gathered the news of the world!

In the case of the November 17, 1888, telegraph with Kumblety being arrested on suspicion, Greaves' news source could not have been the London papers. Three of the four stories were exclusives, never having been published in any London dailies: Sir George Arthur's arrest on suspicion, the Kumblety story, and Leon Rothschild offering a lifetime reward for information leading to the capture of the murderer. This leaves the probable source for Francis Tumblety's arrest on suspicion the very same organization that arrested him—the police—and indeed the article itself has sentences phrased to that effect, such as, "It occurred to two policemen that Sir George answered very much to the description of Jack the Ripper," "The police say this is the man's right name," and "A score of men have been arrested by the police this week." Further, the following is a record of the *New York World* correspondent not only using the police as a news source for the Whitechapel investigation, but also having an informant at police headquarters—Scotland Yard:

*The World (Evening Edition), Tuesday, October 9, 1888*
*A STARTLING THEORY.*
*(SPECIAL CABLE TO THE EVENING WORLD.)*
   *LONDON. Oct. 9.—I am informed by a gentleman, who stands in close relations at Scotland Yard, that several of the leading detectives have thrown over the clues and ideas heretofore taken up a dare working on an entirely new and most remarkable theory. . . . My informant tells me that a well-known, prosperous resident of Grosvenor square is the man thus under police surveillance. He moves in the best of society and is completely removed from derogatory suspicion among those who are his daily associates. This man, however, as I am assured, has been tracked and traced . . .*

*Chicago Tribune, Sunday, 7 October 1888,*
*THE WHITECHAPEL HORRORS.*
*SPECIAL CABLE DISPATCH TO THE TRIBUNE.*
*(Copyright, 1888, by the Press Pub. Co., N. Y. World.)*
   *LONDON, Oct. 6.— . . . I learned today from a Scotland Yard man working on the case that the mysterious American who was here a few months ago offering money for specimens of the parts taken from the bodies of the victims has been discovered . . .*

In view of this, the source for the story of Francis Tumblety being arrested on suspicion likely came from the Metropolitan Police Department, i.e., the reporter's Scotland Yard informant. This is significant, since it demonstrates credibility that Tumblety was arrested for the Whitechapel crimes just as reported. The informant was at Scotland Yard on London's West End, so he was probably not directly involved with Tumblety's arrest and was merely reading a general report of the Whitechapel investigation to the *New York World* reporter. It may very well have been the informant who misread the local police report and relayed Tumblety's name as Kumblety. An expressively hand-written capital T with a deep dip in the center—as was done on occasions—certainly could resemble a capital K.
   While it is very likely the source for the news of Tumblety's arrest came from Scotland Yard, at the same time, it is highly unlikely Tumblety had a chance to speak to the *New York World* reporter and spin the story before the dispatch was sent off to US

papers on November 17, 1888. With respect to the claim that Tumblety spoke with the reporter from inside a police station jail cell, the newspaper reports contradict this. This interview could only have taken place on November 7 or before, since after the November 7 remand hearing Tumblety would have been transferred to Holloway Prison. Of the multitudes of newspaper articles reporting on Tumblety's arrest on suspicion, not one reported a date this early, and some even reported an initial arrest on suspicion around November 16 to November 18. The Scotland Yard informant told the reporter of the arrest, but not when it occurred. Additionally, the *New York World* reporter only learned of the story *after* his November 14 committal hearing, as evidenced by the following statement in the article, "has been committed for trial in the Central Criminal Court under a special law passed soon after the modern Babylon exposures . . ."

The reporter would not have known about Tumblety's November 14 committal hearing either. While the British press generally reported police court cases in excruciating detail, they never reported Tumblety's hearing. The American journalist would have been completely ignorant of Tumblety's case, especially since police courts around London were only attended by British journalists. By extension, the reporter would not have known that Tumblety was in Holloway Prison until his bail on November 16. There is actually evidence that the reporter did not receive the information on "Dr. Kumblety of New York" until the end of the week, Friday, November 16 or Saturday, November 17. Note the following (author-emphasized) phrase in the dispatch, "A score of men have been arrested by the police *this week* on suspicion of being the murderer . . ." The report could not have stated this until the week was over, likely on Saturday, November 17, 1888. Confirming this is the following *New York World* article sent by E. Tracy Greaves' office four days after Tumblety posted bail:

*The World (Evening Edition), Nov. 21, 1888*
*EXTRA, 11 O'CLOCK TEN!*
*The Whitechapel Fiend Uses His Knife Once More.*
*Copyright, 1888 by The Press Publishing Company (New York World).*
*SPECIAL CABLE DESPATCH [sic] TO THE WORLD.*
*LONDON, Nov. 21.—Another Whitechapel murder. . . . Coming at a time when people were beginning to think that the Dr. Twomblety now in custody might really prove to be the Whitechapel fiend . . .*

The reporter still believed Tumblety was in custody. This also contradicts any claim that Tumblety sought the reporter out when he was released on November 16, since the report had no idea of this event. Even the idea that the *New York World* reporter happened to see Tumblety at Marlborough Street Police Court has problems. First, American journalists took advantage of the British reports in the dozen or so police courts around London, since they were reported on in detail. Second, the *New York World* reporter was collecting news on the Whitechapel investigation, so a West End police court would be the last place he would spend the day.

### Tumblety's Escape

When *New York World* London correspondent E. Tracy Greaves wired the Whitechapel murder investigation stories off to New York headquarters on November 17, 1888, partnering newspapers published the dispatch in its entirety, but the *New York World* opted not to publish the subordinate story on "Kumblety" arrested on suspicion. As evidenced by the November 19, 1888, reports on Francis Tumblety, they decided to discover the identity of this New Yorker first before publishing. As was the practice of collecting news on people in trouble with the law across the Atlantic, the New York City newspapers sent reporters to New York City Police Department's detective division in order to find out who this Dr. Kumblety was. Heading the detective division was Chief Inspector Thomas F. Byrnes, and Byrnes had informed the press two years earlier that his department and Scotland Yard made it a practice to keep each side of the Atlantic informed of mutual prisoners. According to researcher Joe Chetcuti, Inspector Byrnes was interviewed in January 1886 by *New York World* reporter, Isaac White (the same person who interviewed Tumblety three years later).

*NY World, January 1886—*
   *. . . Of course, it is a great help to a man in my* [Inspector Byrnes'] *business to keep well posted on the movements of all the big criminals, not only in this city but all over the United States and part of Europe. Now, here, for example, is a letter from our correspondent from London. It contains, as you see, details of the movements of several well-known American crooks who have found New York too dull a field and went to England a few months ago. . . . The same system of correspondence follows their movements there,*

*and I can tell almost to the day where they have been. When they make up their minds to return to America I know by what steamer to expect them, and my men are ready to meet them at the steamer's pier and keep an eye on them as long as they remain in New York.*

In support of Byrnes' office being earlier informed by Scotland Yard of Tumblety's arrest on suspicion, the reporters were immediately told that the Dr. Kumblety was in fact the notorious Indian herb doctor, Dr. Francis Tumblety (or Twomblety):

*New York Herald, Nov 19, 1888—*
*Dr. Tumblety's Queer Antics in this City—Known to the Police.*
*An odd character is the New Yorker Dr. Francis Tumblety, who, according to a cable dispatch, was arrested in London on suspicion of being concerned in the Whitechapel murders and held on another charge for trial under the special law passed after the 'Modern Babylon' exposures. . . . The prisoner has been known to Inspector Byrnes for over twenty years . . .*

If the reporters approached Byrnes' office with a request for the identify of a "Dr. Kumblety from New York" and Byrnes' office was not tipped off by Scotland Yard, they would never have connected Kumblety with Francis Tumblety. Searching for a Kumblety in New York would have been futile. In effect, the very first time readers discovered that Francis Tumblety, the infamous Indian herb doctor from New York, was arrested on suspicion for the Whitechapel murders was by the New York City Police Department, specifically Inspector Byrnes and his detectives.

Again, the specific date of his initial arrest on suspicion is unknown; only that it occurred on or before November 7, 1888. There is evidence of approximately when Tumblety's initial arrest on suspicion occurred—the evening after the Double Event murders:

*The World (Evening Edition), October 1, 1888,*
*IS HE THE FIEND?*
*BY CABLE TO THE PRESS NEWS ASSOCIATION.*
*LONDON, Oct. 1.—A man was arrested at midnight last night on suspicion of having committed the terrible murders in Whitechapel.*
*He is a tall man, with a dark beard. He wore an American slouch hat, by which he was traced from the*

*locality of the last murder, where it is reported he was seen on Saturday night, to Albert Chambers on Union street, in the Borough, South London, where he was found. The Borough is across the river and far away from the Whitechapel quarter. When arrested he was unable to give any account of himself during the previous night. He assumed a defiant attitude. The police are investigating his antecedents and movements, of which it is said he refuses to give any information. Several other suspicious persons have been arrested. The Financial News has offered a reward of £300 for the capture of the murderer.*

The London correspondent of the *Press News Association*, or *Associated Press*, was the seasoned James Mclean. A correspondent from the London newspaper, the *Echo*, actually visited Albert Chambers that morning, giving many details:

*Echo, London, U.K., 1 October 1888,*
    *A VISIT TO ALBERT CHAMBERS.*
    *. . . From this house I went to Albert-chambers. It is a very respectably-conducted house, in Gravel-lane, off Union-street, Borough. The object of my visit was to ascertain the truth of the statement that an American had been arrested in that house on suspicion . . .*
    *THE MYSTERIOUS AMERICAN.*
    *A diminutive individual appeared upon the scene, and explained that the deputy was 'not up yet.' He, however, offered any information I might require. After repeated questioning he stated that yesterday a tall dark man, wearing an American hat, took a bed in the house. He was in the house all day, associated with the other lodgers, entered into their various amusements, but somehow seemed to be rather reserved, and, at times, absent-minded. Towards evening he commenced conversing about the latest horrors in the East-end. He entered very vigorously into the details as supplied by the Sunday papers, and expressed an opinion that the police would never capture the murderer, who would remain at large until he gave himself up.*
    *'Oh,' said he, 'he's a lot too "cute" for these London detectives.'*
    *The 'deputy's' attention was attracted to this mysterious individual by the singular amount of excitement he displayed while discoursing upon the subject. There were*

*about twelve men in the room—a long, scrupulously clean, though somewhat scantily furnished, apartment. Each one seemed afraid of the individual, and ultimately the police were summoned, and the luckless American was marched off in custody as a 'suspect.'*

*DISCHARGED BY THE POLICE.*

*He told the police he spent the previous night on Blackfriars-bridge, and appeared unable to account for his previous movements. Accordingly, he was conveyed to Stones-end Police-station, in Blackman-street, Borough.*

*'But he came back this morning,' said my informant.*

*'Came back?' I essayed in surprise.*

*'Yes,' was his cynical reply, 'and he's in bed now.'*

*My informant went on to say that the police, after conveying him to the station, at once instituted inquiries, but could find nothing whatever against the man, who they accordingly allowed to leave. I then called at the police-station in Blackman-street, but from the officer there could get no information. He so stolidly obeyed the 'orders' he said he had received, that he refused to answer—'Yes' or 'No'—whether the man had gone or not, and even to say whether he had really been in custody.*

This particular suspect was a tall man with a dark beard who wore American slouch hats; he admitted to wearing them on the streets of Whitechapel to the *New York World* reporter on January 29, 1889.

Not only do the description and abnormal mannerisms of the man match Francis Tumblety, but Tumblety also admitted to have been in the area and wearing the American slouch hat. Additionally, note that the police purposely held back information on the Albert Chambers suspect's arrest. The reticence of the police seems to imply they did not want this suspect in the newspapers. If this was a significant person of interest requiring further investigation, not wanting him reported in the press is perfectly understandable.

There is another suspicious event that also occurred immediately after the double murders, not only fitting the Albert Chambers suspect but also implicating the very same suspect: Francis Tumblety. As stated earlier, when Tumblety visited a location for an extended period of time he was known to take residence in posh hotels, but he would also find temporary quarters in local boarding houses as he visited different parts of a geographic area, including slums. The following newspaper story discovered by Stewart Evans records such a temporary non-English lodger in the *Daily News*, October 16, 1888:

> *According to a Correspondent, the police are watching with great anxiety a house at the East-end which is strongly suspected to have been the actual lodging, or a house made use of by someone connected with the East-end murders.*
>
> *Statements made by the neighbours in the district point to the fact that the landlady had a lodger, who since the Sunday morning of the last Whitechapel murders has been missing. The lodger, it is stated, returned home early on the Sunday morning, and the landlady was disturbed by his moving about. She got up very early, and noticed that her lodger had changed some of his clothes. He told her he was going away for a little time, and he asked her to wash the shirt which he had taken off, and get it ready for him by the time he came back. As he had been in the habit of going away now and then, she did not think much at the time, and soon afterwards he went out. On looking at his shirt she was astonished to find the wristbands and part of the sleeves saturated with wet blood. The appearance struck her as very strange, and when she heard of the murders her suspicions were aroused. Acting on the advice of some of her neighbours, she gave information to the police and showed them the blood-stained shirt. They took possession of it and obtained from her a full description of her missing lodger. During the last fortnight she has been under the impression that he would return, and was sanguine that he would probably come back on Saturday or Sunday night, or perhaps Monday evening.*
>
> *The general opinion, however, among the neighbours is that he will never return. On finding the house and visiting it, a reporter found it tenanted by a stout, middle-aged, German woman, who speaks very bad English, and who was not inclined to give much information further than the fact that her lodger had not returned yet, and she could not say where he had gone or when he would be back. The neighbours state that ever since the information has been given two detectives and two policemen have been in the house day and night. The house is approached by a court, and as there are alleys running through it into different streets, there are different ways of approach and exit.*

*It is believed from the information obtained concerning the lodger's former movements and his general appearance, together with the fact that numbers of people have seen the same man about the neighbourhood, that the police have in their possession a series of most important clues, and that his ultimate capture is only a question of time.*

Notice that the reporter's information came from neighbors who gave the landlady advice, meaning they had knowledge of the incident with the landlady as their source. The police clearly told the lady not to speak with the press, as evidenced by her taciturn behavior, which was coincidentally similar to the behavior of the police in the Albert Chambers incident. The Batty Street lodger arrived "very early" Sunday morning from being out all night; the same evening as the double murders. He changed his clothes, quickly gave the landlady his wash, then left. This event conforms quite nicely with the Albert Chambers incident, where the suspect rented a room the morning after the murders.

Evans then discovered that the location of the house was 22 Batty Street, near the Elizabeth Stride murder site, in additional reports, such as reported in the *Manchester Evening News* on October 17, 1888:

*. . . The German lodging-house keeper could clear up the point as to the existence of any other lodger absent from her house under the suspicious circumstances referred to, but she is not accessible, and it is easy to understand that the police should endeavour to prevent her making any statement. From our own inquiries in various directions yesterday afternoon a further development is very likely to take place.*

*With regard to the statements current as to finding a bloodstained shirt at a lodging house in Whitechapel, the Central News says: 'The story is founded on some matters which occurred more than a fortnight ago. It appears that a man, apparently a foreigner, visited the house of a German laundress at 22, Batty-street, and left four shirts tied in a bundle to be washed. The bundle was not opened at the time, but when the shirts were afterwards taken out, one was found to be considerably bloodstained. The woman communicated with the police, who placed the house under observation, the detectives at the same time being lodged there to arrest the man should he return. This he did last Saturday, and was taken to Leman-street Police Station*

*where he was questioned, and within an hour or two
released, his statements being proved correct.'*

The suspect returned to 22 Batty Street the following weekend
on a Saturday. Other reports stated that the police claimed the
Batty Street lodger's account of the bloodstains was satisfactory,
but if the police were continuing their clandestine investigation on
the man, it would not be a surprise that they would attempt to
muffle the curiosity of the press. Scotland Yard certainly would
not have wanted the suspect aware of their continued interest.

When Stewart Evans co-wrote his first edition of *The Lodger*
(1995), which appeared in the United States as *Jack the Ripper:
First American Serial Killer*, he saw enough evidence to link the
Batty Street lodger with Francis Tumblety. The German-speaking
woman lived in England, so an American like Tumblety would
have been classified as a foreigner. Tumblety was known for
taking up lodgings and suddenly disappearing, even leaving
clothing behind. As Evans points out, it would also explain why
the month of October saw no attacks.

Furthermore, after the publishing of *The Lodger*, Evans
discovered another piece of evidence linking Tumblety to the Batty
Street lodger suspect. In 1996, he purchased a bound scrapbook
with press cuttings on famous murders. In it was an article in the
*Yarmouth Independent*, of February 25, 1911, from famous British
journalist George R. Sims, titled "Adventures of a Journalist, Part
VIII 'On the Track'":

*JACK THE RIPPER.*

*The crimes of Jack the Ripper are still debated and from
time to time the discussion as to his identity is revived in the
Press.*

*. . . Three years ago, when the discussion as to Jack's
identity cropped up again in the Press, I wrote on the
subject. Soon afterwards a lady called upon me late one
night. She came to tell me that the Whitechapel fiend had
lodged in her house. On the night of the double murder he
came in at two in the morning. The next day her husband,
going into the lodger's room after he had left it, saw a black
bag, and on opening it discovered a long knife, and two
bloodstained cuffs. The lodger was a medical man, an
American. The next day he paid his rent, took his luggage
and left. Then the police were communicated with but*

*nothing more was heard of the American doctor with the suspicious black bag.*

*'But,' said my lady visitor, 'I have seen him again this week. He is now in practice in the North West of London.'*

*She gave his name and address and the names of two people who were prepared to come forward and identify him as the lodger with the black bag, the knife, and the incriminating cuffs. The next day I took the information, for what it might be worth, to the proper quarters. But the doctor was not disturbed in his practice. There was ample proof that the real author of the horrors had committed suicide in the last stage of his maniacal frenzy.*

Notice the similarities between the two accounts. Both involve a female landlady and a male renter; the renter is identified as a lodger; the incident occurred on the night of the double event murder; the lodger was out during the night and only returned in short time intervals; and lastly, the landlady noticed bloodstained "wristbands," sleeves, or cuffs. Also, the slight differences in the accounts might not be differences at all. First, they come from different sources. The 1888 *Daily News* account came from the neighbors, while the 1911 Sims account came directly from the landlady. Second, both are reporting on slightly different events. The *Daily News* account describes when the lodger came in on the evening of the murders then asked the landlady to wash his clothes. The Sims account reports on the man's return on the night of the murders at two in the morning but mentions nothing about an interaction with the landlady, only what occurred after the man left. The neighbor's account suggested she received the bloodstained clothes directly from the suspect that night, differing from the Sims account, but the *Manchester Evening News* story of the Batty Street lodger clarifies that it was later, "The bundle was not opened at the time, but when the shirts were afterwards taken out . . ."

It is true the lady told Sims she believed she saw him practicing in Northwest London in 1908, but after two decades this could easily be a case of mistaken identity. Sims clearly believed in the drowned doctor theory, so his rejection of the story is irrelevant.

If the Albert Chambers suspect was indeed Francis Tumblety, then this October 1 arrest was Tumblety's initial arrest on suspicion. The *Evening Post* report stated Tumblety's illegal rendezvous with young men was discovered by a piece of correspondence on his possession, thus, the dates of each rendezvous are telling if the Albert Chambers affair was Tumblety.

According to the court records, the illegal acts with Albert Fisher were on July 27, Arthur Brice on August 31, James Crowley on October 14, and John Doughty on November 2, 1888. The correspondence found on his person would have been Albert Fisher and/or Arthur Brice, and the subsequent investigation would have later uncovered James Crowley and John Doughty. Within five days of his rendezvous with John Doughty on November 2, 1888, Tumblety was arrested and charged.

A claim has been raised that Scotland Yard certainly did consider Francis Tumblety a Whitechapel suspect, but they quickly rejected this possibility because of insufficient evidence. They then realized this man was guilty of gross indecency and indecent assault, so by November 7, 1888, they shifted their attention solely upon convicting him of this misdemeanor charge. Conflicting with this claim is the fact that three Scotland Yard officials commented upon Tumblety as a Ripper suspect *after* he was committed to Central Criminal Court for gross indecency on November 14, 1888. Head of the Whitechapel investigation, Assistant Commissioner Anderson, sent private cable communications to US chiefs of police requesting information on Ripper suspect Francis Tumblety:

> *The Brooklyn Citizen, November 23, 1888*
> *'Is He The Ripper?'*
> *A Brooklynite Charged With the Whitechapel Murders.*
>     *Superintendent Campbell Asked by the London Police to Hunt Up the Record of Francis Tumblety—Captain Eason Supplies the Information and It Is Interesting.*
>     *Police Superintendent Campbell received a cable dispatch yesterday (November 22) from Mr. Anderson, the deputy chief of the London Police, asking him to make some inquiries about Francis Tumblety, who is under arrest in England on the charge of indecent assault . . .*

A second Brooklyn journalist from a competing newspaper corroborated the story and the connection to the Whitechapel murder case:

> *Brooklyn Standard-Union, November 23, 1888*
>     *. . . the London Police are evidently doing their level best to fasten the Whitechapel murders upon Dr. F. T. Tumblety. Today Police Superintendent Campbell received a telegram from Assistant Police Commissioner Anderson . . . in*

*reference to Tumblety. Mr. Anderson wants some information
as to his life in Brooklyn . . .*

In Chief Inspector Littlechild's letter to Sims written in 1913,
he stated Tumblety was "amongst the suspects":

I never heard of a Dr D. in connection with the
Whitechapel murders but amongst the suspects, and to my
mind a very likely one, was a Dr. T. (which sounds much
like D.) He was an American quack named Tumblety . . .

It would be a stretch of logic to suggest Littlechild, a chief
inspector at Scotland Yard at the time of the murders, would have
remembered Francis Tumblety as amongst the suspects—and a
very likely suspect—if he was not a significant suspect.

Lastly, when a Toronto newspaper reporter interviewed
Scotland Yard Inspector Walter Andrews about Francis Tumblety
after Tumblety's escape back to the United States and asked
about him being a Whitechapel murder suspect, Andrews stated,
". . . we would like to interview him [Tumblety], for the last time
we had him he jumped his bail. He is a bad lot" (*The Evening
World*, December 21, 1888). Why would Andrews want to
interview Tumblety if he was not still considered a suspect? An
interview for only the gross indecency case would not have helped,
since nothing discovered in that interview would have made the
misdemeanor case extraditable. Divulging information about the
Whitechapel crimes did have the power of Tumblety's extradition
back to England.

Recall, on November 14, 1888, Police Court Magistrate Hannay
issued a warrant of committal on Francis Tumblety to Holloway
Prison with bail set at £300, and on November 16, two men paid
the sureties on Tumblety's behalf. He was now free from custody
while awaiting trial. On November 20, Tumblety successfully had
his trial rescheduled for December 10, 1888, and within a couple
days he was out of the country, never to return. According to the
Certificate of Indictment on Tumblety, the "recognizances of
defendant" were estreated; in other words, Tumblety officially
jumped bail and his sureties were kept.

Tumblety skipped the country not because he feared being
prosecuted for the Whitechapel murders, but to avoid
incarceration for the unbeatable gross indecency and indecent
assault case. Interestingly, key events in his sneaking out of the
country demonstrate with certainty Tumblety was on Scotland
Yard's short list for the murders. The following *New York World*
article published on December 2, 1888, was the very first account

of Tumblety absconding, which actually occurred one week earlier:

*TUMBLETY IS MISSING*
*The American Charlatan Suspected of the Whitechapel Murders Skips from London*
*HE WAS LAST SEEN AT HAVRE*
*Is He On His Way Home Over the Ocean to New York?*
*HE HAD A BITTER HATRED OF WOMEN*
*Copyright, 1888, by the Press Publishing Company (New York World).*
*SPECIAL CABLE DESPATCH [sic] TO THE WORLD.*
  *London, Dec. 1.—The last seen of Dr. Tumblety was at Havre, and it is taken for granted that he has sailed for New York. It will be remembered that the doctor, who is known in this country for his eccentricities, was arrested some time ago in London on suspicion of being concerned in the perpetration of the Whitechapel murders. The police, being unable to procure the necessary evidence against him in connection therewith decided to hold him for trial for another offense against a statute which was passed shortly after the publication in the Pall Mall Gazette of 'The Maiden Tribute,' and as a direct consequence thereof Dr. Tumblety was committed for trial and liberated on bail, two gentlemen coming forward to act as bondsmen in the amount of $1,500. On being hunted by the police today, they asserted that they had only known the doctor for a few days previous to his arrest . . .*

This being a special cable "despatch" to the *World*, owned by the *World* with a London origin line, means the origin of the report was from their London correspondent. When Tumblety stepped off of the *SS La Bretagne* in New York Harbor on December 2, 1888, it was proof he sneaked out of the country and sailed from the ship's origin, Havre, France, but the absconding story actually broke one day earlier. Even so, the London correspondent was absolutely correct with two significant facts; Tumblety left England *and* he escaped to Havre, France. This had to have been inside police information, and thus, likely came from his Scotland Yard informant.

Scotland Yard officials certainly were aware Tumblety escaped at least one week earlier, as evidence by Inspector Byrnes stating this fact to a *New York Sun* reporter December 2, 1888. The

London police knowing of Tumblety's escape prior to him leaving Havre on November 24, 1888, is also confirmed by the head of Scotland Yard's Special Branch in 1888, Chief Inspector Littlechild. Because Tumblety made his way to Havre, France, he must have taken a ferry either out of Liverpool on the West Coast straight to Havre or on the East Coast in the English Channel from Dover to Calais or from Folkestone to Boulogne. Per Littlechild, it seems he took the Folkestone to Boulogne route:

> Tumblety was arrested at the time of the murders in connection with unnatural offences and charged at Marlborough Street, remanded on bail, jumped his bail, and got away to Boulogne. He shortly left Boulogne and was never heard of afterwards. (Littlechild Letter, 1913)

After Littlechild mentioned Boulogne—all preceding comments quite accurate and surprisingly detailed—he mixed the Tumblety events up with the events surrounding suspect Montague John Druitt. It should not be a surprise that Sir Melville Macnaghten was Littlechild's future immediate superior who was convinced of Druitt's guilt. Regardless, the Boulogne statement is part of the accurate information he presented to Sims.

Note how Tumblety was "first seen" out of England in Boulogne, and according to the *World* article, he was "last seen" in Havre, a day's train ride along the French coast. For Scotland Yard to have reported his last sighting in France, it implies an all-out search for him weeks before he officially jumped bail, which occurred when he was a no-show at Central Criminal Court on December 10, 1888. Would a law enforcement department, still responsible for their normal daily duties and having any available resources allocated to the embarrassing Whitechapel murder investigation, spend the time searching for a nobody New Yorker on a mere misdemeanor case when it was lawfully postponed into December? Knowing Tumblety's whereabouts indicates high priority.

Tumblety was supposed to appear in Central Criminal Court on Tuesday morning, November 20, 1888, but his legal counsel, Mr. Bodkin, attended in his stead and successfully applied for a postponement to December 10, 1888. If Tumblety intended on jumping bail at the outset, then this application for postponement is a red flag. Whatever postponement plan was formulated between Tumblety and Bodkin, such as Tumblety claiming to be too sick to attend court, this possibly occurred the day before, on November 19, three days after being released on bail, or in the very early morning of November 20. Coincidentally, Tumblety requested £260 1s. 6d. from his New York bank on November 20! He reprinted his bank's response letter in his 1889/1893 autobiographical pamphlets:

> No later than November of last year Dr. Tumblety received a letter from Drexel, Morgan & Co., which contained the subjoined passage, quoted here to show the pleasant business relations existing between them.
>
> 'In accordance with your order of the 20th inst., we have forwarded you by this mail our sterling letter of credit for £260 1s. 6d., upon Messrs. Drexel, Morgan & Co., of New York.
>
> We are, etc.,<br>J. S. Morgan & CO.'

Tumblety certainly embedded lies in his pamphlets, but they are also filled with accurate information. In this case, Tumblety continued to have a business relationship with Drexel, Morgan & Co. Further, the fact that this is a wiring of money the day Tumblety was in London and needing money is just too coincidental. Tumblety knew he could purchase a transatlantic ticket out of Havre in London at the Langham Hotel, and he certainly needed money to purchase it.

We know Tumblety absconded within a five day window between November 17 and November 22, and the evidence suggests this occurred on November 20, especially since Tumblety was required by law to instruct his counsel for the postponement. Unsurprisingly, police constables were reassigned to watch train stations on November 20. Researcher and biographer Andrew Cook, in his book, *M:MI5's First Spymaster* (2011), reported a correspondence between Scotland Yard senior official Lieutenant Colonel Pearson and the home under-secretary, which pertained to deploying twelve extra constables at two train stations on November 20, 1888, in order "to examine the belongings of passengers arriving from America." Scotland Yard never admitted Tumblety was a suspect in the Whitechapel murder case (although it was later confirmed by the statements of three Scotland Yard officials) and they certainly did not want his name on any official correspondence to the home officer. The timing of this reassignment combined with the fact that the American would likely escape on the train is certainly suggestive that the deployment of extra constables was for Tumblety.

When in Toronto in December 1888, Inspector Andrews was asked by a *Mail* reporter about Whitechapel murder suspect Francis Tumblety, and he admitted they still wanted to interview him about the case. This further demonstrates that Tumblety was still a Ripper suspect on November 20 and that not making court likely caused detectives to pay him a visit; they would have found his room empty. Scotland Yard, fearing Tumblety was attempting to leave the country, would have not only populated the train stations with constables, they would also have searched the harbors. In view of this, Littlechild's statement of Tumblety being sighted out of England in Boulogne was likely on November 20, 1888.

It should not be a surprise that Chief Inspector Littlechild, head of the division responsible for monitoring the violent groups of the Irish Nationalist movements, such as the Fenian and Irish Republican Brotherhood, knew of the rich American-Irish Francis Tumblety. He was known to be sympathetic to Irish causes, especially in Canada in the 1850s. In his memoirs, Littlechild stated, "it fell to my duty to arrest many dynamiters [from New York City] and to be brought into contact with men whose names stand out prominently in the history of the 'physical force' policy, adopted by the extreme wing of the Irish party. . ." Tumblety lived in New York City and, in fact, at around the same time he began his trips to England in 1869 he roomed at the Northern Hotel on Cortland Street in New York—occurring in 1871—which was a hotel managed by Irish Nationalist and Fenian sympathizer Jeremiah O'Donovan Rossa.

The large dossier on Tumblety that Littlechild referred to likely had, at least in part, information on his involvements with the Irish Nationalists. Researcher and historian Christopher T. George suggested the adventurer/traveler Dr. Tumblety would have been the perfect candidate as a courier or bagman for the Fenians, and indeed he made biannual trips from New York to England in the 1880s.

Interestingly, a report in the *Brooklyn Eagle*, April 27, 1890, supports this assertion,

> He [Tumblety] was last heard of a couple of years ago in New York, where for a time he was under suspicion on account of his supposed connection with the advance branch of the Irish national party.

Researcher Roger Palmer noted in a private correspondence that the route taken by Tumblety to exit the country across the English Channel was the same route taken by Irish Nationalists sneaking out of the England. Scotland Yard knew of this escape route and had a detective from Special Branch Division in France, responsible for the French ports in Boulogne and Le Havre; it stands to reason they would have involved him in the chase. The detective assigned to monitor the French ports in November 1888 was Inspector First Class William Melville, soon to become head of Special Branch and eventually the first chief of the British Secret Service. Melville spoke fluent French. Andrew Cook contacted the descendants of Melville's son, William John, who immigrated to New Zealand around 1900. One of the descendants told Cook that William John was interviewed on radio station 2YA (Wellington) about his father's experiences around 1935. In those interviews, William John revealed that William Melville found himself involved in the Whitechapel murder case. Researcher Roger Palmer then discovered in the *Evening Post,* a Wellington, New Zealand newspaper, the record of nine "talks," or "lecturettes" made by Captain W.J. Melville: 21 July 1933, 8:40 p.m.—"Scotland Yard Celebrities" by Captain W. J. Melville; 2 December 1933, 8:39 p.m.—"The Secret Service" by Captain W.J. Melville; 5 December 1833, 8:40 p.m.—"Chief Constable Wensley, O.B.E." by Captain W.J. Melville; 28 February 1935, 8:40 p.m.—"More Scotland Yard Personalities," a twenty minute lecturette by Captain W.J. Melville; 5 March 1935, 8:40 p.m.— Captain W.J. Melville; "Heroes of the British Secret Service" and 13 December 1938, 8:40 p.m.—talk by Captain W.J. Melville, "Superintendent Froest Gets His Man." The three talks by Melville were on espionage and/or military matters: 13 July 1935, 8:40 p.m., "Steinhauer, The Kaiser's Master Spy"; 19 July 1935, 8:40 p.m., "Aerial Espionage"; and 26 April 1938, 8:40 p.m., "With the Australians in Palestine."

Almost all of these talks had the potential to discuss Melville's involvement in the Ripper case. Might Melville have possibly been involved in the Whitechapel murder case at any other time, meaning it was not about Tumblety? Prior to November 1888, Melville was still in France. When he returned to London in December 1888, the last murder had already occurred. Although Scotland Yard believed subsequent murders were at the hands of Jack the Ripper, early 1889 saw a reduction of inspectors involved in the Ripper case down to one. In fact, the inspector heading the case, Inspector Abberline, left the case in early 1889, leaving only Inspector Moore to continue. To suggest Inspector Melville became involved in the case in 1889 would be inconsistent with the actions of Scotland Yard.

Noting that if Scotland Yard realized Tumblety was in Boulogne, France, around November 21, assumed to be on his way back to the United States as the report stated, we only need to find transatlantic steamships available after this date and arriving in New York by December 2, 1888. According to the *St. Paul Daily Globe* (December 1, 2 & 3, 1888), the following steamships arrived in New York on December 1 or 2: steamer *Scotsman*, from Cardiff (seven day crossing); *City of Berlin* from Liverpool; *Germanic* from Liverpool (left on November 21); the steamship *Bolivia*, from Liverpool, which arrived, had one case of mild varioloid among the steerage passengers; steamers *Umbria*, Liverpool (departed on November 24, 1888, and arrived in New York on December 2); and *Bohemia*, Hamburg, via Havre.

With Scotland Yard taking the time to track Tumblety through France, it should not be a surprise that they continued the effort across the Atlantic. The following events were published in the *New York World* on 4 December 1888,

> . . . *It was just as this story was being furnished to the press that a new character appeared on the scene, and it was not long before he completely absorbed the attention of every one. . . . He could not be mistaken in his mission. There was an elaborate attempt at concealment and mystery which could not be possibly misunderstood. Everything about him told of his business. From his little billycock hat, alternately set jauntily on the side of his head and pulled lowering over his eyes, down to the very bottom of his thick boots, he was a typical English detective . . .*
>
> *Then his hat would be pulled down over his eyes and he would walk up and down in front of No. 79 staring intently into the windows as he passed, to the intense dismay of Mrs. McNamara, who was peering out behind the blinds at him with ever-increasing alarm . . .*
>
> *His headquarters was a saloon on the corner, where he held long and mysterious conversations with the barkeeper always ending in both of them drinking together. The barkeeper epitomized the conversations by saying: 'He wanted to know about a feller named Tumblety , and I sez I didn't know nothing at all about him; and he says he wuz an English detective and he told me all about them Whitechapel murders, and how he came over to get the chap that did it.'*

The *World* reporter's impression of the man being an English detective corroborates the barkeeper's comment that, "he says he wuz an English detective," and the reporter witnessing the detective staking out Tumblety's residence corroborates the barkeeper's comments about him being interested in Tumblety. The barkeeper also brought up Tumblety's name to the reporter, clearly evidence that he received the information from the detective. There is no reason to assume the barkeeper's account of the English detective's Whitechapel murder mission as the product of a barkeeper's lie. Additional evidence confirming the veracity of the barkeeper's statement comes from a second, separate eyewitness, a *New York Herald* reporter:

> I found that the Doctor was pretty well known in the neighborhood. The bartenders in McKenna's saloon, at the corner of Tenth street and Fourth avenue, knew him well. And it was here that I discovered an English detective on the track of the *suspect*. This man wore a dark mustache and side whiskers, a tweed suit, a billycock hat and very thick walking boots. He was of medium height and had very sharp eyes and a rather florid complexion. He had been hanging around the place all day and had posted himself at a window which commanded No. 79. He made some inquiries about Dr. Tumblety of the bartenders, but gave no information about himself, although it appeared he did not know much about New York. It is uncertain whether he came over in the same ship with the suspect. (*New York Herald*, Dec 4, 1888)

Note how the *Herald* reporter spoke to multiple bartenders who corroborated each other. Lastly, according to the *World* reporter, the English detective told the barkeeper he just came over from England, and the *Herald* reporter's assessment of an inexperienced New Yorker matches this statement.

Some claim the English detective was a private detective hired by the two bondsmen seeking to recoup their £300 ($1,500) sureties. Problems arise with this claim. First, the barkeeper revealed the detective's specific Tumblety agenda: the Whitechapel murders. The bondsmen would have had little interest in solving the case. Second, according to the December 2, 1888, *World* article, the bondsmen were informed of Tumblety absconding on December 1, only one day before the detective was seen in New York. Third, Tumblety did not officially forfeit the bail until December 10, 1888, when he was a no-show at court. There is absolutely no evidence the bondsmen went after Tumblety while in New York, so if the private detective claim were true, their total losses would have been the initial $1,500 bond plus the excessive funds they spent to hire an English private detective to sail across the Atlantic then follow Tumblety for an untold amount of time. Additionally, since Tumblety violated no New York state law, what would an English private detective have done to bring Tumblety back to England—illegally arrest a man wealthy enough to afford the best lawyers?

The decision to send a detective off to New York to follow Tumblety also conforms to Inspector Andrews' comment to reporters in Montreal. He stated that there was no need to hire American detective agencies in the Whitechapel murder case, since "we can do that ourselves, you know" (*New York World*, December 21, 1888).

Interestingly, in the *New Northwest*, November 30, 1888, it was reported that the eastward transatlantic trip by the *SS Umbria* was the fastest eastward transit by any steamship on record at six days, two hours, and twenty-two minutes. With Scotland Yard knowing Tumblety absconded to France as early as November 20 or 21, likely on his way back to New York via Havre on Saturday, November 24, sending a detective off from Liverpool on the fastest ship in the Atlantic on November 24 makes sense.

An argument challenging the English detective in New York being a Scotland Yard detective is that he was not specifically identified in a Scotland Yard correspondence request to Home Office for funding. Recall, in Inspector Andrews' case to escort Barnett to Canada, Scotland Yard communicated extensively with Home Office. But of course, Andrews was a different case, since the English authorities attempted to have Canada pay his bill on an extradition mission, so should we expect to see Assistant Commissioner Anderson requesting funding to pay for one of his detectives to sail off to New York and haunt Tumblety? The answer is no. Anderson did not have to create a paper trail of vouchers and accounts to Home Office. Note the following 1889 legal report out of San Francisco, which published a *Chicago Tribune* reporter's interaction with Special Branch Detective H. Dutton,

> . . . *They (CID) were formerly attached to each station. Now they are under the central control. . . . They form a division by themselves called the 'C.O.' and are under the immediate command of the Assistant Commissioner of Police of the Home Office (Anderson). . . . About twenty of the men are employed on political matters solely, and of these ten have made a specialty of Irish affairs both in Ireland and America. The political detectives have the best of it. They are*

*intrusted [sic] with the spending of the secret service moneys, and much of it of course is expended without vouchers or accounts . . .*

*'It is a case of fighting the devil with fire,' said Detective H. Dutton, one of the Scotland Yard men now stationed in Dublin, to the writer while in that city last winter . . .*

*Beside the salary there is always a liberal traveling allowance, and all expenses incurred in the line of duty are paid without question. Vouchers are seldom asked for, nor even itemized accounts. Sometimes these expense bills are heavy, especially when there are ocean voyages to be made. The ordinary traveling expenditure is about £2 a day.*

*As the secret service is largely political, one function of Scotland Yard is the foreign correspondence, which is carried on invariably in the language of the country to or from which the letters are directed. . . . There are also employed expert cryptologists who are supposed to be able to unravel the blindest of ciphers. . . . The cipher used by Scotland Yard itself is the old movable key-word, the key generally being the name of the place to which the message is sent. . . . In cabling a code cipher is used, which, of course, defies unravelment. A specimen of this steganograph received in New York last winter runs thus:*

*'Able – desert – ocean – Chicago – manly – revolution – silver – Ireland – pretense.'*

*All that is known about this dispatch is that it certainly came from Scotland Yard to an English detective in New York and that it preceded by a few weeks Le Caron's departure for London (December 8, 1888).*

*Most of the English detective work in America is done through the Pinkertons; but there are always three or four Scotland Yard men in the country watching the 'dynamite' societies, so called, and looking after their Irish friends in different parts of the country. These men are chosen with great care, and have privileges and pay beyond their fellows. One of them who was stationed in New York last year is said to have been paid $5,000 a year and expenses. . . . In some cases shadows have accompanied the dynamitards from the quay in New York to the jail door in England, as was the case with Dr. Gallagher.*

Not only does the above 1889 account state that Anderson did not have to go to Home Office and request sending a detective off to New York, it also shows a Scotland Yard detective being stationed in New York in 1888. Also, the above cryptic message was sent around the same time Inspector Byrnes received a cable from Scotland Yard about Tumblety. Even though the reporter assumed the message was about Le Caron, Anderson's spy, the timing certainly fits a cable message warning a detective stationed in New York that Tumblety was on his way. It may even have been reporting the fellow "English detective" en route.

It is true that the open account for Anderson was specific to Special Branch, but it certainly demonstrates that Anderson had the latitude and authority to send a detective off to New York without informing Home Office. Keep in mind, this is the same top Scotland Yard official who performed illegal activities in the Parnell fiasco without the approval of Home Office, justifying it for the benefit of England. Anderson confidentially sending a detective off to New York under the guise of Special Branch was certainly justified in his mind.

# 7

# TUMBLETY AND ANATOMICAL MODELS AND MUSEUMS

Once the world knew New Yorker Francis Tumblety was arrested on suspicion of the Whitechapel crimes, investigative reporters from major North American city newspapers searched for anyone who knew him in the past:

*San Francisco Chronicle, 20 November, 1888*
*DR. TUMBLETY.*
*MORE ABOUT THE SUSPECTED WHITECHAPEL FIEND.*
*Clement R. Bennett, the well-known stenographer of the Circuit Court, knew Dr. Tumblety of New York, who has been arrested in London on suspicion of being the Whitechapel murderer. In conversation yesterday in regard to the case he said:*
*'The first time I ever saw Tumblety was at the Jerome Park fall races in 1870. I was then living in that fashionable suburb, Fordham. Tumblety, in company with a flashily dressed man, passed by our house, which was the short cut from the park to the Fordham depot, on the New York and Harlem Railroad. The men stopped, and Tumblety, who acted as spokesman, asked me a great many questions about the resident . . .'*

In New York City, the *New York World* discovered a number of former acquaintances of Francis Tumblety, such as Martin McGarry, William H. Carr, and New York lawyer William P. Burr. They discovered another New York City lawyer who knew Tumblety in both New York in the recent decades and Washington DC at the beginning of the Civil War. Shockingly, this man witnessed not only Francis Tumblety's professional anatomical museum but his unusual interest in his collection of uterus specimens—the same internal organ Jack the Ripper collected from two of his victims. His name was "Colonel" Charles Dunham, the man who met him at the onset of the Civil War:

> *Col. C. S. Dunham, a well known lawyer who lives here Fairview, N.J., was intimately connected with Twomblety for many years and, in his own mind, had long connected him with the Whitechapel horrors. 'The man's real name,' said the lawyer, 'is Tumblety, with Francis for a Christian name. I have here a book published by him a number of years ago, describing some of his strange adventures and wonderful cures, all lies, of course, in which the name of Francis Tumblety M.D., appears. When, to my knowledge of the man's history, his idiosyncrasies, his revolting , his antipathy to women, and especially to fallen women, his anatomical museum containing many specimens like those carved from the Whitechapel victims . . .*
>
> *'At length it was whispered about that he was an adventurer. One day my Lieutenant-Colonel and myself accepted the 'doctor's' invitation to a late dinner—symposium, he called it—at his rooms. He had very cosy and tastefully furnished quarters in, I believe, H street. There were three rooms on a floor, the rear one being his office with a bedroom or two a story higher . . .*
>
> *'Then he invited us into his office where he illustrated his lecture, so to speak. One side of this room was entirely occupied with doors, outwardly resembling wardrobes. When the doors were opened quite a museum was revealed—tiers of shelves with glass jars and cases, some round and others square, filled with all sorts of anatomical specimens. The 'doctor' placed on a table a dozen or more jars containing, he said, the matrices of every class of woman. Nearly a half of one of these cases was occupied exclusively with these specimens.' (New York World, Dec 1, 1888)*

According to Dunham's story, we see "Dr." Francis Tumblety—who was in his early thirties at the time of the Civil War—having his own professional anatomical museum, similar in content to the museum at the London Hospital. It raises questions as to how he received these specimens. With the wealth he had already acquired, he could easily have afforded purchasing these specimens through the body snatching business, a practice occurring in the city he lived in, New York City. In *A Traffic of Dead Bodies: Anatomy and Embodied Social Identity on Nineteenth*

*Century America* (2002), author Michael Sappol states that in 1819, New York made grave robbing illegal, but body snatching for the resupply of medical institutions became so prevalent afterward that the "Bone Bill," or the "Act to Promote Medical Science and Protect Burial Grounds," was passed in 1854 in an attempt to control the business. Note the connection to infamous Burke and Hare, displayed in London's chamber of horrors wax museums.

How intriguing that Whitechapel murder suspect Tumblety's early obsession was over the same internal specimen that Jack the Ripper harvested from two of his victims, an organ that is unique to a woman, the particular gender Tumblety had such an aversion to even be near.

Charles Dunham could have lied to the reporter, and indeed during the Civil War thirty years earlier, the New York lawyer was a reptile journalist, purposely spreading deception in the papers—but for a reason. Foremost expert on Charles Dunham, Carmin Cumming, author of *Devil's Game: The Civil War Intrigues of Charles A. Dunham,* explains Dunham had a clear agenda in his deceptive activities, which even included a hint of altruism. Cumming claims if one takes all of the available evidence into account, a pattern within Dunham's actions emerges of a brilliant, crafty, often unscrupulous and charismatic man who skillfully utilized the art of deception as required by his job description: an agent provocateur for the Union. It is certainly true that Dunham created a series of elaborate faked stories in New York newspapers during the Civil War under different aliases, but it was for the purpose of "damaging the Confederates and Northern Peace Democrats." In effect, Dunham participated in reptile journalism "for the better good." Dunham once stated when referring to his deceptive tactics, "I do not believe in fighting the Devil with fair play and honesty, and claim the right to use his own weapons."

Dunham certainly did have it in him to lie in the daily newspapers, and like his comments about Tumblety's marriage, there is no concrete evidence Tumblety ever was married. Was that a Dunham lie or a Tumblety lie? Being once married would have been the perfect excuse for Tumblety explaining to a group of military officers he was attempting to impress as to why he had no interest in women. Throughout Tumblety's life he publicly denied his homosexual activities. Knowledge of this would have adversely affected the reputation and business of a "highly respected" doctor. Surprisingly, the Tumblety origin of the marriage story has two corroborating pieces of evidence. The first comes from an article in the *New York World* on December 4, 1888:

> Everybody in the neighborhood seemed to have heard of Dr. Twomblety's arrival, and he is well known in all the stores and saloons for several blocks. One merchant who knows him well said: 'Mrs. McNamara is a queer old lady, very religious and kind-hearted. The doctor began stopping with her years ago and he has lived there ever since he was in New York. He used to explain his long absence at night, when he was prowling about the streets, by telling her he had to go to a monastry [sic] to pray for his dear departed wife.'

If his story was false, Francis Tumblety was concealing his evening activities from Mrs. McNamara. His excuse was about his wife since passed, which clearly supports the possibility that the origins of the Tumblety marriage story in the 1888 interview came from Tumblety himself and not Dunham. Tim Riordan, author of *Prince of Quacks*, comments on page 170, "It is likely that Tumblety used the idea of being a widower as a way to mask his true orientation."

The second piece of evidence is Tumblety's death certificate, issued by the City of St. Louis Health Department upon his death on May 28, 1903 at St. John's Hospital. Crime historian Stewart Evans obtained a copy of Tumblety's death certificate in 1995. On it, it states that Francis Tumblety's conjugal condition was "widowed." The *St. Louis Republic*, May 29, 1903, reported that Tumblety checked himself into St. John's Hospital about one month prior, on April 26, and "selected St John's as a convenient place to die." It also stated that he died "without a relative or intimate friend at his bedside." In view of this, it is highly likely that the source for the physician having knowledge of his conjugal condition was Tumblety himself.

The preponderance of the evidence demonstrates that the marriage story did not come from the imagination of Charles Dunham. Dunham was telling the truth as far as he knew. Dunham questioning Tumblety in 1861 about his hatred of women indicates that this issue was significant enough to have Dunham ask the question in the first place. Instead of Tumblety stating he had no issues with women, he gave an explanation as to why he hated them. This would certainly explain why the lawyer Dunham was convinced that Tumblety had motive to be the Whitechapel killer.

Specific to Dunham's comment that Tumblety's offices were on H Street, there is further evidence where Tumblety lived and practiced in the capital in 1861. Ontario's *St. Thomas Weekly Dispatch* reported on March 20, 1862:

> The Washington Republican, reporting the trial of the case, says: 'The Doctor stated that he had already been injured in his business, one of his patients [a lady] having ordered him to leave her house, and that he had been treat [sic] with disrespect at his boarding house . . .

The Willard Hotel, the hotel Tumblety lived at the following year, was a high-end hotel and was likely not referred to as a boarding house. In both Washington DC newspapers, the *Evening Star* and the *National Republican*, every day from Monday, December 2, 1861 to the following Monday, December 9, the Canterbury Hall's ads published a comedy act titled, *Tumblety Outdone*. This was playing at a time when Tumblety was not living in the Willard Hotel.

There is an excellent reason why Tumblety would have chosen to have his practice on H Street in 1861, as opposed to Pennsylvania Avenue. Tumblety was attempting to gain the attention of a man who lived on H Street, Major General George B. McClellan. According to Civil War researcher John O' Brian, General McClellan frequently wrote to his wife, Ellen, in Cincinnati, Ohio, several times a week. McClellan stated in his letter dated August 13, 1861:

> I am living in Com. Wilkes's house [on H Street], the northwest corner of Jackson [sic] Square, close by where you used to visit Secretary Marcy's family. It is a very nice house.

The *Philadelphia Inquirer* reported in its August 9, 1861, issue:

> Gen. McClellan has taken for two months for himself and his staff, the handsome private dwelling to the eastward of Lafayette Square, of Commander Wilkes, of the Navy, and formerly occupied by Mrs. Madison. The business headquarters of the General will be on Pennsylvania Avenue, corner of Nineteenth street, as usual.

O'Brian also reported that on November 8, McClellan wrote to friend Sam Barlow, stating that his new house, the former residence of Bayard Smith on H Street at 15th—now the site of the Sofitel Hotel—was ready to accommodate him.

There really is no evidence Dunham lied about his wartime experience with Tumblety, other than his past penchant to deceive. He also had the ability to tell the truth, as evidenced by the majority of his recollections in the interview being true. Dunham certainly did have a commission as a colonel at the time (although he lost it soon after). Some researchers have argued that Dunham was not in the capital at the same time as Tumblety in 1861, thus, Dunham could not have seen Tumblety's illustrated medical lecture. This is untrue. Cumming states, "He [Charles Dunham] is known to have visited the capital at least three times in 1861—in July, August, and November—and may have been there more often."

The following *Cleveland Morning Leader* article, November 18, 1861, shows Tumblety was indeed flourishing in the capital in November 1861 when Dunham was there:

*DR. TUMBLETY REDIVIDUS. The Buffalo Courier has it from good authority that the original Dr. Tumblety is flourishing about Washington with the original dog, as large as life and a good deal more natural. Also, that he had been attached to Gen. McClellean's Staff as a Surgeon. The first part of the story is correct, and the last is perhaps a good joke. The Dr., dressed in a sort of half military suit, with his great hound behind him, gallops up Pennsylvania avenue in a style that causes half the people in town who don't know better to mistake him for one of the foreign Princes. The Dr. is a living illustration of what small means, joined to faith, can accomplish.*

Further evidence shows Tumblety was in the capital even earlier, supporting Dunham's claim of seeing him in late July 1861. The *Rochester Daily Union and Advertiser* published an article on April 5, 1881, seven years before Tumblety was implicated in the Whitechapel murders, explaining how Tumblety visited a local Rochester regiment in 1861:

When the 13th Regiment was at Fort Corcoran, Tumblety came around mounted on a fine Arabian horse, and when the men who knew him asked where he got it his answer was 'My friend [Secretary of State] Billy Seward gave it to me.'

This regiment, the 13th Regiment of New York Volunteers, was only stationed at Fort Corcoran from June 3 to October 1, 1861. They left Western New York in May 1861 and arrived at Fort Corcoran on June 3 with the understanding they had only a three month enlistment contract. After fighting in the First Battle of Bull Run on July 21 at Manassas, they returned to Fort Corcoran. On August 14, 1861, instead of returning to Rochester at the expiration of their enlistment contract, they were sworn into national service for a further two years. On or about the first of October, 1861, the regiment received new orders, being assigned to Martindale's Brigade, Porter's Division; still part of the Army of the Potomac. They were detailed on special guard duty at the aqueduct and ferries opposite Georgetown until March 8, 1862. The entire brigade, including the 13th Regiment, was stationed at Hill's Hall in Eastern Arlington County, not Fort Corcoran.

Just as important to the veracity of Dunham's story is Tumblety's reason for presenting his professional anatomical collection to a group of military officers. In Dunham's words, they "illustrate his lecture." Tumblety was acting as an anatomy teacher to the officers. Recall the statement of A.W. Bates, PhD, MD, at the Department of Histopathology in the Royal Free Hospital, London, England: "Anatomy teachers assembled their own collections or 'museums' of material with which to illustrate lectures."

Dunham even stated he and his lieutenant colonel were invited to a combination social gathering and a professional lecture—what he called a "dinner-symposium." Tumblety invited the officers to a party and took the time to demonstrate his expertise. Sappol stated that the professional anatomical museum was an integral part of the nineteenth-century medical profession from students in medical school to even seasoned practices of established physicians. Bates affirms this point and explains it was the same in mid-Victorian England. He states:

Ownership of a museum indicated that a teacher was likely to be financially solvent and, in the 1820s, possession of a museum worth more than 500 pounds was suggested as a prerequisite for an anatomy teacher to be recognized by the College of Surgeons.

Specific to the individual doctor, professional anatomical collections were a visible testimony of their medical expertise and legitimacy, and Tumblety would have had some expertise. Tumblety was intimately aware of the credibility battles between his quack medical profession and the established medical profession in 1861. He even acknowledged the importance of anatomical knowledge in quality medicine. Note that he quotes Thomas Jefferson on page 42 of his 1866 autobiography:

'The only sure foundations of medicine are an intimate knowledge of the human body, and observation of the effects of medicinal substances on that. The anatomical and clinical schools, therefore, are those in which the young physician should be formed.'

When Tumblety was in his thirties, his lucrative traveling/advertising business was in full swing, and the reason he went to Washington DC was to make money. That is why he established an office there. In view of this why did he invite not only Dunham, but all of the officers?

The image that Francis Tumblety was attempting to portray in DC was not only of a credible medical professional but also of a surgeon. It would have been a tremendous business advantage if he received a personal endorsement from the man in charge of the Army of the Potomac, General McClellan, and received special access to the thousands of men under his command. If the general believed Tumblety was a valued surgeon, then Tumblety could take advantage of this for his medical practice—at least until he was actually required to perform surgery. The problem for Francis Tumblety would have been to convince General McClellan that he was the real deal, and in the mid-nineteenth century being in possession of a professional anatomical museum would have done just that.

This explains why he had a symposium for McClellan's officers. He wanted to convince General McClellan, a person few had access to for obvious reasons during a time of war, so the best way to convince him was to convince his readily accessible subordinate officers. Not only were the general's officers assigned to carry out his orders, they were also the eyes, ears, and advisors to him. Colonel Dunham was an important subordinate officer to

General McClellan, since he was supposed to have been the commanding officer of a newly forming regiment. The regiment never did successfully form, but that is immaterial. At the time that Tumblety invited Dunham and Dunham's second in command to his office, Tumblety believed they were important subordinate officers to General McClellan.

Because it was most likely a financial reason for Tumblety to be in DC in the first place, Tumblety was strategically allowing McClellan's officers a peek at his "professional anatomical museum" in hopes the general would receive word that Tumblety was a credible surgeon. It was only after this meeting that General McClellan discovered Francis Tumblety was a detriment to his forces and ostracized him.

Recall Sappol's statement: "Doctors were known to keep a few specimens or a cabinet of material on display in their offices as trophies and, more broadly, as objects that advertised a medical vocation (as did diplomas, weight medical tomes, medicines, and instruments)." Tumblety did this very thing. Note the following article in the *Chicago Tribune*, November 25, 1888:

*DR. TUMBLETY'S CAREER.*
*Where His Office was and What He Did In and Around New York.*

*New York, Nov. 24.—(Special.) Police Superintendent Campbell of Brooklyn has been investigating a little of the life of Dr. Tumblety, now under arrest in London on suspicion of being 'Jack the Ripper.'*

*The Superintendent finds that during the few years that Tumblety spent in Brooklyn he conducted himself properly and attended strictly to business, but was regarded by the more sensible portion of the community as a sort of humbug who palmed off his nostrums on those who are always ready to patronize every mountebank who comes along. The doctor was a tall, well-built man, with a big flowing mustache, which was a good walking advertisement, for everybody used to ask when he appeared on the street who he was. He wore a short sack velvet coat, a velvet cap, and high top patent leather boots with his trousers tucked inside. He had a herb store at Fulton and Nassau streets with a glass case in front. Among other things in this case was a sort of glass siphon with a red liquid running through a thin glass tube to indicate blood. He was known as 'The*

*Great Pimple Banisher,' and he used to promenade Fulton
street with two large greyhounds and a valet.*

Tumblety clearly had a display of the circulatory system in
order to convince patients visiting his office that he understood
the circulatory system, and thus, was a credible doctor. Glass
tubes and containers representing the circulatory system were
certainly in anatomical museums as far back as the 16th century.
Note the following description in *The Lancet* of Rackstrow's 16th
century Museum of Anatomy and Curiosities in London, England:

> Rackstrow specialised in wax models of the human
> reproductive system, and visitors to his museum were
> shown case after case of distended wombs, syphilitic
> genitalia, and a selection of preserved and bottled fetuses.
> But his pièce de résistance was a wax sculpture of a
> pregnant woman, partially dissected, with claret running
> through glass tubes representing the circulation of her
> blood . . .

In addition to the Rackstrow Museum, the Victoria and Albert
Museums contained models of the circulatory system composed of
a red substance flowing "through glass veins and arteries," as
well.

Besides possessing one particular apparatus likely found in an
anatomical museum, note that the *London Daily Post* reporter
stated it was "among other things," suggesting Tumblety displayed
multiple items. Multiple items imply a collection. But this was
years later. Is there evidence of any anatomical museum during
the Civil War? The following is an article from the *Evening Star*
(Washington DC), Wednesday, November 20, 1888:

*DR. TUMBLETY.*
*A Naval Officer Tells Some More About Him While in
Washington.*
   *In speaking this morning of the recent arrest of 'Dr.
Tumblety' in London on suspicion of being 'Jack, the
Ripper,' a naval officer said to a STAR reporter:*
   *'I met that man in 1861 in this city. I was standing in
front of a toy store looking at a mechanical toy in the
window, when this man, who stood beside me, began to
talk about it. He afterward invited me to his room to see an
arrangement of his to show the circulation of the blood. I*

*then thought that either he was a fool or regarded me as a fool, but after listening to him for some time came to the conclusion that he was a decided crank on the subject of medicine. He pretended to be practical, but I soon saw that he knew almost nothing about anatomy. Among other things he had a patent preparation for skin diseases, which seemed to have some merit. He rode a magnificent horse, a bay with white spots, and used to dash up the avenue. At certain points boys would run out from the curb with notes for him, thus giving folks the impression that he was doing a driving business. He did not last very long here, and in '69 I met him again in San Francisco, where he was doing very poorly . . .'*

Tumblety personally showed the naval officer first a medical apparatus followed by other items in order to demonstrate his medical credibility—the identical purpose of a professional anatomical museum. This is exactly what Colonel Dunham claimed Tumblety was trying to do with him and his second in command. It may not be a coincidence that at the same time Charles Dunham saw Tumblety's anatomical museum another military officer reported seeing "an arrangement of his to show the circulation of the blood . . . among other things." Tumblety was also observed to have a glass circulatory apparatus in his New York office in 1888, which suggests he continued the practice of using medical items in order to demonstrate medical expertise.
Lastly, there is another account of Francis Tumblety giving medical lectures—as he did with Charles Dunham—and this account also occurred at the beginning of the Civil War soon after he left Washington DC for Buffalo, New York.

*Buffalo Courier, May 31, 1914*
*One particular week that will ever remain notable in local history was in July, 1863. . . . In fact quite an intimacy sprang up between him [John Wilkes Booth] and a Dr. Tumblety—or Tumulty. He drove around selling cure-alls for everything, giving lectures with Thespian emphasis.*

The significance of this cannot be overstated. It demonstrates Tumblety was in the habit of giving lectures for the purpose of his medical profession, corroborating Dunham's claim of the lecture where Tumblety revealed his uterus collection. Anatomical specimens were part of medical lectures. Finally, the following

August 31, 1861, *Vanity Fair* article shows Francis Tumblety in the possession of anatomical images in the very same year Dunham observed his anatomical collection:

*Vanity Fair, August 31, 1861*
*A CASE FOR THE POLICE—IF POSSIBLE*
   *. . . But if one quack is thus happily thwarted in his attempts to outrage decency and insult the public, why should another be quietly suffered to hang out his disgusting banners in our very midst? In a central part of Broadway—we forget the exact Spot, there are so many there to confuse the eye—the passers by are daily outraged by the exhibition of certain anatomical pictures, which look as if they might once have formed part of the collection of a lunatic confined in a leper hospital. . . . He is generally accompanied by a large greyhound—a well-bred animal, but wearing a dejected look, as if ashamed of the company into which it has fallen. The man's name is TUMBLETY . . .*

The most obvious connection between anatomical models and the Whitechapel murder case is the amazing similarity between the Anatomical Venus display and the Mary Kelly crime scene; both the Venus and the victim were portrayed lying in bed, nude, on their backs, with their abdominal organs methodically exposed and their breasts removed. There is also a connection between the Anatomical Venus and Tumblety. Recall that three of the four New York popular anatomical museums in the Bowery were destroyed by law enforcement officials in the same year as the Whitechapel murders. Coincidentally, this was just a few months before Francis Tumblety made his way to England. Tumblety lived near these museums. In fact, researcher Roger Palmer pointed out that the owner of many of these anatomical museums, Louis Jordan (a.k.a. Dr. Ricord & Dr. Kahn) operated his business out of 7 University Place, New York City, up until 1881, early 1882. This is the exact same address Tumblety moved into after "Dr. Ricord" moved out.

These same New York popular museums had as one of their main attractions the Anatomical Venus—which bore a striking resemblance to the display of Mary Kelly's mutilated body. The New York newspaper, *The Sun*, January 22, 1888, reported on the anatomical museums being destroyed by a police raid. Recall, Dr. Hamilton pointed out that anatomical museums have made weak-minded people lunatics.

How coincidental was Dr. Hamilton's warning that these types of wax museums may affect the weak-minded into becoming lunatics, when in the same year of their destruction, the Ripper murders occurred. Not only this, but we have Francis Tumblety, a Jack the Ripper suspect, connected to anatomical museums, living next to these destroyed operations. It certainly does suggest a possible motive—i.e., anger.

# 8

# TUMBLETY
# THE WOMAN HATER

In Chief Inspector Littlechild's 1913 private letter to George R. Sims, he stated,

> . . . in connection with the Whitechapel murders but amongst the suspects, and to my mind a very likely one was a Dr. T. (Which sounds much like D.) He was an American quack named Tumblety and was at one time a frequent visitor to London and on these occasions constantly brought under the notice of police, there being a large dossier concerning him at Scotland Yard.

He then explained why Tumblety was "amongst the suspects," stating that ". . . his feelings toward women were remarkable and bitter in the extreme, a fact on record."

Littlechild explained that Francis Tumblety was suspected of being Jack the Ripper—per his record—and he had an unusual hatred of women. Note a number of other sources reflecting his misogyny:

'He was known as a thorough woman-hater and as a man who never associated with or mixed with women of any kind.' (William Pinkerton, November 19, 1888)

'. . . and in New York his behavior was that of a man who had no liking for women.' (San Francisco Chief of Police Patrick Crowley, *San Francisco Examiner*, November 23, 1888)

When asked about Dr. Tumblety's aversion to women, McGarry said: 'He always disliked women very much. He used to say to me: "Martin, no women for me." He could not bear to have them near him . . .' (*New York World*, Dec 5, 1888)

'You are accused of being a woman-hater. What have you to say to that?' (*New York World* reporter interviewing Tumblety, January 1889)

It has been proposed that Tumblety was not suspect because of his misogyny, but for the less than credible reason of him being gay. The argument goes that even though Francis Tumblety was considered a "woman-hater," in the nineteenth century, this expression meant one thing: homosexual, or lover of men, therefore, it had nothing to do with him truly hating women. In support of this, a broadsheet ballad in 1707 titled, "The Women-Hater's Lamentation'," about a group of gay men was used to point out that the term "woman-hater" meant homosexual. Other evidence demonstrated that this meaning was used even into the twentieth century. On the surface, this conclusion seems very plausible, but it actually breaks down when weighed against the evidence.

The ballad in question was written almost two centuries before the Ripper murders, and the English language is a living, dynamic language. Although the expression "woman-hater" was still being used in this way at the time of the killings, another definition crept into the lexicon. A major social movement began to take hold in England and the United States just prior to the Whitechapel murders—a feminist movement called the woman's suffrage movement, which pushed for improving women's rights in a male dominated society. Men who were absolutely opposed to this feminist movement were at times labeled as "woman-haters," because they had such a hatred of women and women's rights. For example, in *Mencken: A Life*, author Fred Hobson states:

Depending on the position of the reader, he [H.L. Menchen, author of *In Defense of Women* (1918)] was either a great defender of women's rights or, as a critic labeled him in 1916, 'the greatest misogynist since Schopenhauer,' 'the country's high-priest of woman-haters.'

The term for this kind of hatred of women is known as misogyny, which was also used in the mid- to late nineteenth century. According to sociologist Allan G. Johnson:

> Misogyny is a central part of sexist prejudice and ideology and, as such, is an important basis for the oppression of females in male-dominated societies. Misogyny is manifested in many different ways, from jokes to pornography to violence . . .

Thus, the expression "woman-haters" had two definitions at the time of the Whitechapel murders: homosexuality and misogyny. Henry Havelock Ellis (1859 – 1939), a British physician and psychologist, focused his research on homosexuality in the late nineteenth and early twentieth century, and in 1897 published a book called *Sexual Inversion*. Prior to Chief Inspector Littlechild's woman hater comments about Tumblety, one of Ellis' case study homosexual subjects stated this:

> Even their [women's] physical beauty has little or no charm for me, and I often wonder how men can be so affected by it. On the other hand, I am not a woman-hater, and have several strong friends of the opposite sex.

Note the clear distinction this man made between his homosexuality and the misogynist term of woman hater. Here's yet another example. At the time of the Ripper murders, a theatrical play was being performed called *The Woman Hater*, by David Demarest Lloyd, featuring actor Roland Reed. It was advertised in the papers as "THE WOMAN HATER. Reed as the Misogynist, Reed as the Bigamist, Reed as the Trigamist." Reed played the bachelor, Samuel Bundy, who involves himself in no less than three distinct love affairs with "mature widows." The focus was not his homosexuality but his misogyny.

The evidence demonstrates that both connotations of woman hater were used around the time of the murders. Of the countless times Tumblety was called a woman hater, which connotation were they insinuating? Most importantly, did Chief Inspector Littlechild mean hatred of women? Analyzing his letter, Littlechild never used the term "woman-hater," so we really do not have to figure out which definition he meant. Instead, he made a statement about Tumblety's "feelings toward women." It being modified with "remarkable and bitter in the extreme" can only refer to his hatred of women. If Littlechild merely meant gay, then he was stating that Tumblety was not just gay, but really, really gay. This makes no sense. Also, Littlechild did comment about Tumblety's homosexuality, but instead of using the term woman hater he used the term "Sycopathia Sexualis." He was stating that Tumblety was both a man lover *and* a misogynist. Littlechild seems to have had the opinion that men with "contrary sexual instincts" are prone to violence, but he was not saying Tumblety's man lover desires made him a suspect but that his hatred of women did.

We also see Tumblety being reported as a misogynist in the British press, as well. The newspaper *Sheffield and Rottherdam Independent*, December 5, 1888, picked up the following cable dispatch from a foreign correspondent of a London paper, the *Daily Telegraph*. Even though Tumblety's name was not used, note the clear references to him:

> It is reported by cable from Europe that a certain person, whose name is known, has sailed from Havre for New York, who is famous for his hatred of women, and who has repeatedly made threats against females of dissolute character.

The reporter highlighted two particular reasons for Tumblety's fame in connection with the Whitechapel murders, and if true, the information likely originated from Scotland Yard. In view of this, the reporter was informing the readers that Scotland Yard had perfectly plausible reasons for suspecting him of the murders. The use of both reasons make sense, only if hatred of women meant exactly that: hatred of women.

The following *Buffalo Courier* article is not only an excellent example of the woman hater reference—to Tumblety having a true hatred of women and not to homosexuality—but the timing and location of the event connects him to the Whitechapel murders:

*Buffalo Courier, December 7, 1888*
*A reporter of The Courier chanced to overhear the above statements and soon learned the following story from Mr. Bloom:*

*'I have known this Dr. Tumblety for the past fifteen years. The first time I ever met him was at the Burnett house in Cinncinnati [sic], years ago. I travel for the Royal Baking Powder Company, and since that time I have met him in nearly every city in the United States. My business takes me into nearly every quarter of the commercial world. During the past summer and early fall I was in London, England, for three months. One pleasant day in October, in*

company with my wife and another lady, I was going down Regent street. At Oxford street I was greatly surprised to see this same Dr. Tumblety enter the omnibus. I spoke to him but his greeting did not seem to be as cordial as it had always been here in America.

'But what surprised me was his actions when he found that I was in company with the ladies. When I introduced my wife to him his actions were so strange that she has spoken about it several times since and has asked me what I knew about him. He seemed to be very ill at ease and never raised his eyes from the floor after he had learned that the ladies were with me. As I told you, he got on at Oxford street, and only went as far as Piccadilly, when he left the omnibus very hurriedly without any word or sign.

'All this seemed very strange to me at the time. It was only a very short distance from Regent street to Piccadilly—about as far as from here to the Central depot—and I am very sure that he intended to ride much farther when he got into the omnibus. About the only talk that I had with him was to ask where he was stopping, and he simply replied that he should spend the winter in southern France or Italy, and thought that he should probably go to Monte Carlo. He was dressed in his usual gaudy manner, with his heavy watch fop dangling from his coatpocket, but never before had I seen him so uncongenial and restless.

'I have frequently met him here at the Mansion, and we were quite well acquainted. One curious thing about him was that he always had plenty of money and usually carried several diamonds in his pocket done up in a chamois skin. Once when I met him on the train between here and Rochester he showed me letters that he had from Lincoln, Grant & Seward. Soon after I met him in London I heard that he had been arrested, but somehow he got away from the authorities, went to France and from there to America.'

'Did you visit the Whitechapel vicinity during your stay in London?'

'Yes, out of curiosity, I went there several times. It is a tenement district, and a place one would never expect that anybody but a ruffian would frequent.'

'What is the most popular belief concerning the murders among the London people?'

*'Nearly every person there has his own theory, but I think the most popular belief is that these murders are the work of some religious monomaniac.'*

A valid argument against the possibility of Francis Tumblety being Jack the Ripper is that he *was* homosexual, and male homosexual serial killers almost always victimize men. This generalization may be correct about certain male homosexual serial killers—as evidenced by Jeffrey Dahmer killing and eating his young male lovers—but in Tumblety's case, the generalization is irrelevant if we base our conclusion upon actual contemporary reports. According to the FBI, there are multiple motives behind serial killings including homosexual serial offenders. The following is the FBI list of motives of serial offenders based not upon interviews but upon offender actions and crime scene evidence:

- Anger (rage or hostility towards a certain subgroup of the population)
- Criminal Enterprise (benefiting in status or monetarily in a criminal group)
- Financial or personal gain ('black widow')
- Ideology (to further a goal due to prejudice against subgroups based upon race, ethnicity, gender, such as racism and misogyny)
- Power/thrill (offender feels empowered and/or excited when he kills)
- Psychosis (severe mental illness like paranoia, grandiose, or bizarre delusions)
- Sexually-based (driven by sexual desires).

The FBI makes clear that these are non-inclusive general categories not intended to discount other possible motives. They also make it clear that serial killers may be driven by multiple motives, which can even evolve throughout time. If Francis Tumblety was Jack the Ripper, the available evidence indicates that his motive was not at all sexually-based, but was a combination of other motives: the first being ideology, specifically misogyny, and the second being anger directed toward women.

As reported in a previous chapter, *The Liverpool Leader*, January 9, 1875, reported on the recent appearance of a "doctor" setting up shop within their community, who was advertising miraculous cures of Liverpool citizens, but with some investigative journalism, the paper believed they had exposed a fraud. Their investigation of the doctor, who was none other than Francis Tumblety, apparently revealed not only a misogynist, but a violent misogynist when the reporter noted all young and unmarried women fled in alarm from his premises because of his language and dangerous conduct.

Prior to the Civil War, Tumblety was single-minded in his goal of making money through his nefarious advertising Indian herb doctor business, and it worked. A few years after the Civil War, Tumblety seemed to have gone into semi-retirement but continued his traveling, even into Europe, especially England. Thus began his practice of hiring very young men as assistants and even travel partners, obviously for the primary purpose of sexual relations. Examples are Isaac Golliday (*Evening Star*, Nov 21, 1888), Thomas Henry Hall Caine (private collection of Tumblety letters once owned by Caine) in England, a young man named Joseph Lyons (*Rochester Democrat and Republican*, Dec 3, 1888) in the 1870s, and Martin McGarry (*New York World*, Dec 5, 1888) in 1882. In true misogynist fashion, Tumblety was notorious for warning these young men about women, stating to McGarry that all women were imposters and the cause of the trouble in this world.

In 1874 while in Liverpool, England, Tumblety began a relationship with young Thomas Henry Hall Caine, which lasted until 1876. Caine was in the habit of saving everything, including all of his letters and correspondence, and historian Neil Storey received special permission to look through the huge volumes of his material. In his newly published book, *The Dracula Secrets: Jack the Ripper and the Darkest Sources of Bram Stoker*, Storey reveals twenty new letters written by Tumblety to Caine. One of them gives a clue as to why he had such a hatred of women, especially prostitutes:

> The Chinamen are as nasty as Locust, they devour everything they come across, rats and cats, and all sorts of decomposed vegetable matter, they are a species of the Digger Indian. Grass hopper is a luxury which they partake with delight. This is not all, the Chinese that are now being landed on the Pacific shelf are of the lowest order. In morals and obscenity they are far below those of our most degraded prostitutes. Their women are bought and sold, for the usual purposes and they are used to decoy youths of the most tender age, into these dens, for the purpose of

exhibiting their nude and disgusting person to the hitherto innocent youths of the cities.

Notice the ideological prejudice Tumblety displayed against the Chinese and "Digger Indians" (indigenous peoples in the Great Basin), and he then compared the Chinese to "our most degraded prostitutes." The clear inference is that Tumblety had a prejudice against prostitutes, most likely referring to female prostitutes. He further revealed his misogynist ideological beliefs as he then narrowed the subject to "their women." Of particular interest is what he stated about these women being "used as decoys" on his preferred sex partners, "innocent youths" "of the most tender age."

Recall what young McGarry said Tumblety told him, "all women were *impostors*, and he often said that all the trouble in this world was caused by women." By itself, the use of the term "impostors" is confusing, but when we realize what Tumblety stated about Chinese female prostitutes, that they were used as "decoys," it begins to make sense. If you think of duck decoys in hunting, the decoy is a duck impostor designed to lure the prey. In Tumblety's mind, females, especially prostitutes, were "sex partner" impostors, designed to lure young males away from their intended sex partners: older males. They did this by confusing young males at an impressionable age, making them have, as Tumblety considered it, unnatural sexual desires for the wrong gender.

Tumblety was accused of decoying, as well. In 1873, eighteen year-old Paddington, England, resident Henry Carr was asked by Tumblety to be his secretary and move to Liverpool. In the *London Times*, December 1, 1873, it states: "[Henry Carr's] parents objected to his doing so, but eventually he went to Liverpool with the gentleman . . . [Henry's father Charles] said that this was the person who had decoyed his son away."

We now know Tumblety understood the use of duck decoys. One particular Liverpool article published by Joe Chetcuti discusses how Tumblety hired people as similar decoys and placed them in his office waiting room. When a new customer would enter Tumblety's waiting room, the decoys would impersonate actual satisfied customers. In other words, they were impostors, paid by Tumblety to spin a web of lies in order to convince new customers of how effective his treatments were.

So, a thorough evaluation of the available evidence suggests that the reason why Francis Tumblety had such a hatred of women, especially prostitutes, was two-fold. First, he had a deep-seated misogynist *ideology* clearly evident in his letters and actions, and second, he displayed much *anger* that women—especially prostitutes—acted as decoys, or impostors. Note that these are two of the motivations behind serial killings identified by the FBI, and in Tumblety's case, both of these motivations are directed toward the exact type of person Jack the Ripper mutilated. If we look at how the Whitechapel victims were mutilated, a common conclusion is that the motivation behind Jack the Ripper was sado-sexual, since the killer spent so much time attacking the reproductive organs in the abdominal region. Keep in mind, though, no one really knows who the Whitechapel fiend was, so this is an educated guess made by qualified persons using the available evidence. The killer's motivation may also have been one or more of the others if the evidence supports this conclusion.

Sociologist Dr. Allan Johnson did state that the ideological belief of misogyny can manifest itself through violence, and the focus of the Ripper mutilations were upon *the areas that identify one as female*. This could easily have been the result of someone with a deep-seated hatred of women, blaming them for all the woes of the world. The ferocity of the attacks also suggests a tremendous buildup of anger being released through the blade. It should now not be a surprise as to why Scotland Yard took Francis Tumblety so seriously as the possible Whitechapel fiend, and it also shows why students of the Whitechapel case today should still take him seriously.

### The Aggressive Narcissist

Tumblety tried desperately to keep his private life private, but researchers have done an impressive job discovering the details of his nefarious side, thanks in part to his legal troubles making the daily newspapers. If Tumblety was Jack the Ripper and his motive was, at least in part, anger and hatred, did he have it in him to commit such gruesome murders? Let's start with the traits of an aggressive, or malignant, narcissist. The Hare Psychopathy checklist for traits of an aggressive narcissist is as follows:

1. Glibness/superficial charm
2. Grandiose sense of self-worth
3. Pathological lying
4. Cunning/manipulative
5. Lack of remorse or guilt
6. Shallow affect (expressing emotions deceptively)
7. Callous/lack of empathy
8. Failure to accept responsibility for own actions

The following are Hotchkiss' seven deadly sins of narcissism:

1. Shamelessness
2. Magical thinking
3. Arrogance
4. Envy
5. Entitlement (Defiance of their will is a narcissistic injury that can trigger narcissistic rage)
6. Exploitation
7. Bad boundaries (societal norms do not pertain to them).

Dr. Anthony Benis, ScD, MD, states in his book, *Toward Self & Sanity* (1985, 2nd edition 2008):

*When reduced to the subdued state NA (Narcissist-Aggressive) this individual strongly resembles the self-flaunting UNAGGRESSIVE narcissistic personage. Of course, he 'plays the game', and with his hyperactivity and tendency toward 'hypersexuality' he would involve himself in many compulsive dependencies, usually as the subjugator but sometimes as the subjugated individual. As is often the case in the dependency of subjugation, he may become overtly sadistic, especially in frustrating and in playing on the emotions of his subjugated companions, of which there may be several at one time. And he too, if opposed, seeks retribution in the self-justified vindictive triumph. This individual when frustrated can be incited to a narcissistic rage, an aggressive-vindictive rage, or a combined narcissistic-aggressive rage (NA rage).*

The above descriptions of a classic aggressive narcissist fit Francis Tumblety like a glove—grandiose, superficial charm, pathological lying, manipulative, lack of remorse, failure to accept responsibility, bad boundaries, etc. Benis goes on to say that aggressive narcissists love to travel, and countless contemporary eyewitness testimonies about Tumblety discuss his ubiquitous nature.

This leads to Hotchkiss' narcissistic rage and the triggering of this rage due to narcissistic injury, a trait the deceptive/manipulating Tumblety would certainly have wanted hidden in keeping an approachable public image. Is there any evidence of Tumblety exhibiting this particular behavior? Note Francis Tumblety's reply to a *New York World* reporter interviewing him soon after he arrived back in the United States from the Whitechapel district. When asked how long the police put him in prison, he stated: "Two or three days; but I don't care to talk about it. When I think of the way I was treated in London, It makes me lose all control of myself." There are multiple incidents reflecting Tumblety's aggressiveness. As stated earlier, the *Liverpool Leader*, January 9, 1875, reported he anger and aggression toward young and unmarried women.

Tumblety was once reported to have hired thugs to beat up an actor. Researcher Joe Chetcuti has written about four other instances where Tumblety was personally accused of rage/violence, though it should be kept in mind that those instances are classified as accusations and not outright convictions. He was accused of kicking an asthmatic patient down a stairwell in 1864:

> *Brooklyn Daily Eagle, 10 May 1864*
> *THE INDIAN DOCTOR IN COURT.—The case of the Indian Doctor, Francis Tumblety, or as the Court spelled it, Tumbletoe, was called on before Justice Perry yesterday afternoon. The Doctor appeared in his usual resplendency, his mustache having a slight upward curl of defiance. He was accompanied by his cane and friend Parmenter. The 'yaller dorg' was still missing. Fenton Scully, the asthmatic complainant, being placed in the stand, swore that the Doctor promised to cure him complete for $20; that he paid $14 on account and received a liberal supply of medicine. He took the medicine home and applied it internally, but got worse instead of better; he then came to Brooklyn to see the Doctor again, and told him that the medicine made him worse; that the Doctor refused to have anything at all to say to him, and finally kicked him several times in the ribs and knocked him down stairs . . .*

Tumblety initiated a physical fight against an editor named Ralston:

> *New York Herald, November 19, 1888*
> *WHIPPED BY AN EDITOR.*
> *Sixteen or seventeen years since Tumblety had some difficulty with Editor Ralston, of Frank Leslie's Weekly. The outcome of this trouble was a full exposure of his doings in Nova Scotia and also in this city. Some days after this*

*exposure the Doctor met Editor Ralston in the barroom of the Fifth Avenue Hotel. Mr. Ralston was at the time chatting with Supervisor Briggs and Central Office Detective Timothy J. Golden. Tumblety assaulted Ralston and a lively fight was the result, in which the editor came off first best. Tumblety afterward wanted Mr. Ralston to fight a duel, but the latter said that the fellow was really not worth fighting with. Detective Golden arrested Tumblety for assault, but Ralston declined to make any complaint and the prisoner was let go. This occurred about 1872.*

Tumblety getting angry at an attorney on the witness stand in 1880, nearly losing control over the questioning, and becoming threatening:

*Rochester Democrat and Republican, December 3, 1888*
*. . . William P. Burr, of No. 320 Broadway, speaking of the man yesterday, said: 'I met him in July, 1880. He brought a suit against a Mrs. Lyons, charging her with the larceny of $7,000 worth of bonds, and I was retained to defend her . . .*

*'James D. McClelland was his lawyer, and I went into history of the doctor's life. I remember well how indignant he became when I asked him what institution had the honor of graduating so precious a pupil. He refused to answer, and was told the only reason which he could refuse was that the answer would tend to humilate [sic] or criminate him. He still refused to answer, and I thought he would spring at me to strike. There was quite a commotion in court. The case fell through and the old lady was not held. The son returned and brought a suit against the doctor, charging atrcious [sic] assault, and the evidence collected in this case was of the most disgusting sort. The lawyer who had the matter in hand is now dead, but I remember that there was a page of the Police Gazette as one exhibit, in which the portrait of the doctor appeared, with several columns of biography about him. This suit was not pushed . . .'*

Charges were brought against Tumblety on June 4, 1889 for striking in the face with his cane a young man named Davis at a location in Manhattan known for male prostitution. Tumblety approached Davis and began a conversation, which apparently upset Davis. After Davis objected, Tumblety apparently struck him in the face.

Although none of these cases were resolved in court, i.e., Tumblety was not convicted, the pattern shows these attacks did indeed occur. These were the only incidents that made the papers, making it likely that Tumblety's aggressive side came out on numerous other occasions.

Recall that forensic pathologist Dr. William Eckert and forensic scientist and criminal profiler Brent Turvey concluded that the Whitechapel killer was not sadistic since the victims' bodies showed few signs of sexual assault. Turvey explained that the mutilation and overkill was consistent with anger-retaliatory behavior, specifically toward what is female—the uterus and breasts. As mentioned, this type of extreme hatred of women is called misogyny. Also exhibited were reassurance-oriented behaviors, such as the collection of organs and the displaying of the bodies, likely caused from feelings of inadequacy. He also stated that there was psychopathic coolness, anatomical knowledge yet not skill, and there was not necessity of geographically local knowledge. This profile conforms perfectly with the misogynist Francis Tumblety.

Note the connections between this serial offender behavior, the anatomical, or Florentine, Venus, and with Francis Tumblety. The Roman goddess Venus was the goddess of love, beauty, sex, fertility, prosperity, and desire. This desire was pure seduction; the persuasive erotic female charm, which united men with women. Francis Tumblety—hating women, especially prostitutes, for decoying his impressionable young men away from him and toward a life of heterosexuality—would have hated the paintings of the reclining Venus, something he had clearly seen. In his autobiographies, Tumblety claimed to have visited famous art galleries in his European travels, such as the Louvre:

> The Louvre was once a royal palace, but it is now the most extensive museum in the world . . . the great picture gallery, filled with rare paintings, sculpture and curiosities, is said to be about ten miles, affording one of the costliest and most celebrated of collections. Chief among these is the Grand Gallery, filled with works by the great painters of antiquity, scarcely a notable name unrepresented, and the whole rivaling the galleries of the Vatican at Rome and Escurial at Madrid.

The Louvre had numerous reclining Venus paintings, such as the *Venus and Cupid with a Satyr* (1528) by the Italian late-Renaissance artist Antonio Allegri da Correggio. The *Sleeping Venus* (1510) in Dresden, Germany, is an erotic reclining Venus by Giorgione, but he died before completion, so Titian completed it. Tumblety claimed to have visited Dresden as well:

> Dresden is so complete in situation, shade, walks and laying out as to hold the name of the 'Northern Florence'; and it is considered by many the equal of any other capital in Europe, while in works of art, and especially in antique jewelery and fine sculptures, it is certainly unequaled.

The *Rokeby Venus* displayed in London's National Gallery was easily accessible to Tumblety in 1888. This particular painting clearly represented the seductive power of women over men.

Just as Tumblety would have hated the erotic reclining Venus, representing the epitome of decoying men through physical love, he would have loved the Anatomical Venus, an image of the goddess of seduction being eviscerated. In terms of mythology, killing the goddess of heterosexual erotic desire would have allowed Tumblety to take control over what he hated most.

Of particular significance related to the Anatomical Venus, triggering anger-retaliatory behavior in Tumblety in 1888 is the destruction of anatomical Venuses very near his New York residence in January. The official website of the Library Company of Philadelphia states,

> . . . In 1888 New York City authorities, with Comstock's urging, raided several anatomical museums in the Bowery, seizing over 200 wax figures valued at over $37,000 that they destroyed with great ceremony. Comstock's prurient prudery was not lost on local news reporters, who reported that he stood by as the figures were dismembered, 'and only once did his antipathy to nudity get the better of his judgment, when he tore from her soft couch a sleeping damsel with such force as to dislocate one of her nether extremities.'

Another significant event related to both the Anatomical Venus and a possible anger-retaliatory trigger for Tumblety occurred *just two days before Mary Kelly was murdered on November 9, 1888, in London*. In the February 16, 1889, *Evening Post*, it stated that

Tumblety was released after being initially arrested on suspicion and Scotland Yard had begun an investigation on him for gross indecency and indecent assault. The detectives would have purposely hid this fact from Tumblety, and indeed Tumblety later stated in his interview with the *New York World* reporter, ". . . and did not know that all the time I was being followed by English detectives." Tumblety discovered this fact when he was arrested on November 7, 1888, then taken in front of Police Court Magistrate Hannay for a remand hearing—a hearing to consider Tumblety being jailed until his trial. Tumblety the aggressive narcissist, a man who had horrible experiences in prison, would have been shocked and infuriated. Mary Kelly was murdered on November 9, 1888. Once Tumblety was released, either on November 7 or 8, it is quite conceivable he retaliated by murdering Mary Kelly—and did so in her apartment to avoid getting caught.

# 9

# THE ELIXIR OF LIFE

Criminal profiler Dr. Brent Turvey, PhD, as mentioned, explained that the murders were not only consistent with anger-retaliatory behavior, but they were also consistent with reassurance-oriented needs, suggesting personal inadequacy. He states that souvenirs—in this case anatomical souvenirs—are collected as a "token of remembrance that represents a pleasant experience." Turvey also states that souvenirs are collected by serial offenders for other reasons, depending upon the motive. If Tumblety was Jack the Ripper, evidence suggests he may have also been driven by a third possible serial offender motive listed by the FBI: personal gain.

I was surprised to learn that there is very little information online about a specific Jack the Ripper theory involving an "elixir of life," yet Scotland Yard was well aware of it and even acted upon it in early October 1888. Notice the following October 8, 1888, *Bridgeport News* article:

> *An American who used to live in New York, and who now keeps an herb shop in the Whitechapel district, was visited by a detective at his place this week. The detective asked him if he had sold any unusual compound of herbs to a costomer [sic] since August. Similar inquires [sic] have been made at other shops in the neighborhood. The basis for this investigation has a startling Shakespearian [sic] flavor. An eminent engineer in London suggested to the police the theory that the murderer was a medical maniac trying to find the elixir of life, and was looking for an essential ingredient in parts taken from murdered bodies; that, like the witches in Macbeth, he spent time over bubbling caldrons of hell broth, made gory by the ingredients, and looking for the charm. The fact that police are spending time looking up wild theories like this, only shows the utter absence of anything like a clew. The wildest rumors are*

*credited to the exclusion of sound ideas. The Whitechapel
district is swarming with detectives, some disguised as
laborers, talking with loose women and endeavoring to find
out from them something to give the police a tangible basis
to work on . . .*

The article states that a theory proposed by an "eminent
engineer" in London "suggested to the police that the murderer
was a medical maniac trying to find the elixir of life, and was
looking for the essential ingredient in the parts taken from the
murdered bodies." The opinion of the reporter was that this theory
is ridiculous, but this is merely a personal opinion from someone
with only limited information on the investigation. Notice in the
article that Scotland Yard officials took the theory seriously
enough to question multiple shop owners about a compound of
herbs collected for the elixir of life. Apparently, additional
essential ingredients for the elixir are to be found in the parts of
the murdered female bodies, logically, fluid from the female uterus
where life begins and forms—an appropriate ingredient for an
elixir of life. The concoction seems to have been a combination of
ingredients from both the plant kingdom, purchased at an herb
store, and the animal kingdom, taken from the bodies of
prostitutes. Notice also that Scotland Yard was looking for a
customer who may have been purchasing these ingredients since
August, or around the time of Martha Tabram's murder on August
7, 1888.

The description the reporter gave for the store owner is an
excellent fit for Francis Tumblety: "An American who used to live
in New York and now keeps an herb shop in Whitechapel."
Tumblety was an American who came from New York, was
considered an herb doctor, and set up herb shops everywhere he
went. Tumblety himself admitted to being in the Whitechapel
District during the murders. It would not at all be surprising if he
had a shop in this district. Notice how the reporter phrased his
words, ". . . now keeps an herb shop in Whitechapel." This clearly
suggests the owner of the shop did not live at the store location,
and we know Tumblety lived elsewhere and used trains and cabs
for transportation. In an article in the *Bucks County Gazette*,
December 13, 1888, titled *AH THERE! TUMBLETY*, it states:

. . . His 'herb doctoring' finally became unprofitable in
America; so he went to London, located near the
Whitechapel road and for a while did a big business. His

oddity of manner, dress and speech soon made him notorious as the 'American doctor'; but he enjoyed notoriety and turned it into money, till the Whitechapel horrors caused a general overhauling of suspicious characters.

Near Whitechapel Road is in the Whitechapel district, just as the *Bridgeport News* article states.

Significant in the case of Francis Tumblety is that he, more than most, had a motive for finding an elixir of life or health. He contracted a progressive disease of the heart in 1863, which plagued him until his death in 1903. Tumblety actually talked about his deteriorating health in his 1872 autobiography, nine years after he contracted it:

> . . . About this period [while in Washington DC in 1863] I experienced a decline of health of an alarming character, which induced me to abandon my project . . . I have alluded to the great injury of my health from the incarceration, privation, and horror I experienced in the Washington bastile, better known as the 'Old Capitol Prison.' [This conflicts with his earlier statement that he was ill prior to leaving Washington for St. Louis.] Compensation for this is beyond all price, for health is an inestimable jewel, that cannot be purchased with gold; and I feel that I shall never again realize the hardy and robust physique for which I was distinguished previous to my arrest in St. Louis. But the pecuniary loss I have sustained, and the disarrangement of my business, are other matters, for which I have a clear claim upon a Government by whose authority I have been so outraged and despoiled. I will here just adduce one instance as a sample, and it will be seen how my professional reputation has been trifled and tampered with . . .

This particular comment was made close to nine years after the initial contraction, which means whatever he contracted in 1863 had caused multiple years of a loss of hardiness and robustness.

In support of his own comments are the following newspaper articles showing the nature of his illness:

*New York World, November 19, 1888, HE IS 'ECCENTRIC' DR. TWOMBLETY*

*His own face is covered with pimples, and although his features are otherwise regular, his appearance on this account is somewhat repulsive.*

*New York World, 26 November 1888, HE IS A MYSTERY TO ALL, WHO AND WHAT IS 'DR' TWOMBLETY, THE WHITECHAPEL SUSPECT?*
*'I have known Dr. Twomblety by sight for thirty years,' said William H Carr, . . . 'I never saw any one who could tell anything about him, though hundreds of people knew his name and had seen him in cities all over the country. I have not seen him for several years and the last time he came into the hotel I noticed that he was aging rapidly . . .'*

*The New York World, January 29, 1889, HE WORE A BIG SLOUCH HAT (Interview to a New York World reporter)*
*The pictures that have been published of Dr. Tumbley in London and New York give a very good idea of him. He is a powerfully built man and stands 6 feet 2 inches in his stockings. His long black mustache has been trimmed close and reaches down in the shape of a thick growth of beard around his chin, which he keeps smooth shaven. His face is ruddy* [reddish or rosy crimson color] *and he has blue eyes. If he ever dressed sensationally in the past, he does not do so now. Yesterday he wore a dark suit which was by no means new, and a little peaked traveling cap. Altogether, he gave the appearance of a prosperous Western farmer. He wore no jewelry.*

*Atchison Daily Globe, Kansas, 15 December 1888, OH! DR. TUMBLETY., He Was Charged with Being the Whitechapel Fiend—Where Is He Now?*
*. . . and was an extremely well built though homely featured man. His face was very red, and his mustache dyed a jet black.*

*Newark Advocate, Ohio, 30 May 1903, Kept Identity A Secret*
*St. Louis. . . . Dr. Tumblety was suffering from valvular disease of the heart. He came to the hospital under the assumed name of Mr. Townsend. He was unmarried. He amassed a fortune as an advertising physician 40 or 50 years ago, when that line of medical practice was rare. Dr.*

*Tumblety refused absolutely to tell anything about his life or relatives.*

Note that the very first time Tumblety visited Europe was *after* he contracted the illness, and more importantly he reveals that his illness was the reason why he went to Europe, specifically London, per his 1872 autobiography:

> . . . About this period [while in Washington DC in 1863] I experienced a decline of health of an alarming character, which induced me to abandon my project of entering the army and seriously contemplate a trip to Europe . . .

He then gave one additional and important detail:

> . . . Since the publication of the foregoing [1872] I have visited far off places, including the golden regions of California, Great Britain and Ireland, and the European continent. My tour was not one of mere pleasure, but rather research on behalf of my profession . . .

When Tumblety had to "seriously contemplate a trip to Europe," it was because of his illness, so this "European research" seems to have been research for a cure—in other words, an elixir of health.

In the very same year as the Whitechapel murders, notice what Tumblety stated to a Toronto reporter:

> *The Mail , November 23, 1888*
> *THE UBIQUITOS TUMBLETY*
> *The Travelled Doctor Who Was Suspected of the Whitechapel Murders.*
> *Dr. Francis Tumblety, who was arrested in London recently on suspicion of being implicated in the Whitechapel murder, was in Toronto for a few days in January last. That was his last visit to this city. While here he informed a reporter of THE MAIL that he (the doctor) was suffering from a kidney and heart disease, and that he was constantly in dread of sudden death.*

So, before Francis Tumblety left for London, England, just prior to the Ripper murders, he was in constant dread of sudden

death. If there was a motive for discovering the elixir of life in the
most irrational manner, fear of sudden death would be it.

Amazingly, Tumblety discusses an elixir of health in his 1872
autobiography. He quotes Dr. A.R. Porter's address in the
*Botanical Medical Reformer*:

> . . . In the vegetable kingdom there may be found the elixir
> of health—there may be found the healing balm. Would to
> Heaven that the study of this extensive division of natural
> objects was more generally pursued and appreciated;
> because, if it were, and the medicinal properties of plants
> better understood, disease might be more easily and
> successfully treated . . .

The aforementioned *Bridgeport News* article talks about a
concoction of both the vegetable kingdom and the animal
kingdom. Tumblety had available to him the knowledge that
Victorian London was a location where people were attempting to
discover an elixir of life. The following article was in *UrologyToday*
on elixir of life ideas from London in the late nineteenth century.

> *M. L. Miller discussed the use of 'Injection, Ligation and
> Transplantation: the Search for the Glandular Fountain of
> Youth.' She began with the Emerson quote: 'All diseases run
> into one: old age.' So everyone seeks the fountain of youth.
> She believes that modern endocrinology began with Brown-
> Sequard, who self-injected crushed testicles and 'got new
> vigor.' Physicians soon tried this on their patients. Then, (as
> noted above), the Steinach rejuvenation procedure of
> vasectomy also became popular. Voronoff went a step
> further by transplanting sliced ape/monkey testes into the
> abdominal wall. This became so popular that the French
> government eventually had to ban primate hunting in their
> colonies. So all forms of searching for the elixir of youth have
> been tried. Today, we have hormones of all types that can
> be given to males or females: androgens, estrogens, growth
> hormone, etc. Thus, we continue our search for the perfect
> 'anti-aging medicine.'*
>
> *C. Nicholson continued the ideas of rejuvenation by
> filling out the discussion of Brown-Sequard's Elixir of Life:
> Pioneer Andrology and Genitourinary Endocrinology. The
> famous physician received his MD degree in 1846 and
> subsequently held positions in London, Paris and the USA.*

*He is most famous for the description spinal cord hemi-
transection and its resulting neurologic syndrome. But he
also pursued the 'Elixir of Life' and in 1889 reported on his
studies of injection of a mixture of dog blood of the testicular
veins, semen and juices of the testis. This resulted in
increased strength, stronger limbs, better urination and so
forth. Soon, over 12,000 physicians accepted and used his
treatment on patients. However, reanalysis of this treatment
in 2002 led to the determination that most probably little
testosterone entered the human blood after this treatment,
and that there must have been a significant placebo effect.*

At the same time Charles-Edward Brown-Sequard was
searching for an elixir of life in Victorian London there were also
Londoners actively involved in the Middle Age practice of alchemy
and the search for a chemical elixir of life. Freemasonry was
rumored to be involved in alchemy due to the influence of
*Rosicrucianism*, which is the theology of a secret society of mystics
involved in discovering insights into nature. Secret societies, such
as Freemasonry, were alive and well in the wealthy parts of West
End Victorian London. According to Dr. Andrew Prescott, director
at the Centre for Research into Freemasonry, University of
Sheffield:

One of the engines behind the development of Victorian
middle class culture was the multiplicity of clubs and
societies in both London and the provinces. One of the
largest and most influential of these was freemasonry.
Mainstream craft freemasonry in England was governed by
the United Grand Lodge, a descendant of the first Grand
Lodge established in London in 1717. Victoria's reign saw
an astonishing boom in freemasonry. In 1840, there were
just over a hundred lodges in London and 340 in the
provinces. By 1894, the number of London lodges alone
had increased to 382, and the provincial lodges showed a
similarly large increase. There were also English masonic
lodges throughout the Empire, and by 1894 there were
altogether 2543 lodges on the register of United Grand
Lodge.

Famous actor and manager of the Lyceum Theatre, Sir Henry
Irving, was a Freemason. Regarding this, Prescott states:

Biographies of Victorian worthies frequently list their masonic honours with other social attainments, and in reporting details of Sir Henry Irving's involvement with freemasonry in his *Life of Irving*, Austin Brereton was following these precedents in order to emphasise Irving's respectability. The information given by Brereton is confirmed by the register of membership held by the United Grand Lodge of England and available for consultation at the Library and Museum of Freemasonry. There are three degrees in craft freemasonry: entered apprentice; fellow craft; and master mason. Irving was initiated and became an entered apprentice in the Jerusalem Lodge No. 197, which met at Freemasons' Hall in London, on 27 April 1877. Irving was initiated by the master of the lodge, the organist Sir William Cusins.

There was another secret society, an offshoot of the Freemasons, called the Order of the Golden Dawn, whose central philosophy was Rosicrucianism. Interestingly, Bram Stoker was associated with this order. (Being a practicing Catholic, an organization strongly opposed to Freemasonry, Stoker would not have become a direct member.) According to Jeff Dannes of Washington and Lee University:

*The Hermetic Order of the Golden Dawn (G.D.) was a secret fraternal organization dedicated to the study (with practical focus) of occult and esoteric practices. The organization was founded in the late 1880s by prominent Freemasons, and drew heavily on the tradition of Victorian Freemasonry, and from the German Rosicrucian movement. The Order also based much of its ritual practice on ancient texts, particularly the Egyptian 'Book of the Dead' and the Hebrew Kabbala, but G.D. never identified itself as a religion or substitute for religion. Like Rosicrucians and some Kabbalists, G.D. adherents (called adepts) sought to 'penetrate the mysteries of nature,' that is, to reform philosophy and science to reveal divine truths. The Order used alchemy, astrology and other such practices to reveal a member's 'true life.' Golden Dawn adepts could be of any religious persuasion and any gender. The group recruited members from all sections of European Society, though many were members of Britain's intellectual elite: W.B.*

*Yeats, Aleister Crowley, and Bram Stoker all belonged to the Order . . .*

As Francis Tumblety was socializing with the military elite in Washington DC, would he have possibly come in contact with the idea of Rosicrucianism? When Francis Tumblety was in the nation's capital during the Civil War, so was a General Ethan Allen Hitchcock (May 18, 1798–August 5, 1870), special advisor to the secretary of war. Hitchcock was a high member and author of an American Rosicrucian society called the *Fraternitas Rosae Crucis* and was the leader of a Washington-based Rosicrucian club associated with the society. Note what he stated about the elixir of life:

> I am convinced that the character of the Alchemists, and the object of their study, have been universally misconceived; and as a matter of fact [proven such by experience], the subject is of such importance to the seeker for truth, that the mystery should be revealed. . . . The opinion has become almost universal, that Alchemy is a 'pretended science by which gold and silver were to be made by the transmutation being called the Philosopher's Stone.' Those who professed this Art are supposed to have been either impostors or under the delusion created by impostors and mountebanks. . . . It was in that midnight of darkness that a light from heaven was discussed in books for the initiated, as the Elixir of Life, the Water of Life, the Universal Medicine, and the Philosopher's Stone.

General Hitchcock was also closely associated with the European Rosicrucian societies. He was a member of the Order of the Rose of England, and of *L'Ordre du Lis* of France, and even patterned the Rosicrucian Club of Washington somewhat after the two. He also was a member of the Order of the Double Eagle of Austria.

Another Rosicrucian that Francis Tumblety may have met prior to his London trip was the founder of the *Fraternitas Rosae Crucis,* Paschal Beverly Randolph (October 8, 1825–July 29, 1875). He was an American medical doctor and writer. According to A. E. Waite, he was the first person to introduce Rosicrucianism and sex magic into the United States. In the 1840s and 1850s, Randolph traveled to Europe to meet with the European Rosicrucians. In 1858 in London, he was made the

Supreme Grand Master of the Western World and Knight of the L'Ordre du Lis. He was a close friend of President Abraham Lincoln and was even at Lincoln's funeral. Coincidentally, Francis Tumblety was also at the funeral.

In "Knocking on Pall Mall's Door" (*Ripperologist*, January 2008) Joe Chetcuti writes about West End clubs, especially the Beefsteak Room and the associated Beefsteak Club:

> . . . illustration of the Beefsteak Room. This private dining area was located inside the famous Lyceum Theatre in London's West End. Beginning in early August 1888, American actor Richard Mansfield performed in 'Dr Jekyll and Mr. Hyde' on the Lyceum stage, . . . the vast majority of these patrons were never given the opportunity to step foot on the carpet of the exclusive Beefsteak Room. Entry into this chamber was by invitation only—an invitation sent by Sir Henry Irving himself—the manager of the theatre.

Many West End clubs were a playhouse for the elite. Bram Stoker was an active member of the Beefsteak Club. Chetcuti then states, "Writer Thomas Hall Caine was part of the inner circle of this social setting and would consistently receive an invitation from Irving to enter through the Lyceum's rear entrance." Bram Stoker was frequently seen with Thomas Hall Caine.

The following is a paragraph from Casebook.org, an online forum for enthusiasts of the Whitechapel crimes:

> After these fiascos Tumblety wisely chose to leave the U.S. for London in the late 1860s, soon after travelling to Berlin, then to Liverpool in 1874. It was there that he was to meet the not-yet famous Sir Henry Hall Caine (then 21), who was bisexual and almost certainly carried on a homosexual affair with the 'doctor.' The two carried on their romance until 1876, when Tumblety returned to New York City. While in New York, Tumblety aroused suspicion through his 'seeming mania for the company of young men and grown-up youths.'

Chetcuti also points out that literary critic Elaine Showalter spoke of "the shadow of homosexuality that surrounded clubland," such as the Beefsteak Club. With Tumblety's ex-boyfriend a member of the elite Beefsteak Club and it having a shadow of homosexuality, it seems likely that this would have attracted Tumblety. Notice what he states to the *New York World* reporter on January 29, 1889:

> . . . If it were necessary I could show you letters from many distinguished people whom I have met abroad. I am a frequenter of some of the best London clubs, among others the Carleton Club and the Beefsteak Club . . .

At around the same time the eminent engineer proposed the theory that Jack the Ripper was searching for ingredients to an elixir of life as reported in the above October 8, 1888 article, the eminent Colonel (F.C.) Hughes-Hallet of London was convinced that Jack the Ripper was a wealthy London West End club man:

> *Reno Evening Gazette, Nevada, 8 October 1888, LONDON HORRORS, A New Theory Relative to the Whitechapel Murders, New York, Oct. 6.*
> *Colonel (F.C.) Hughes-Hallett of London, formerly of the Royal Artillery and a member of Parliament, is in this city. He says that he disguised himself and investigated the Whitechapel case just after the second murder—that of Martha Turner. He said to-day: 'I had made up my mind, and I have seen no reason to change it, that the perpetrator of the atrocities is a West End man, a gentleman, a person of wealth and culture perhaps, but certainly of intellectual qualities, (finesse) and keen discrimination. I was convinced that my man left his club, as I was then doing, and disguised himself for his hideous nocturnal revel, as I was then about to do. My theory is that the Whitechapel murderer is an army doctor, or medicine student, or a gentleman who has read medicine and studied anatomy as a fad or simply as part of a liberal education. I have no idea that he is practicing physician or hospital student. I believe him to be a gentleman and a man of leisure, or perhaps a retired army surgeon. He is a man of the world . . .'*

When Colonel F.C. Hughes-Hallet stated, ". . . as I was then doing," in reference to him leaving his club just as the killer was, he was explaining to the reporter that the West End was his world, and he understood how they think. It seems plausible that the colonel knew of the shadow of homosexuality at certain clubs, especially those connected to the entertainment community, and had this in mind when he was interviewed.

Recall that Bram Stoker was closely associated with the Order of the Golden Dawn, an order known for its alchemy and search for an elixir of life. As an active member of the Beefsteak Club during the time of the Whitechapel murders and a friend of Tumblety's ex-boyfriend, Hall Caine, it would not be a big stretch for Tumblety to know about the Order of the Golden Dawn and their goals.

This leads us back to the original *Bridgeport News* article. Was the eminent engineer who proposed the elixir of life theory also a member of the West End clubs? Was he a Freemason, thus, "in the know" about orders such as the Order of the Golden Dawn and their search for the elixir of life? He was certainly considered one of "Britain's intellectual elite," as explained by Jeff Dannes, thus eligible for membership in the West End clubs. Was it mere coincidence that investigators ended up in what may have been Tumblety's herb store when Tumblety claimed he socialized in the same West End circles?

Enter Sir Charles Hutton Gregory (1817–1898), an eminent British civil engineer who was president of the Institute of Civil Engineers from 1867 to 1869. He was appointed a knight commander on the Order of Saint Michael and Saint George in November 1884. Notice what Dr. Prescott states about civil engineers involved with freemasonry:

> The Jerusalem Lodge in which (Sir Henry) Irving had been initiated was one of London's oldest and most prestigious. It had been founded in 1771 and was one of the nineteen 'red apron' lodges which were entitled to nominate one of their members as Grand Steward. Jerusalem Lodge was the first private masonic lodge in England which the Prince of Wales visited after becoming a mason. The membership of the lodge was dominated by civil engineers and architects, including Sir Charles Hutton Gregory, President of the Institution of Civil Engineers, Charles Barry, the eldest son of the architect of the Palace of Westminster and a distinguished architect in his own right, John Whichchord, President of the Royal Institution of British Architects, and the general managers of the Midland Railway and the London and North Western Railway.

Sir Charles Hutton Gregory, an "eminent" engineer, was a freemason in an order that was not only dominated by civil engineers but also had Sir Henry Irving as a member. Irving had social interaction with Hall Caine and Bram Stoker at the same time he was involved with eminent engineers. Is it not out of the realm of possibility that the engineer mentioned in the *Bridgeport News* article was Gregory? Interestingly, Gregory's future wife was a British actress, who frequently played at the Lyceum theatre. She was the famous Mary Anne, or Fanny, (Clifton) Stirling. Among other occasions, Fanny Stirling played at the Lyceum theatre in 1857 in *A Wolf in Sheep's Clothing,* and in 1884 she played in *Romeo and Juliet.* It is ironic that the *Bridgeport News* reporter stated, "The basis of this investigation has a startling Shakespearian flavor," a comment perfectly suited for a theory involving the Lyceum Theatre.

Notice the following news report:

*Te Aroha News, December 1, 1888*
*ANOTHER LETTER FROM 'JACK THE RIPPER.'*
*EXCITEMENT IN PARIS.*

*The 'Daily News' correspondent telegraphs: The Whitechapel murders have not only been a newspaper sensation of the first magnitude, but have go on weak brains and set madmen and lovers of practical jokes writing to the Prefect of Police. M. Gauren, the head of the Criminal Investigation Department, receives letters written from both. The following was received by him recently: 'Sir, You must have heard of the Whitechapel murders. This is the explanation of their mysterious side. There are partners—I and another—in this business; one is in England and the other in France. I am at Brest, and am going to Paris to operate as does my London colleague in London. We are seeking in the human body that which the doctors have never found, and you will try in vain to hunt us down.'*

"We are seeking in the human body that which the doctors have never found" certainly sounds like a search in the body for the key to immortality. The author claims Jack the Ripper, the collector of female internal organs, especially the life-giving uterus, is searching for that which doctors have never found.

There was indeed a Ripper-like murder in France three years later:

*Le Crime de Saint-Lumine-de-Coutais: Jack l'Eventreur*
*French Broadsheet, August 14, 1891*

*This broadsheet is currently held at the Bibliothèque Nationale in France. It describes a 'Ripper-like' murder committed August 14th, 1891, in Saint Lumine de Coutais, France. Marie-Anne Mignonneau's throat was slashed, and her body mutilated from her groin to her chest. Her intestines were torn out and scattered upon the ground. A pork butcher named Joseph Pacaud was suspected of having committed the murder, which was eerily reminiscent of the Jack the Ripper murders of three years before.*

This particular murder may or may not have been a medical maniac attempting to create the elixir of life, but the point is, few today knew about this murder. There may have been other unknown French Ripper-like murders that did involve an elixir of life agenda.

Interestingly, there is a report of Francis Tumblety planning to travel to Europe, including France, after his London stay:

*Buffalo Courier, December 7, 1888*
*About the only talk that I had with him [Tumblety] was to ask where he was stopping, and he simply replied that he should spend the winter in southern France or Italy, and thought that he should probably go to Monte Carlo.*

Tumblety never made the European excursion to southern France, although he did make his way to the port city of Le Havre on his way back to back to New York after jumping bail. Interestingly, Tumblety seems never to have left the United States after this abrupt return.

# 10

# CONCLUSION AND COINCIDENCES

Francis Tumblety purposely hid his decades-long habit of frequenting the slums of large cities and seeking the company of young males; this was never to be written in his autobiographical pamphlets. Because his secret side was not well documented, any evidentiary evaluation of him would naturally lead to a biased perception. Additionally, if Scotland Yard was indeed suppressing the facts surrounding their investigation of Tumblety in the Whitechapel case, this would further bias conclusions. From a historical perspective when dealing with limited evidence, coincidences and correlations can play a role in discovering the truth, and in the case of Tumblety, the number of coincidences is extraordinary.

The trail of evidence connecting the very first news cable report of Francis Tumblety being implicated in the Whitechapel murders—the November 17, 1888, *New York World* London dispatch—with their European correspondent E. Tracy Greaves, demonstrates that his news source was the same organization that arrested Tumblety in the first place: Scotland Yard. Additionally, the story could not have come from Tumblety himself spinning a lie to the reporter since the exclusive came after Tumblety posted bail. Both of these realities confirm that Tumblety was indeed arrested on suspicion. Further reinforcing this were the corroborative investigations made by competing US newspapers, the Associated Press, and the London press.

Once Scotland Yard received word that their officers had arrested a New Yorker named Dr. Tumblety, they searched their files on him and found that he had an "extensive dossier" filled with his past run-ins with the law in England. The information it contained caused them to take seriously the possibility that Tumblety was Jack the Ripper. Knowing they had nothing on him for the Whitechapel crimes, they had to release him, but an incriminating correspondence found on his person offered them the opportunity to eventually re-arrest him on the misdemeanor charge of gross indecency and indecent assault. Corroborating this chain of events surrounding the arrest and re-arrest of Francis Tumblety, as spelled out in US newspaper reports, was the fact that three Scotland Yard officials commented upon him as a Ripper suspect *after* he was committed to Central Criminal Court for the misdemeanor case. Head of the Whitechapel investigation, Assistant Commissioner Robert Anderson, sent private cable communications to US chiefs of police requesting information on Ripper suspect Francis Tumblety. Chief Inspector Littlechild wrote a private letter to famed London journalist George R. Sims in 1913 stating Tumblety was "amongst the suspects." Lastly, weeks after Tumblety had escaped back to New York, Scotland Yard Inspector Walter Andrews commented to a Toronto reporter that we—meaning Scotland Yard—still wanted to interview Francis Tumblety about the Whitechapel murder case.

On December 1, 1888, the day before Tumblety pulled into New York Harbor after jumping bail in London, New York City lawyer Colonel Charles Dunham claimed to a *New York World* reporter that in Washington DC in 1861, he witnessed Tumblety illustrating a medical lecture with his anatomical collection, specifically, numerous favored uterus specimens. Colonel Dunham claimed that many of General McClellan's officers were also invited to the lecture. The importance of this is that Jack the Ripper harvested the uterus organs from two of his victims. Coincidentally, near the same time as Tumblety's lecture in the capital, a *Vanity Fair* reporter complained of Tumblety displaying images of anatomical specimens just outside his New York office, before he left for Washington DC. Just months after Tumblety completed his two year sojourn in the capital, it was reported in the *Buffalo Courier* that Tumblety was giving medical lectures.

Suspicion at Scotland Yard about Tumblety being Jack the Ripper ended when prostitutes were murdered in Whitechapel after he had jumped bail and fled to the United States. Most experts today agree, though, that these particular victims were not murdered by Jack the Ripper; these later murders are not included in the canonical five.

Just months before the murders began, Francis Tumblety told a *Toronto Mail* reporter that he was suffering from kidney and heart disease, and that he was constantly in dread of sudden death. This certainly sounds like the comment of a desperate man. He himself stated that his health began to deteriorate years earlier and was always in search of an elixir of health from the botanical world. Coincidentally, personalities in England and

Europe were searching for the elixir of life, just as coincidental as Tumblety then traveling to London and planning on traveling to France and Italy afterward.

Semiretired Tumblety resided on the wealthy West End of London, had ample time on his hands, and he enjoyed the theater, as evidenced by his history with actor John Wilkes Booth. The following was in the *Buffalo Courier*, May 31, 1914:

*Friend of Surrat's.*

   *Tom Kean, the notable critic of The Courier and regarded at that time by professional people as the best in the country, said—'. . . Booth made a very singular acquaintance while in Buffalo [August 1863]. In fact quite an intimacy sprang up between him and Dr. Tumblety—or Tumulty. He drove around selling cure-alls for everything, giving lectures with Thespian emphasis. He frequently located himself on the Terrace, where he would draw a big crowd by distributing bags of flour. He was particularly susceptible to the allurements of the theatrical profession. He sought Booth and they were seen together treating each other with familiarity . . .'*

In the *New York World*, December 5, 1888, Martin H. McGarry admitted to being a young traveling companion hired by Tumblety. He stated:

'He took a liking to me, and that day I was employed by him. My duties were not hard. I was always to be near him. He got up at 11 o'clock when he would usually send out his jug for a pint of old ale. He breakfasted in the house and then walked around town. Usually he went up to the Morton House, where he pointed out the actors to me and told me who they were and what they did. Sometimes in the afternoons we would drop in to the matinees.'

Tumblety clearly had a taste for the theater, and the top theater in London was the Lyceum Theatre. His comment about the Lyceum's private Beefsteak Club is a testament to him having knowledge of the theater. How coincidental that those who worked at this theater were members of the Order of the Golden Dawn, whose goal was to discover the elixir of life. How coincidental that the business manager of the Lyceum Theatre was Bram Stoker, close friend to Tumblety's old boyfriend, Henry Hall Caine. How coincidental that the proprietor of the Lyceum Theatre was the famous actor Henry Irving, a man who was a member of the Masonic Order, whose other members were eminent engineers. How coincidental that it was an eminent engineer who approached Scotland Yard about a medical maniac searching for the elixir of life, mixing ingredients from the botanical world with ingredients found inside the female gender—the same ingredients Francis Tumblety was claimed to have collected years earlier.

Continuing with the series of coincidences, the day before the Martha Tabram murder in early August, Mansfield's *Dr. Jekyll and Mr. Hyde* played at the very same Lyceum Theatre, the character Dr. Jekyll developing a formula he believed to answer one of life's greatest mysteries. The theory brought to Scotland Yard was one of a number of Jekyll and Hyde-Ripper theories, an eminent physician by day and a medical maniac murdering women by night. If desperate Francis Tumblety was the medical maniac the eminent engineer heard about, regardless if he was indeed the killer, did this show give him the idea of mixing a botanical concoction with fluids from the uterus where life is created?

Curiously, there were three different organs taken from the Whitechapel murder victims: the uterus, the kidney, and lastly, the heart. All three connect Francis Tumblety with the elixir via his uterus collection and his progressive kidney and heart disease.

Tussauds Chamber of Horrors was showcased in the same British paper as Mansfield's *Jekyll and Hyde*, demonstrating that this popular haunt may have been visited by Tumblety, especially since he likely enjoyed popular anatomical museums in New York, which were reported to have displayed wax models of murderers. In the Chamber of Horrors was the execution of the resurrectionists, Burke and Hare. How intriguing that this could have given him the idea to harvest ingredients from women. Recall that in 1907 George R. Sims referred in the *Sunday Referee* to a particular theory he received from Scotland Yard officials; note his comment about having some curious information:

*The other theory in support of which I have some curious information, puts the crime down to a young American medical student who was in London during the whole time of the murders, and who, according to statements of certain highly-respectable people who knew him, made on two occasions an endeavour to obtain a certain internal organ, which for his purpose had to be removed from, as he put it, 'the almost living body.'*

*Dr. Wynne Baxter, the coroner, in his summing up to the jury in the case of Annie Chapman, pointed out the significance of the fact that this internal organ had been removed.*

*But against this theory put forward by those who uphold it with remarkable details and some startling evidence in support of their contention, there is this one great fact. The American was alive and well and leading the life of an ordinary citizen long after the Ripper murders came to an end.*

As explained earlier, the papers clarified that the American medical student was actually an established and eminent physician from Philadelphia, yet Sims—a man who was a journalist in London at the time of the murder—ignores this. With this mix-up in stories twenty years later, Sims may also have been a referring to the elixir of life theory Scotland Yard investigated, especially when he stated, "the almost living body." Tumblety certainly was an American who was leading a life of an ordinary citizen after the Ripper murders. Sims' statement, "was leading a life," suggests the person was no longer alive at the time of this article, and Tumblety certainly did pass away four years earlier.

If Tumblety was inspired by the Burke and Hare effigy in Tussauds, and if he found it difficult to obtain internal organs from an almost living female body through purchasing them, Whitechapel prostitutes would have been the perfect donors. These women were not only forgotten human beings, likely not important enough to initiate an expensive investigation, but Tumblety also had an unusual hatred for them, considering them cattle—just another animal bred for mutilation.

Continuing further with coincidences, as he visited Tussauds Chamber of Horrors he would also have gazed upon the wax presentment of Henri Pranzini's execution and the story of how he murdered three women in Paris, Ripper-style: deep cut to the neck and abdominal mutilations. How intriguing that this wax display may have given the killer the idea of *how* to mutilate his victims. Recall that the very first of the canonical five victims, murdered Pranzini-style, was just yards away from Whitechapel's chamber of horrors and their own presentment of the Pranzini execution.

Recall that immediately after Polly Nichols, the first of the canonical five victims, the proprietor of the Whitechapel chamber of horrors wax museum put on display inside Jack the Ripper's hunting grounds wax effigies of the mutilated bodies of both Tabram and Nichols. With hundreds of patrons visiting the display each night, it should not be a surprise that the museum was visited by the killer himself, revisiting his bloodthirsty agenda along with horrified visitors. How intriguing the possibility that the display further incited his murder spree.

How coincidental that the last of the canonical five murders, Mary Kelly, was displayed almost identically to the Anatomical Venus, and how coincidental that the Venus was showcased in the popular anatomical museums where Tumblety lived in New York City and that they were destroyed in the same year as the Whitechapel murders. With the mutilation and position of Mary Kelly's body in her bed being nearly identical to the Anatomical Venus display, their connection would not at all be implausible, especially in the case of misogynist Francis Tumblety. The Anatomical Venus exhibited the seductive nude pose, lying in a bed and staring at the viewer, which was a recreation of the famous paintings of the reclining Venus. Venus was the goddess of physical love, the uniter of men and women through sexual passion. Tumblety blamed women, especially fallen women, for decoying young men away from their intended lovers: older men. He hated all that the erotic reclining Venus stood for, but the Anatomical Venus on the other hand depicted the goddess eviscerated, in the throes of death. Tumblety would have liked nothing more than to see the divine power of heterosexual love eliminated.

The haunts likely visited by Francis Tumblety—professional anatomical museums, such as the London Hospital's anatomical and pathological museum; popular anatomical museums in the Bowery District of New York; Tussauds' and Whitechapel's chamber of horrors wax museums; and the theaters, specifically, the Lyceum Theater—fit a pattern of coincidences that suggest he may have been involved in the Whitechapel murders. Although we cannot say for sure if Francis Tumblety was Jack the Ripper, Scotland Yard suspecting him based upon evidence they acquired, his actions conforming quite well into three of the FBI serial offender motives, and this pattern in his haunts, the theory certainly does seem convincing.

A question amongst Ripperologists has been, "Why were there no murders in the month of October 1888?" As demonstrated, there is evidence that Francis Tumblety was arrested on suspicion for the Whitechapel crimes just after midnight, October 1, 1888, the day after the Double Event murders. If Tumblety was Jack the Ripper, he would have immediately realized he was now on Scotland Yard's radar screen. Modern experts agree that psychopathic serial offenders can be quite intelligent, and the very bright Dr. Francis Tumblety would have postponed any murderous agenda in order to avoid getting caught. Once Tumblety was arrested for gross indecency and indecent assault on November 7, 1888, likely shocking this aggressive narcissist and infuriating him, this may have triggered his anger-retaliatory behavior. Mary Kelly was murdered on November 9, 1888, explained by modern experts as an anger-retaliatory murder.

After posting bail on November 16, 1888, he was released from incarceration, but he had no intentions of making his court date in early December. He jumped bail and sneaked out of the country, a practice he was very experienced at. Interestingly, his usual point of departure from and entry into England was on the West Coast in Liverpool, where his sister lived, but instead, he stealthily made his way easterly to Folkestone Harbour and crossed the English Channel to France. On November 24, 1888, he boarded the transatlantic vessel, *La Bretagne*, in Le Havre under the alias Frank Townsend, en route to New York Harbor, where he landed on December 2.

Once he arrived in New York, Tumblety was met at the pier by New York City detectives. Because his official charge in England was for misdemeanor crimes, Scotland Yard had no authority to extradite him back to England, thus, the detectives had no grounds to make an arrest. New York City Superintendent Byrnes purposely made this clear to the press. Tumblety then made a quick exit and spent the next month keeping a low profile. Even so, both Scotland Yard and the New York Detective Division attempted to keep an eye on him.

Although Tumblety consistently visited Toronto up until 1888, he never stepped foot on Canadian soil again. He knew perfectly well that England had extradition authority in Canada. Even though he traveled within the United States, he maintained his residence in New York, finding himself in front of a New York City judge on two separate occasions for the usual homosexual encounters with young men. He was even arrested in Washington DC in 1890 for similar circumstances.

Because of his kidney and heart condition, he took periodic travels to Hot Springs, Arkansas, where on April 21, 1891, his room at the Plateau Hotel was burglarized, losing thousands of dollars in cash and diamonds. There is no evidence that he stayed in Hot Springs, now penniless after losing all his money and valuables. Curiously, New York City prostitute Carrie Brown was murdered Ripper-style in the slums on April 24, less than a mile away from his New York residence. Although, there were suspects, it remains unsolved to this day. Researchers rejecting the claim that Brown was a victim of Jack the Ripper focus upon certain dissimilarities to the Whitechapel victims and crime scenes, yet no two London cases were alike. If Tumblety did find himself penniless in Hot Springs on April 21, his New York residence was only a day's train ride away.

Tumblety continued to travel for the next decade, finding himself in slums of many of the major cities, such as New Orleans. He no longer worked and seemed to prefer evenings in the slums. From 1899 to 1902, he spent much of his time in Baltimore. In 1903, he took one last trip to Hot Springs, Arkansas, but went immediately to St. Louis to St. John's Hospital for the purpose of dying. Note the following newspaper report:

*St Louis Republic, 29 May 1903*
*Leaving an estate estimated to exceed $100,000, Doctor Francis Tumblety, 82 years old, died at St John's Hospital yesterday afternoon without a relative or intimate friend at his bedside. Legacies of $10,000 each to Cardinal Gibbons and Archbishop Ireland for charitable purposes were among his bequests. Coming to St Louis under an assumed name, Doctor Tumblety, as he expressed it to the attendants of the hospital, 'selected St John's as a convenient place to die.' For some time he had been suffering from valvular disease of the heart, and after a stay at Hot Springs, Ark., he decided to come to St Louis and prepare for the end, having amassed a large fortune as an advertising physician, forty or fifty years ago, when that life of medical practice was rare, Doctor Tumblety has in later years travelled about the world. He was unmarried, and as he aged he developed a reticence about himself and his affairs that almost amounted to a mania.*

*Introducing himself as 'Mr. Townsend,' he engaged a room at St John's Hospital on April 26. Gradually the malady from which he was suffering developed to a serious stage and calling for a lawyer, Doctor Tumblety made known his identity. Even within the shadow of death he exacted from the lawyer, and the Catholic priest whom he called to administer to his spiritual welfare, a promise of secrecy. Of his past life he would not speak except in a general way and it was only through his will that his wealth was made known to those who cared for him. Although he realized that the end was near, Doctor Tumblety insisted upon going about whenever his condition would allow. Monday last he requested to be dressed, saying that he wished to take a walk. An attendant was assigned to assist him, but the doctor wished to be left alone. After walking about the street for some time he returned to the hospital and sat on the steps of the building. While sitting there he went to sleep and fell forward on his face, breaking his nose and sustaining a shock from which he never recovered . . .*

Even the end of Tumblety's own life has coincidences connected to the Whitechapel crimes. When he entered St. John's Hospital for the purpose of dying, instead of giving his real name, he gave an alias, the same alias he used escaping England in 1888—Frank Townsend. Those were the only two recorded incidents where he used that particular alias. Found within his personal possessions were the usual set of diamonds and jewelry he always had on him, likely purchased after he was robbed of his original precious travel companions in 1891. Included were two cheap rings, arguably similar to those stolen off of Annie Chapman by Jack the Ripper.

According to the FBI, a major misconception about serial offenders is that all serial killers continue to kill. Continuing to murder is motive-specific. Many sadistic serial killers, such as Jeffrey Dahmer, do indeed continue to murder due to an impulsive sexual desire. Still, sadistic serial killers have been known to stop. Once caught, it was revealed that these serial offenders who stopped continued to have a sexual impulse but channeled the drive through other sexual avenues. Even so, if Francis Tumblety was Jack the Ripper, his motive was not sadistic, but anger-retaliatory against females with an additional possible motive of personal gain, i.e., harvesting organs for the creation of an elixir. His reported fear of sudden death from kidney and heart disease in early 1888 paints a picture of a desperate man willing to try anything to survive, such as the creation of an elixir. Recall, he himself wrote in his autobiographical pamphlets about the probability of an elixir to cure all ills. Forensic scientist and criminal profiler Brent Turvey concluded that Jack the Ripper was an extreme misogynist exhibiting psychopathic behavior with anger-retaliatory and reassurance-oriented motives. This is classic narcissist Francis Tumblety with the inability to feel remorse.

One of the foremost modern day researchers of the Whitechapel mystery, Stewart Evans, stated that we will never know, conclusively, who Jack the Ripper was. Even if someone found an old confession letter tucked away in some descendant's attic, we'd merely add it to a list of other claimed confessions. The Whitechapel murder file is classified, which prompted theories of a royal conspiracy, but Evans explained a perfectly valid reason for "the Special Branch file being closed, or lost, to this day. Actions of an ancestor resulting in arrest or police action against terrorist suspects could mean that reprisals may be taken against descendants in order to show that the criminals have a long memory which can reach beyond the grave for revenge," or words to that effect. In view of this, modern researchers have only a limited amount of evidence to work with. This invariably leads to multiple plausible theories, all fitting the preponderance of the evidence. Any new information involving the Whitechapel murder mystery, as in the contents of the preceding chapters, must be added to the pool of reliable knowledge in order for the experts to gain a truer picture. Dr. Francis Tumblety may not have been Jack the Ripper, but explaining away the facts and coincidences presented here with a cogent explanation would be a monumental task.

# APPENDIX

## JOTTINGS OF A RIPPEROLOGIST

Although the following two published research articles are not directly related to Tumblety's haunts, they do involve Francis Tumblety and the Whitechapel investigation. [These articles appear in their original published format; they have not been re-edited before being printed in this book.]

### Article One: Tumblety's Rings

Two days after Scotland Yard Assistant Commissioner CID Robert Anderson personally cabled Brooklyn's Chief of Police Patrick Campbell about Whitechapel murder suspect Francis Tumblety on November 22, 1888, Tumblety had successfully made his escape out of England. He did not use his usual port of entry and exit at Liverpool on the west coast where his niece lived, but he unexpectedly took the back way on the east coast across the English Channel to La Havre, France, and boarded the transatlantic steamship *La Bretagne*. When he arrived on the New York docks on December 2nd wearing a long English cloth ulster and a derby hat, he had with him only an umbrella, two canes tied together, and a "small steamer trunk," most likely leaving behind many personal items in order to make a quick and quiet exit. What he did not leave behind, and regularly kept on his person, were his usual pair of large diamond rings and his gold watch. During the later years of Tumblety's life, he rarely travelled without having in his pockets his complement of jewelry, cash, and a few letters from important people attesting to his character and social class. Upon his death fifteen years later in St. Louis, Missouri, at St. John's Hospital, an inventory of his personal possessions revealed his usual jewelry/cash travel companions, but two other items were also cataloged that had never been associated with Francis Tumblety before; a set of relatively inexpensive imitation rings. In 1903, Scotland Yard no longer had any interest in Francis Tumblety and this fact went unnoticed until nearly a century later when Stewart Evans had rediscovered this Ripper suspect in the

163

early 1990s. It was soon realized that Ripper victim Annie Chapman had similar rings stolen off her body by the killer, thus, the connection was made. Could Tumblety's two imitation rings be the same rings as Annie Chapman's? Arguments for and against were made within the Ripperology community and the latter eventually won the day, and the issue seems to have been settled. Thanks to a number of new discoveries pertinent to this issue, it is now prudent to re-examine these arguments, opening up the possibility that it was premature to reject the idea of Tumblety possessing Chapman's rings *for these reasons.*

A number of the most persuasive arguments against the idea of Tumblety possessing Chapman's rings center mainly upon differences in assessed values between the two sets. Research on Francis Tumblety's rings and their assessed 1903 value was accomplished by Tim Riordan. On April 26, 1903, Francis Tumblety checked into St. Johns Hospital in St. Louis, Missouri, *incognito,* under the alias Frank Townsend, for the purpose of dying, which occurred one month later. Once he desired to make out a final will and testament, it required him to finally reveal his true identity, but he then requested that no family members be informed and be at his side. The state of Missouri required that if no family members were available to take charge of a deceased's assets and personal items, a public administrator assumed that role. In 1903 Gerrard Strode was the public administrator for St. Louis and he ensured that Tumblety's estate was handled properly. Specific to the rings, Strode assigned a group of three people to arrange the inventory of Tumblety's possessions. Riordan states:

> *To do so, he [Strode] had to get three 'disinterested householders' to view the goods and provide a monetary value for them. There was no set procedure for selecting these men nor any information on their knowledge of what they were valuing. Arthur Marshall was a law clerk and had been a collector in the assessor's office. Strode had also been in that office and may have known him. A second man, Samuel H. Batavia, seems to have left no record of himself. These two names were filled out on the form before the inventory and they may have accompanied Strode to the hospital. The final man, A.B. Walker, was a retired school janitor and may have been associated with the hospital. While he signed the form, his name is not listed in other parts. None of these men can be shown to have any*

*experience in valuing jewelry nor is there any indication
how they came to the assigned values.*

Riordan then published the results of the personal inventory
and their conclusion to the assessed values of the jewelry:

The personal possessions that these men viewed were few:

- One cluster ring of 17 diamond stones, $75.00
- One five stone diamond ring, $60.00
- Two imitation set rings, $3.00
- One old gold watch, $10.00.

Note that Riordan's presentation of the three responsible for
assessing the monetary value of Tumblety's jewelry items casts
doubt upon its credibility. First, the one and only requirement for
viewing the personal goods and assigning a monetary value was
that the three assigned to this task be merely "disinterested
householders." This might effectively eliminate bias or favoritism,
but it gives no assistance to obtaining an accurate monetary
assessment. The three questionable householders selected by
Strode certainly support this point. Marshall was only a law clerk
in the office likely having no background in jewelry, Batavia was
an unknown, and Walker was a retired janitor.

Another argument forwarded by Riordan suggests that since
the diamond rings were so undervalued as compared to previous
assessments of Tumblety's diamond rings—from thousands of
dollars to hundreds of dollars—that the $3.00 value for the
imitation rings is correspondingly drastically undervalued:

The value of the jewelry is considerably less than reported
at other times but there is no way to know if those were
inflated values or if these are deflated. When arrested in
Washington, 13 years before this, Tumblety had on two
diamond rings, each valued at $2,500, as well as a smaller
ring worth $200. In certain circles, a great deal had been
made of the two imitation set rings which have been
suggested as 'trophies' taken from one of the Ripper
victims. As Tumblety was known to wear many rings and
the inventory seems to undervalue these, it is more likely
that they were part of his own adornment . . .

Riordan confirms his undervaluing/credibility arguments about the 1903 St. Louis inventory assessment in a comment on Casebook.org on February 18, 2009. Riordan stated: "Tumblety's jewelry was seriously undervalued by the public administrator of St. Louis. There were some strange problems with the assessment, including enlisting the janitor of the hospital as one of the assessors . . ."

Besides Riordan's arguments, another persuasive argument negating the possibility of Tumblety's rings matching the Ripper victim's rings states that $3.00 for any kind of ring during the Victorian Era is not cheap and would have been out of the price range for an unfortunate like Annie Chapman. Wolf Vanderlinden used this argument on the same Casebook thread on February 18, 2009: "The two 'cheap' brass rings found among his possessions are a bit of a non-starter. They were appraised at being worth $3 so they were hardly 'cheap' for their time and were probably more expensive than Annie Chapman could afford (or afford to keep without hocking)."

These arguments have been very convincing to the Ripper research community as evidenced by very little discussion about this issue since, but additional evidence has come to light, which may alter this perception. First to evaluate is the "credibility of the 1903 assessors" argument. Note what the Missouri Association of Public Administrators states: "Public Administrators serve as court appointed Personal Representatives in decedent's estates, and as guardians and/or conservators for individuals who are unable to care for themselves or their property when there is no one else to serve."

The fact that public administrators are court appointed means the results of their assessments are legal issues and might be argued in probate court. Even though the only mandate for assigning someone to personally handle and assign monetary values to personal items was that they be "disinterested householders," the public administrator—Gerrard Strode in Tumblety's case—was still ultimately responsible for the accuracy of the results. With competing arguments on both sides of any case, accuracy and verifiability in jewelry assessment values is critical. Assigning Arthur Marshall, the first householder, with his experience as a legal clerk in the Public Administration office now makes perfect sense, especially when the Tumblety case actually did make its way into court.

Riordan then dismisses the second householder, Samuel H. Batavia, as insignificant since there is no record of him. Record of him has now been discovered and even his occupation. Note the following October 29, 1902, *St. Louis Republic* article:

*Tale of Treasure Secreted in Tarrieu Homestead To Be Told in Court Since Old House is Dismantled. Heirs of Mrs. Frances Roberts Seek to Recover Hidden Treasure.*

*In the walls of the old Larrieu residence Mrs. Roberts is supposed to have secreted $4,000 years ago. The building was recently demolished by William Lohrengel who discovered some of the money, which he says, 'has been chewed up by rats.'*

*What has become of $4,000 in gold, Mexican dollars and currency which Mrs. Frances Roberts is said to have secreted in the old Larrieu homestead at No. 6715 Water street at a time when the presence of Indians in that neighborhood made her cautious? Is a question that will be asked in the courts.*

*William Lohrengel, a contractor and builder living at No. 6714 Pennsylvania, who was arrested Monday on a warrant sworn out by Samuel H. Batavia of the Public Administrator's office charging that he found the treasure and failed to turn it over to Mrs. Roberts's heirs, will sue Mr. Batavia for damages . . .*

It seems that Samuel H. Batavia had enough experience and credibility that Gerrard Strode trusted him with swearing out warrants, an action which could ultimately be on the other end of a lawsuit, as in this case. This certainly suggests that Batavia was up to the task of properly handling Tumblety's personal items.

Riordan then claims that the third householder, A.B. Walker, was just a retired janitor. A search for all "A.B. Walkers" living in St. Louis, Missouri, around the time of Tumblety's death did not reveal a retired janitor, but it did reveal a person involved in St. Louis hospitals (such as the hospital Francis Tumblety died in) who had experience in handling documents, and personnel and administrative issues. Near the same time as Tumblety's death in St. Louis, an "A.B. Walker" held the position as a hospital clerk and chief clerk,

*Annual report of the Health Commissioner for the year ending . . . Volumes 5-6*
*St. Louis City Hospital year ending 1873,*

> *A.B. Walker, Clerk*
> *Mayor's Message, St. Louis, MO, to the Municipal Assembly of the City of St. Louis, for the Fiscal Year Ending April 12th, 1897*
> *City Hospital—Miscellaneous.*
> *A.B. Walker, Chief Clerk (temporary)*

Notice that the "A.B. Walker" registered in health commissioner's report and the mayor's message not only lived in St. Louis, Missouri, just as the "disinterested householder" did, but he also lived there at the same time, was involved with St. Louis hospitals, and had his first and middle name published in initial form as "A.B." Chances are this A.B. Walker and the disinterested householder involved with Tumblety's possessions were the same person. Thus, it is perfectly plausible and appropriate for a hospital clerk to be selected by the public administrator, especially if he worked in the same St. Louis hospital that Tumblety died in.

In view of the above series of revelations, the "disinterested householders" were actually well qualified for the task of completing an inventory of Tumblety's jewelry. How about being credible in assessing the value of the jewelry? Since the assessment was still the responsibility of the public administrator *and* the results were intended to be used in court, thus crucial to be accurate, how difficult would it have been for one of the "disinterested householders" to suggest taking the jewelry to a local jeweler for a qualified opinion?

Next to evaluate is the "undervaluing" argument. Riordan points out that the 1903 public administrator value assessment of the diamond rings were only in the hundreds of dollars, while all other value assessments of Tumblety's diamond rings were ten-fold greater, in the thousands of dollars. His unquestioned assumption is that the thousand dollars assessments were the correct assessments. Is he correct? We need to take a closer look at the thousand dollar assessments, beginning with the assessment Riordan himself referred to in *Prince of Quacks*. Riordan states that when Tumblety was arrested in Washington DC thirteen years before this, he had on two diamond rings, each valued at $2,500, as well as a smaller ring worth $200. The following is the *Washington Post*, November 18, 1890, newspaper report Riordan references:

*DR. TUMBLETY IN TOWN*
*At the station the doctor was searched, and an*
*unexpectedly large number of valuables were secured from*
*him, amounting in worth to several thousand dollars. There*
*were $250 in greenbacks, a check for $160, and two*
*magnificent diamond rings, each worth, he claims, about*
*$2,500. The brilliant glitter of the diamonds dazzled the*
*eyes of the officers. The doctor also had a gold watch and a*
*ring of rubies, set with small diamonds, worth about $200.*

Note that the person who assessed Tumblety's jewelry in this
article was Francis Tumblety himself. Riordan is suggesting we
trust Tumblety's value assessment of his jewelry over the
assessment of the St. Louis public administrator's office. Since
Tumblety would have every reason to inflate the assessed values,
it certainly casts a new light upon why the public administrator's
office requires "disinterested householders" to obtain the
monetary values of personal jewelry possibly being contested in
probate court.
The following are a majority of the sources for Tumblety's
diamond rings being assessed in the thousands of dollars or of
extreme value:

*Daily Picayune, March 25,1881, DR. FRANCIS TUMBLETY*
*He was lodged in the Third Station, where he gave his*
*name as Dr. Francis Tumblety. On his person, were found*
*two extremely valuable solitaire diamond rings, two cluster*
*diamond rings, a large amount of money, stocks and bonds,*
*and a magnificent gold chain and a small gold watch.*

*Arkansas Gazette, Little Rock, Arkansas, 19 April 1891,*
*COUPLE OF BURGLARIES*
*HOT SPRINGS, April 18. Thieves went through the Plateau*
*Hotel last night, securing about $8,000 in money and*
*diamonds, Judge A.M. Duffie, of this city, and that well-known*
*mysterious individual, Dr. Frank Francis Tumblety, being the*
*victims. The thieves secured a gold watch and a considerable*
*sum of money from Judge Duffie, and $2,000 in cash and*
*diamonds valued between $5,000 and $7,000 from Dr.*
*Tumblety. It was well known that Dr. Tumblety had the money*
*and valuables and carried them on his person, besides*
*valuable papers. No clue to the identity of the thieves.*

*Oakland Daily Evening Tribune, 8 December 1890, JACK THE RIPPER, HISTORY OF FAMOUS DR. TUMBLETY*

*. . . This description is that of the arrested man, except that now Tumblety's hair is gray and he dyes his moustache to make it black. When arrested at Scotland Yard Tumblety had two or three thousand dollars worth of diamonds and jewelry in his possession.*

*The New York World, January 29, 1889*

*The doctor produced from an inside pocket two magnificent diamonds, one thirteen carats and the other nine carats, both of the purest quality, and a superb cluster ring set in diamonds. He said that, in his opinion, his arrest was due, in a measure, to the police desiring his diamonds and thinking they could force him to give them up.*

In each of the above cases, valuing Tumblety's diamonds in the thousands of dollars most likely did not come from a qualified diamond assessor or even a jeweler. In the case of Tumblety's diamonds supposedly being stolen by thieves, how do we know his diamonds were stolen in the first place? Clearly, Tumblety himself had to have reported this to the authorities, since the diamonds were nowhere in Tumblety's room for the authorities to discover. Tumblety then would have been the source for claiming that the diamonds were valued between $5,000 and $7,000.

How did *The New York World* reporter who gave Tumblety his interview in late January 1889 know that the two diamonds Tumblety pulled out of his pocket were thirteen and nine carats, respectively? The source had to have been Tumblety, especially since the article was put in print so quickly, giving very little time to escort Tumblety to the nearest jeweler in order to receive an accurate assessment.

An argument can now be made that the diamond rings that Francis Tumblety carried around with him for so many years were actually valued in the hundreds of dollars and not in the thousands. So, if it is true that Tumblety's diamonds were correctly valued in the hundreds of dollars, would they have even been diamonds? The answer is most likely, yes. First, the Public Administrator report did not state 'imitation diamond rings', and it certainly mentioned the two set rings as imitation, thus, they understood the classification of imitation jewelry. Second, large diamonds actually were and are valued at various amounts. Note what is stated in *The Practice of Banking* (1883): "The yellow diamond is largely obtained in South Africa, and is of considerably less value than the white diamond . . ." But, the *New York World* reporter claimed the diamonds were of the purest quality. Albeit, a reporter is not qualified to assess the value of diamonds, maybe they did not have a yellow hue to them. Note what *The Law Practice of Banking* was concerned about in 1883:

> The yellow diamond is largely obtained in South Africa, and is of considerably less value than the white diamond, but by introducing the former into a dye of aniline violet (yellow mixed with violet light producing white light) it assumes all the appearance and brilliancy of the latter, as was found to the cost of some diamond merchants who have been recently imposed upon by the trick. A little rubbing with soap and water removed the violet, and the yellow re-appears.

In the Victorian Era, there was a common enough practice of faking the value of diamonds that diamond merchants and jewelers had to be aware of it. The following 1882 newspaper source even explains how this fakery practice can make diamonds valued in the hundreds look as if the were white diamonds valued in the thousands:

> *Lancaster Daily Intelligencer, November 24, 1882,*
> *DIAMONDS, N.Y. Times.*
> *Some very interesting and important experiments with diamonds have lately been made at the Paris Academy of Sciences. An experienced diamond merchant bought not long ago, a fine white diamond for $4,600. One morning he gave it a good washing with soap and water, when what was his consternation to find that it had turned yellow, which sent its value down to $800. The matter was brought to the attention of the academy, and experts submitted a report, which showed that diamond whitening is a fraud easy to accomplish and as easy to detect. By plunging a yellow diamond into an aniline violet dye it becomes white, while at the same time it loses neither its transparency nor brilliancy. In fact, on making the experiment, the experts had in a few minutes transformed several yellow stones into a fivefold value. Take a yellow diamond dip it even into no stronger dye than violet ink, wash it with water to remove*

*any discoloration, and the effect is immediate. The dried*
*diamond remains white . . .*

It would not be a surprise to many that Francis Tumblety
might resort to trickery, such as faking the quality of his large
diamonds. Even though he was wealthy, he was also known for
being very cheap.

Interestingly, the discovery and sale of South African
diamonds mentioned in *The Practice of Banking*, which allowed
the middle class to afford them, occurred in the early 1870s. The
first time Francis Tumblety was reported to possess large
diamonds was in the above March 25, 1881 *Daily Picayune*
article, conforming to the possibility that Francis Tumblety
purchased large South African diamonds valued in the hundreds
of dollars.

Next to examine is the argument stating that $3.00 for
imitation rings are out of the price range for Annie Chapman.
First, note how the 1903 monetary assessment stated the
imitation set rings as compared to the other jewelry:

- One cluster ring of 17 diamond stones, $75.00
- One five stone diamond ring, $60.00
- Two imitation set rings, $3.00
- One old gold watch, $10.00.

It does not say that the two imitation set rings are valued at
"$3.00 apiece," but it only says "$3.00." This could just as easily,
if not more appropriately, mean that both rings added up total a
value of $3.00, and each ring would be worth approximately $1.50
apiece.

Also, missing from these arguments is a detailed account of
Annie Chapman's imitation rings, other than the assumption that
they were imitation rings so cheap that an unfortunate would not
hock them for cash. In order to properly compare the imitation
rings Francis Tumblety owned in 1903 with the imitation rings
stolen off of Annie Chapman's body in September 1888, we will
also need to examine the evidence specific to the physical features
of Annie Chapman's stolen rings. Jane Coram, in her article,
*Doing 'Write' by Annie – A Closer Look at Annie Chapman's Murder*,
she goes into detail about Chapman's rings. She states:

*Edward Stanley, also known as 'The Pensioner,' was a very*
*close friend of Annie's; in fact she shared a bed with him*

*some of the time, although it seems as if Edward had the odd dalliance with Annie's friend Eliza as well. He was, however, in as good a position as any to describe the rings that Annie wore. At the inquest he was quizzed about them by the coroner and his reply was quite illuminating.*

*Q. Coroner: When did you last see her (Annie) alive?*

*A. Stanley: On Sunday, Sept. 2nd, between one and three o'clock in the afternoon.*

*Q. Coroner: Was she wearing rings when you saw her?*

*A. Stanley: Yes, I believe two. I could not say on which finger, but they were on one of her fingers.*

*Q. Coroner: What sort of rings were they—what was the metal?*

*A. Stanley: Brass, I should think by the look of them.'*

The Coroner mentioned additional details in his summary report:

There are two things missing. Her rings had been wrenched from her fingers and have not been found, and the uterus has been removed. There was an abrasion over the bend of the first joint of the ring finger, and there were distinct markings of a ring or rings—probably the latter. If the object were robbery, these injuries were meaningless, for death had previously resulted from the loss of blood at the neck. Moreover, when we find an easily accomplished theft of some paltry brass rings and such an operation, after, at least, a quarter of an hour's work, and by a skilled person, we are driven to the deduction that the mutilation was the object, and the theft of the rings was only a thin-veiled blind, an attempt to prevent the real intention being discovered.

Coram then discusses a report from the Metropolitan Police specific to the value of Chapman's rings:

A Metropolitan Police Criminal Investigation Department report made on the 19th Sept 1888 (52983)16 does help to determine whether or not the rings appeared to be valuable or not: 'The deceased was in the habit of wearing two brass rings [a wedding ring and a keeper] these were missing when the body was found and the finger bore marks of their having been removed by force. Special enquiries have been made at all places where they may have been offered for pledge or for sale by a person believing them to be gold, but nothing has resulted there from'.

In the *The Scotsman*, November 10, 1888, an article titled, *Another Atrocious Murder in London Shocking Mutilation of a Woman in Whitechapel Details of the Crime*, gives additional details about Chapman's rings conforming to the Coroner's comments that they were a wedding ring and a keeper ring:

> . . . The police, on the statement of Farmer, are making a vigilant search for the mother, sister, and brother in law. A man named Chapman, from Oxford Street, has been found, but he proves to be no relation. It has been ascertained that the deceased woman did wear two rings at the time of her death. They were of brass—one was a wedding ring, and the other a keeper of fancy pattern. Both are missing, and the police are still searching for them.

The practice of using a less expensive keeper ring to guard the more expensive wedding ring is an English tradition, which began with King George III in 1761, who presented a keeper ring to his bride, Queen Charlotte. By the late nineteenth century, this tradition spread to 'the common masses'. According to *The Scotsman* article, Chapman's keeper ring had on it a fancy pattern suggesting a value greater than the cheapest of brass rings, and then in turn suggesting an even more expensive wedding ring. Could Chapman have afforded this type of ring set? Generally, a wedding ring and its keeper ring were not purchased by the woman, but given to her as a dowry in a promise of marriage. At the time of her marriage, her husband, John Chapman, was a coachman and had a steady income. Even after their divorce, John Chapman continued to pay Annie ten shillings per week by Post Office order until his death on December 25, 1886. The Annie Chapman wandering the Whitechapel streets in 1888 may have not been able to afford brass rings valued at $1.50 apiece (1903 dollar value), but her employed husband would have been able to.

Would Annie Chapman have hocked her wedding rings in 1888 if they had any kind of value to them? Even though Chapman was separated from her husband for years due to her drinking, he kept on giving her a weekly allowance up until his death, which indicates a continued bond between the two. Annie

Chapman was known for being emotional when discussing her husband's death and earlier married life. If Chapman's rings were her wedding rings, there is evidence that she most likely would have kept them for sentimental value; memories of a better time. According to the Casebook.org article, *Annie Chapman aka Dark Annie, Annie Siffey, Sievey or Sivvey:* "[Amelia] Palmer said that even two years later she seemed downcast when speaking of her children and how 'since the death of her husband she seemed to have given away all together.'"

It has been suggested that Chapman's brass rings were "recently acquired," and if true, the wedding ring and keeper ring did not come from her husband. If the recent acquisition was through theft, then this supports the case for her possessing rings that she could not personally afford, but merely had before eventually hocking them. If she did buy them herself, then she must have spent enough to have a keeper ring covered with a fancy pattern. Conflicting with the 'recently acquired' suggestion is the statement made by the Metropolitan police that "*The deceased was in the habit of wearing two brass rings (a wedding ring and a keeper).*" A habit connotates an extended amount of time, as opposed to a recent acquisition, and her husband had only stopped paying her two years prior to her death.

Even if we accept that Tumblety's imitation rings were very similar to the rings stolen off of Chapman's body, what other logical explanations are there to account for such a flamboyant dandy carrying around cheap imitation rings? One explanation is that the rings were purchased by Tumblety himself as complementary jewelry for his more expensive diamond rings. Assuming that complimentary rings valued at approximately $1.50 a piece would complement diamond rings worth at least hundreds of dollars, a few problems still exist with this suggestion. On the two previous occasions that Francis Tumblety was searched and his personal items were reported—in New Orleans in 1881 and in Washington DC in 1889—there was no mention of additional complementary rings, yet all of his other items were mentioned. Also, every time his expensive diamonds were reported on, the accounts give the impression that he did not wear them on his fingers, but carried them in his pocket. If so, there would have been no need for "complementary rings" in order to accentuate beauty. Few would argue that the purpose of Francis Tumblety carrying around the large diamond rings, gold watch, and the letters from important people was to demonstrate his wealth and importance when needed, whether it was conversing in a hotel lobby or trying to get out of legal problems at a police station. The problem is that a set of two rings valued at $3.00 would not have been useful in this regard, whether they were additional pocket-wear or worn on his fingers.

In the above excerpt, Riordan claims that Tumblety was known for wearing rings on his fingers, but does not produce any supportive evidence. If Tumblety was known for wearing rings on his fingers, then it would have been reported somewhere and most likely in numerous cases. After an extensive search and reviewing of dozens of newspaper articles and reports commenting upon Francis Tumblety, his dress, and his personal jewelry, I have yet to find a comment discussing him wearing rings (other than a fictionalized account of Francis Tumblety's supernatural origins). One just might be found in the future, but Francis Tumblety certainly was not 'known' for wearing rings.

Another proposal suggests that the rings were of sentimental value to him, and they were probably his mother's old wedding rings. According to genealogist and researcher Bill Amos, Tumblety's mother, Margaret, with her husband, James, sired 11 or 12 children in Ireland. James had moved to America first with the older boys and then Margaret and the younger kids—including Francis Tumblety—had finally made their way to America on June 21, 1847, on the famine ship *Ashburton*. All accounts suggest that James and Margaret were poor and would not have been able to afford a nice set of brass imitation wedding rings on their wedding day. If she did receive a wedding ring set, recall that James had moved to America and had left her in Ireland most likely in order to work enough to pay her and the younger kids' way across the Atlantic. Margaret, young Francis, and a number of other children were living in Ireland without James. An article in the *Irish Times*, October 20, 2011, reported on the discovery of a mass Irish potato famine grave from around the same time frame. Of the over 1000 bodies found, only two rings were recovered. This suggests either that wedding rings were sold for food or that these poor families could not afford rings in the first place. Author/writer/researcher Siobhan Patricia Mulcahy explained in a personal correspondence that:

> . . . there was an old tradition/ superstition among poor Irish around that time that only a gold ring could be used at the wedding ceremony as any other metal would bring bad luck and some even believed that the wedding would be illegal if any other metal—other than gold—was used. Poor

people often borrowed a gold ring just for the ceremony. The cheaper ring—brass, copper or whatever—was then worn by the bride to show that she was married after the ceremony.

On the *History Learning Site, The Great Famine of 1845*, it discusses the poor Irish immigrants who sailed on board the *Ashburton*:

Some landlords resorted to forced emigration of their tenants in an effort to 'solve' the problem in Ireland. In October 1847, the ship 'Lord Ashburton' carried 477 Irish emigrants to North America. 177 of these people came from one estate owned by an absentee landlord. They were so poor that they were all but naked for the journey and 87 had to be clothed by charity groups in America before they could leave the ship. On this particular voyage, 107 people died of dysentery and fever. The 'Quebec Gazette'described the 'Lord Ashburton' and all that it represented as 'a disgrace to the Home Authorities.' The absentee landlord who had forced 177 of his tenants onto the ship was Lord Palmerston, the British Foreign Secretary at this time, and one of the most famous of Britain's politicians in the Nineteenth Century.

Margaret Tumblety, who travelled with son Francis to America on this very Irish famine ship on the previous trip, would have fit into this class of poor Irish families, and she would have been dealing with the same starvation pressures for her and her children. Chances are, she was married with a borrowed gold ring, and did not receive a brass ring as dowry because of these atrocious times and conditions. Even if she did acquire a ring, it would have been only a single brass or copper ring since this was not Irish tradition, yet that most likely would have been sold in order to eat. Even if James would have later purchased her a wedding ring, noting he died four years after her arrival to America, it would have been a single ring.

Lastly, Francis Tumblety's mother passed away on May 27, 1873, in Rochester, New York, so if he acquired his mother's rings, it would have been around this time. The problem is Irish tradition holds that wedding rings were passed down from mother to daughter and even granddaughter, not mother to son. When Margaret passed away in 1873, there was at least one daughter still alive. Beneficiaries of Tumblety's will were his niece living in

Liverpool, England, a Mrs. Thomas Bridget Brady, his sister Jane Haynes in Vallejo, California, and two nieces who still lived in Rochester, New York, a Mrs. Barrett and a Mary Fitzsimmons. Also, if the two imitation rings were indeed of sentimental value because they were his mother's wedding rings, why did he not bequeath these to a niece or a sister?

If these rings did not come from his mother, yet they were still of sentimental value, maybe they were from his own failed marriage when he was a young man. Francis Tumblety did claim to his New York City landlord Mrs. McNamara that the reason why he was out late into the evening was to visit the monastery to pray for his dearly departed wife. On his death certificate, issued by the City of St. Louis Health Department, it does state that he was widowed. Lastly, Charles Dunham, a New York City lawyer and Union Army Colonel, did claim Tumblety told him during the Civil War that the reason why he has nothing to do with women is because of his newly married wife to his surprise being an active prostitute. Even so, most researchers agree that Francis Tumblety, a known homosexual, was never married. The story to Mrs. McNamara was most likely a cover up for his usual evening gay interludes, the source for the information on Tumblety's death certificate was most likely Tumblety himself, and the story he gave to Charles Dunham was most likely another cover up in order to explain to military officers why he hated women.

It may very well be true that Francis Tumblety's imitation rings were simply of sentimental value or even from some, as of yet, unknown and insignificant event in what was a highly colorful and eventful life. And it is true that there is no hard evidence, whatsoever, that Tumblety was keeping a trophy in memory of some horrible event, such as the mutilation of a poor unfortunate on the East End of London in 1888. On the other hand, how coincidental it is that, arguably, Scotland Yard's prime Ripper suspect in November 1888, who remained "a likely suspect" in the eyes of Chief Inspector Littlechild even after it was later established that Mary Kelly and not France Coles was the last victim, was found with imitation rings similar to the rings stolen off the body of a Ripper victim by the killer, himself. There is one more tantalizing coincidence. During the "autumn of terror" when Tumblety escaped from England, he used the alias *Frank Townsend*, and the only other recorded time he used this particular alias was checking into St. Johns Hospital with his imitation rings in his pocket knowing full well he was about to die. This coincidence may be just that, a coincidence, but if he truly was the killer and the rings were meant as a reminder, then it would not be a stretch of logic to see this alias coming to the forefront of his mind when the hospital clerk asked him his name when he first walked into the hospital.

### Article Two: Assistant Commissioner Anderson's Furtive Mission in North America

Of all the suspects in the Whitechapel murder investigation, few were ever named by contemporary Scotland Yard officials, yet one was named by three; Francis Tumblety. Stewart Evans' 1993 discovery of the Littlechild letter revealed that the Head of Special Branch at the time of the murders, Chief Inspector John G. Littlechild, not only mentioned Tumblety as "amongst the suspects," but he also mentioned him as a "very likely one" and accurately recollected the events of November and December 1888. In 2015, researcher David Barrat discovered an article in the *Toronto World*, December 12, 1888, edition, where Scotland Yard Inspector Walter Andrews discussed Whitechapel murder suspect "Dr. Tumblety" while in Toronto in December 1888. Heading the Whitechapel murder investigation was the Assistant Commissioner of CID in the Metropolitan Police Force, Sir Robert Anderson. Anderson also mentioned Francis Tumblety in reference to him being a suspect in his cable communications with the US chiefs of police of San Francisco and Brooklyn in November 1888. These Scotland Yard officials referred to the very same suspect and about the very same chain of events, just after the Kelly murder. If Tumblety was indeed a hot item in November 1888 and Assistant Commissioner Anderson was soliciting US chiefs of police for any information on him in order to know more about his American past, it follows that he dug further. The intent of this article is to demonstrate Sir Robert Anderson did indeed have a full-blown, yet clandestine, Whitechapel murder investigation in North America, and he did so for one suspect, Francis Tumblety.

In September 1888, Robert Anderson took over CID, but he immediately left for a much needed one month convalescent leave to Switzerland. The night before departure, on September 8, Annie Chapman was murdered. The top man responsible for the country's internal affairs, Home Secretary Henry Matthews, was receiving increased public and political pressure to apprehend the Whitechapel murderer, so he purposely maintained contact with his vacationing subordinate. When the Double Event murders of Elizabeth Stride and Catherine Eddowes occurred on September

30, Matthews forced Anderson to return to London. In their first meeting upon his return, the Home Secretary told Anderson that they are holding him responsible for finding the murderer, in which he responded, "I hold myself responsible to take all legitimate means to find him." Although Inspector Frederick George Abberline was assigned the investigation, it was Anderson who was ultimately responsible to the Home Secretary. Abberline's efforts were concentrated on the streets of Whitechapel and Spitalfields, so any subsequent investigations outside the East End, especially across the Atlantic, would have been handled by Headquarters, ultimately, Assistant Commissioner Anderson.

Roger Palmer addressed a series of telegraph communications between Assistant Commissioner Anderson and San Francisco's Chief of Police Patrick Crowley, occurring at the end of November 1888. The subject of the communication was Francis Tumblety in connection with the Whitechapel murders investigation. The San Francisco newspapers reporting this correspondence diverged from each other on one fact—who initiated contact with whom? Palmer points out that *The San Francisco Chronicle* insinuated in their November 23, 1888, issue that Chief Crowley initiated contact with Anderson. It stated: "When the news of Tumblety's arrest reached this city, Chief of Police Crowley recollected that the suspected man formerly lived here, and he took the necessary steps to learn all about his career in this city . . ." At the same time, *The San Francisco Examiner* in a more detailed article and on the very same day stated directly that Scotland Yard contacted Crowley:

> The London Detectives ask Chief Crowley about him [Tumblety] . . .there has been considerable telegraphing between the Police Departments of San Francisco and London. . . . When the Chief of Police learned these facts, and that the bank still had several letters written by Tumblety, he telegraphed to the Superintendent of Police of London that he could, if desired, furnish specimens of Tumblety's handwriting. the dispatch was sent on the 19th instant, and yesterday (November 22—three days later) this answer was received: P. Crowley, Chief of Police, San Francisco, Cal.: Thanks. Send handwriting and all details you can of Tumblety. Anderson. Scotland Yard.

One of the newspapers clearly got the fact of the initiator of the correspondence wrong. Palmer points out a huge temporal problem with *The Chronicle's* account. The first news of 'Tumblety' ever being in San Francisco in order for Crowley to make any connection with his city was *The Examiner* dated November 19, 1888, which is on the SAME day that Crowley sent a telegram to Anderson with the results of a completed nineteenth century style investigation by his second in command Captain Isaiah W. Lees. If Anderson initiated correspondence by telegram sometime after Tumblety's arrest and a few days prior to the November 19 telegram by Crowley as suggested by *The San Francisco Evening Post* on November 19, then the temporal problem goes away. *The Evening Post* stated: "When Dr. Francis Tumblety, the eccentric physician, was arrested in London, some days ago, on suspicion of being the Whitechapel murderer, it was telegraphed out here that he had lived in this city for years . . ."

The significance of who initiated the correspondence cannot be overstated. If Assistant Commissioner Anderson, an important man under extreme pressure to discover the Whitechapel killer, spent his own time and energy contacting San Francisco's chief of police for information on Tumblety, then he must have been very high on the list of Whitechapel murder suspects. But if Crowley initiated contact, then Anderson may have been merely accepting the information on Tumblety out of courtesy. This would mean their correspondence had no bearing on whether Tumblety was a serious suspect or not.

Palmer then reveals another, even more convincing piece of evidence that Anderson initiated correspondence with Chief Crowley. At nearly the same time Anderson was in correspondence with Crowley (prior to Tumblety's escape from England) he had initiated contact with another Chief of Police of a major US city that Francis Tumblety was associated with, Brooklyn's Chief Patrick Campbell. Note what *The Brooklyn Citizen* stated on November 23, 1888:

'Is He The Ripper?'
*A Brooklynite Charged With the Whitechapel Murders.*

*Superintendent Campbell Asked by the London Police to Hunt Up the Record of Francis Tumblety—Captain Eason Supplies the Information and It Is Interesting.*

*Police Superintendent Campbell received a cable dispatch yesterday [November 22] from Mr. Anderson, the deputy chief of the London Police, asking him to make some inquiries about Francis Tumblety, who is under arrest in England on the charge of indecent assault.*

Not only does this New York newspaper state that Anderson initiated contact with Campbell, but there were also no other New York newspaper accounts that conflicted with this fact. Keep in mind; this took place at the same time Anderson was in contact with Crowley. Rejecting the reality of Anderson initiating contact with US chiefs of police in two cities known to be connected to Francis Tumblety after reviewing Palmers discoveries must now be considered tenuous.

Some have suggested that Anderson only requested information on Tumblety from the Brooklyn chief of police specific to the gross indecency and indecent assault charges; thus, it had nothing to do with the Whitechapel case. This claim argues that nowhere in Anderson's cable does it specifically state the request being for the Whitechapel investigation. This is a bold claim, especially since no one has seen the original cable. The *Associated Press* articles in the Brooklyn papers only present some of the correspondence. The newspapers do make it clear what the request was for:

*'Is He The Ripper?'*
*A Brooklynite Charged With the Whitechapel Murders.*
*    Superintendent Campbell Asked by the London Police to Hunt Up the Record of Francis Tumblety.*

The following statement, *"who was arrested in England on the charge of indecent assault,"* merely conforms to what the papers had been reporting already, he was initially arrested on suspicion, but was then re-arrested on gross indecency and indecent assault in order to "hold" him. Besides, the San Francisco requests make it clear that Anderson's request for information was for the Whitechapel case. Lastly, why would the man in charge of the Whitechapel investigation worry about a misdemeanor investigation—at the peak of the murders—on a nobody quack doctor from America when any information received in America would be useless in court, anyway? The infraction occurred in London, and to convict, one must satisfy the elements of the charge; gross indecency and indecent assault on four young men in the Marlborough Street District on the West End of London. Lastly, the entire cable Anderson sent was not published, so we don't know what was written specifically. Notice that the editors of the papers interviewing Campbell connected it with the Ripper murders and Campbell rejected the idea Tumblety was the killer. He would have ensured these reporters knew the request was for the misdemeanor charge if it really was, yet he did not do this.

The Assistant Commissioner's personal involvement suggests Francis Tumblety was high on his suspect list in November 1888, a list with few excellent candidates. Other high profile suspects, specifically Kosminski and Druitt, were yet to be seriously considered by Scotland Yard. In Anderson's 1892 interview, there is absolutely no indication he identified Kosminski as the killer. In *Laying the ghost of Jack the Ripper* (1914), Macnaghten stated the suspect—Druitt in his case—was unknown until some years after he killed himself. With no other hot suspects, Tumblety would have been that much more interesting. When pressure was at an all-time high to rid the streets of the killer, it is not a surprise they would invest additional resources into any suspect more suspicious than the usual multitudes they hauled into the stations.

As Roger Palmer explained, it was not unprecedented for Scotland Yard to investigate the history of a suspect in order to possibly gain useful information. In 1891, sailor Thomas Sadler was suspected of killing Frances Coles. Chief Inspector Swanson investigated Sadler's history, attempting to recreate a chronology of his movements throughout the 1870s and 1880s, including his whereabouts during the 1888 Whitechapel murders. Palmer pointed out a second serial offender case in 1892 involving the poisoner Dr. Thomas Neill Cream. On June 18, 1892, Assistant Commissioner Anderson used Inspector Fred Jarvis in North America to discover the history of this killer. Upon the completion of Jarvis' mission, Anderson was satisfied Cream was a credible suspect and on July 18, 1892, he pressed charges.

If Anderson was interested in Tumblety and his American history, it is logical to assume he wired chiefs of police from other cities that Tumblety lived and worked in. The cable communications Anderson had with the chiefs of police in Brooklyn and San Francisco were intended to be private, thus, if the US police did not reveal the correspondence to the press, we would be blind to the correspondence. But still, Anderson may not have privately cabled other chiefs of police about Ripper suspect Francis Tumblety. Is there any evidence Scotland Yard wired police departments in other American cities Tumblety haunted? The best place to start is Tumblety's home of record, New York City.

Even though Francis Tumblety sneaked out of England and boarded the steamship, *La Bretagne*, in France on November 24, 1888, the press had no idea until the day before he arrived in New York City on Sunday, December 2, and reported it on the very same day:

*New York World, 2 December 1888*
*TUMBLETY IS MISSING*
*The American Charlatan Suspected of the Whitechapel Murders Skips from London*
*HE WAS LAST SEEN AT HAVRE*
*Is He On His Way Home Over the Ocean to New York?*
*HE HAD A BITTER HATRED OF WOMEN*
*Copyright 1888 by the Press Publishing Company (New York World)*
*London, Dec. 1.*
  *The last seen of Dr. Tumblety was at Havre, and it is taken for granted that he has sailed for New York. It will be remembered that the doctor, who is known in this country for his eccentricities, was arrested some time ago in London on suspicion of being concerned in the perpetration of the Whitechapel murders. The police, being unable to procure the necessary evidence against him in connection therewith decided to hold him for trial for another offense against a statute which was passed shortly after the publication in the Pall Mall Gazette of 'The Maiden Tribute,' and as a direct consequence thereof Dr. Tumblety was committed for trial and liberated on bail, two gentlemen coming forward to act as bondsmen in the amount of $1,500. On being hunted by the police today, they asserted that they had only known the doctor for a few days previous to his arrest.*

Notice the actions New York City's Chief Inspector Byrnes took as reported in *The Sun* (New York) on December 2:

*TWOMBLETY ARRIVES.*
*Came Away from London in a Hurry Without His Luggage.*
  *'Dr.' Francis Tumblety or Twomblety, who was arrested in London on suspicion of knowing something about the horrible Whitechapel murders, but against whom no direct proof could be found and who was held in $1,500 bail on a charge of dealing in gross literature, arrived in this city on Sunday on the French line steamer La Bretagne. He*

*disappeared from London shortly after his release on bail
and nothing more was heard of him until news arrived from
Havre that he had sailed from there for this country.
Inspector Byrnes said yesterday that he knew of Tumblety's
expected arrival in this city a week ago and had determined
to make sure that his information was correct by having
men who knew on the wharf when the steamer arrived.
Tumblety was short enough of luggage to make it appear
that his departure from the other side was hurried. He was
among the first to leave the steamer, and he went direct to a
house in Tenth street, just west of Third avenue, where
furnished rooms are let. He will probably be an object of
curiosity to the police for some time, but Inspector Byrnes
said that no one has any right to bother him for what
occurred across the ocean, unless the Government becomes
interested and issues a warrant for his detention. He is a
tall fellow, with a sweeping dark moustache, and used to
sell salve, and parade on Broadway with a valet and two
greyhounds.*

Chief Inspector Byrnes could not have received this
information from the press. 'A week ago' conforms to the same
time frame Chief Inspector Littlechild, Head of Scotland Yard
Special Branch in 1888, stated in his letter to George Sims dated
September 23$^{rd}$, 1913, about when they became aware he
sneaked out of England, "Tumblety was arrested at the time of the
murders in connection with unnatural offences and charged at
Marlborough Street, remanded on bail, jumped his bail, and got
away to Boulogne. He shortly left Boulogne . . ."

Did Littlechild, an official not assigned to the Whitechapel
investigation, have direct knowledge of Tumblety in France? There
certainly were Scotland Yard detectives assigned to the west coast
of France, and they worked for Chief Inspector Littlechild. If
Scotland Yard realized Tumblety escaped to the coast of France
and they attempted to intercept him, it would have been
Littlechild's responsibility to coordinate his subordinates to this
task, via, telegraph. If Anderson, Littlechild's superior, wired the
Scotland Yard detectives directly, it would have been professional
courtesy to inform Chief Inspector Littlechild.

Byrnes was prepared for Tumblety to disembark the *La
Bretagne* in New York City and his subordinates were at the docks
waiting for him. This supports the assertion that there was a
private telegraph came from Scotland Yard to Byrnes, about

Ripper suspect Francis Tumblety. This cable would have come to him within a week of Campbell's and Crowley's cable communications and would have been initiated by Scotland Yard. Although, this particular cable may not have had a request for information on Tumblety, it does show there was a line of telegraph communication going on between Scotland Yard and Chief Inspector Byrnes.

In 1888, there was no US federal law enforcement authority, such as today's FBI, and the closest organization operating in this manner was a private US detective company named the Pinkerton Detective Agency. According to Pinkerton biographer, David Ricardo Williams:

*During most of the years between 1866 and 1924, Pinkerton's role was essentially investigative, both in the United States and Canada. In the United States, it filled a void: Pinkerton's was disciplined, incorruptible (though not infallible), and formed, in effect, a national police force . . . By the turn of the century Pinkerton's was regarded in international police circles as the premier law enforcement body in the United States. Sharing and exchanging information about crime with foreign police bureaus, and acting as a clearing house for news of international criminals, Pinkerton's had become the Interpol of its time. William Pinkerton himself was a familiar colleague equal in status to the senior officials of Scotland Yard and the French Suerte.*

*In The Napoleon of Crime: The Life and Times of Adam Worth, Master Thief, author Ben Macintyre states: "One commentator noted in 1888 that 'the Canadian government looks to the Agency entirely, and there is constant correspondence between Robt. A. Pinkerton at the New York office and the police authorities of London, Paris, Berlin and other great European cities.'" In dealing with investigative issues in the United States, Scotland Yard made it a habit to employ the Pinkertons. Note the following excerpt from a contemporary article in the Southland Times:*

*Southland Times, 21 October 1889, SCOTLAND YARD.*
*. . . Most of the English detective work in America is done through the Pinkertons agency; but there are always three or four Scotland Yard men in the country watching the*

*dynamite societies and looking after their Irish friends in different parts of the country. One of them, who was stationed in New York last year . . .*

We do have evidence Scotland Yard requested the assistance of the Pinkerton Agency on the Whitechapel murder investigation; albeit a different suspect. Casebook member "DRoy" posted this on September 26, 2012:

I found an interesting comment in a book called The Record of the Class of 1891 of the University of Pennsylvania. It links Pinkerton's agency with a suspect but it isn't Tumblety. The quote from the book is . . . 'But the expedition will be a complete failure; the English authorities will not allow the champion to land because he has said so many rude things about England, while Bud Hogg will be arrested through the agency of Billy Pinkerton and taken to England on the suspicion of being Jack the Ripper.'

This was not Tumblety, but we see that Scotland Yard did use them for any investigations outside of England. The Pinkertons were aware of Tumblety. As mentioned earlier, William Pinkerton was being interviewed by a *Chicago Daily Inter* Ocean reporter on November 19, 1888 as reported in the November 20, 1888, issue:

*The Chicago Daily Inter Ocean, 20 November, 1888.*
*BILLY PINKERTON'S POINTS.*
*Billy Pinkerton, whose mind is a storehouse of faces, that the rushing world quickly forgets when removed from the immediate arena of its life, late yesterday afternoon, suddenly found without any explanatory introduction, unless a rapt gaze at an evening paper which he had just bought, could be called an introduction, exclaimed as he walked along Clark street with a reporter of THE INTER OCEAN:*
*"Peculiar Dr. Tumblety (looking at the paper, and the description of the supposed Whitechapel murderer.) Tumblety! No, that's not it. Something like that, though. Tumbledy. No! Twombley! That's more like it."*
*'What's more like it,' asked the surprised reporter; astonished at Billy's evolution of the printed murderer's*

*name as given in the London cablegram, into some other name, less peculiar and more directory-form.*

*'What? Why it's the same man. The very same man that I met in Washington long ago.'*

*'Well, but what man. What can your Washington man of long ago have to do with the Whitechapel murders?'*

If the Pinkertons were not already privately communicating with Scotland Yard about Tumblety, then we are seeing the very moment when William Pinkerton realized Tumblety was a Ripper suspect. There is evidence the Pinkertons did indeed privately communicate with Scotland Yard about Tumblety. When Scotland Yard Inspector Walter Andrews arrived in Canada in December and was asked by reporters how many men Scotland Yard had working in America in employment "on the Whitechapel murder case," he stated: "American detective agencies have offered to find the murderer on salaries and payment of expenses. But we can do that ourselves you know."

Is there any record of Scotland Yard detectives coming to American soil specifically for Ripper suspect Francis Tumblety? The following article was in *The New York World* on 4 December, 1888, just a couple of days after Francis Tumblety finally arrived in New York. It goes into great detail about the English detective staking out Tumblety. The assumption has been this particular detective was one who had already been assigned New York and was privately cabled to wait for his ship to arrive, but . . .

*. . . It was just as this story was being furnished to the press that a new character appeared on the scene, and it was not long before he completely absorbed the attention of every one. He was a little man with enormous red side whiskers and a smoothly shaven chin. He was dressed in an English tweed suit and wore an enormous pair of boots with soles an inch thick. He could not be mistaken in his mission. There was an elaborate attempt at concealment and mystery which could not be possibly misunderstood. Everything about him told of his business. From his little billycock hat, alternately set jauntily on the side of his head and pulled lowering over his eyes, down to the very bottom of his thick boots, he was a typical English detective. If he had been put on a stage just as he paraded up and down Fourth avenue and Tenth street yesterday he would have been called a caricature.*

*First he would assume his heavy villain appearance. Then his hat would be pulled down over his eyes and he would walk up and down in front of No. 79 staring intently into the windows as he passed, to the intense dismay of Mrs. McNamara, who was peering out behind the blinds at him with ever-increasing alarm. Then his mood changed. His hat was pushed back in a devil-may-care way and he marched to No. 79 with a swagger, whistling gayly, convinced that his disguise was complete and that no one could possibly recognize him.*

*His headquarters was a saloon on the corner, where he held long and mysterious conversations with the barkeeper always ending in both of them drinking together. The barkeeper epitomized the conversations by saying: 'He wanted to know about a feller named Tumblety , and I sez I didn't know nothing at all about him; and he says he wuz an English detective and he told me all about them Whitechapel murders, and how he came over to get the chap that did it.'*

*When night came the English detective became more and more enterprising. At one time he stood for fifteen minutes with his coat collar turned up and his hat pulled down, behind the lamp-post on the corner, staring fixedly at No. 79. Then he changed his base of operations to the stoop of No. 81 and looked sharply into the faces of every one who passed. He almost went into a spasm of excitement when a man went into the basement of No. 79 and when a lame servant girl limped out of No. 81 he followed her a block, regarding her most suspiciously. At a late hour he was standing in front of the house directly opposite No. 79 looking steadily and earnestly.*

Notice this is a first-hand account by the reporter, and not merely a translation of another newspaper article, which reinforces its veracity. The barkeeper stated the English detective "came over" to get Tumblety, demonstrating Scotland Yard chased Tumblety to the states. The problem was, the English detective had no authority to arrest. In the same *New York Word* article, note what New York's Head of the Detective Division stated:

Inspector Byrnes was asked what his object in shadowing Twomblety. 'I simply wanted to put a tag on him.' he replied, 'so that we can tell where he is. Of course, he cannot be arrested, for there is no proof in his complicity in the Whitechapel murders, and the crime for which he was under bond in London is not extaditable [*sic*].'

English detectives following Tumblety to New York is reinforced in the *Chicago Daily Tribune*, December 9, 1888: "Dr. Tumbetly was the fellow that Scotland Yard detectives followed to New York and who is said to be on his way to Chicago . . ." The English detective following Tumblety to New York suggests Scotland Yard had a continued interest in Ripper suspect Tumblety even after he sneaked out of England. Reinforcing this continued interest is Inspector Andrews' full statement to the *Toronto World* reporter a few days later. Andrews replied: "Do I know Dr. Tumblety, of course I do. But he is not the Whitechapel murderer. All the same we would like to interview him, for the last time we had him he jumped his bail. He is a bad lot" (The Evening World, December 21, 1888).

Andrews stated we would "*like to interview him*", meaning Scotland Yard had interest in continuing their investigation on Tumblety even after he left England. Much issue has been made by Andrews publicly rejecting Tumblety as the Whitechapel murderer, but the fact that Scotland Yard still wanted to interview him shows he was only giving his personal opinion. Those touting this as proof of Scotland Yard not taking Tumblety seriously are the same people who claim Andrews was not involved in the Whitechapel case. If they are correct, then why would Andrews' opinion be significant if he did not know the details of the case? Besides, no one saw the murders take place, so no one knew yet who the murderer was.

Or, is Andrews purposely being disingenuous in his opinion, because he had orders not to speak to the press about Tumblety? Scotland Yard still wanting to interview him certainly supports this assertion. Andrews was not about to reveal Scotland Yard's plans on Tumblety. Andrews even told a *Montreal Daily Star* reporter, who was pressing him on the Parnell issue: "You know I cannot divulge the secrets of my office" (Montreal Daily Star, December 22, 1888). We also see Scotland Yard's North American investigation operating in other cities. The following is evidence of 'English authorities' heading up an investigation on Tumblety in another city he had history in—Cincinnati:

*Cincinnati Enquirer, Dec. 14, 1888, 'Jack the Ripper.' Is He Tumblety's Man Friday?*

*It has been known for some days past that the detectives have been quietly tracing the career in this city of Dr. Francis Tumblety, one of the suspects under surveillance by the English authorities, and who was recently followed across the ocean by Scotland Yard's men. From information which leaked out yesterday around police headquarters, the inquiries presented here are not so much in reference to Tumblety himself as to a companion who attracted almost as much attention as the doctor, both on account of oddity of character and the shadow-like persistence with which he followed his employer. The investigation in this city is understood to be under the direction of English officials now in New York, and based upon certain information they have forwarded by mail. One of the officers whom current reports connects with this local investigation is James Jackson, the well-known private detective . . .*

*The officials at police headquarters declined to talk about the matter or to answer any questions bearing on this supposed discovery of 'Jack the Ripper's' identity.*

Interestingly, the phrase, *"English officials now in New York,"* further corroborates the English detective chasing Tumblety to New York, since it connotes he was not in New York prior to the event.

Scotland Yard had already been informed by William Pinkerton of the Pinkerton Detective Agency about Tumblety having a suspicious past in the United States and Canada pertinent to the Ripper murders, specifically, his extreme hatred of women. Note what William Pinkerton told a *Chicago Daily Inter Ocean* newspaper reporter on November 19, 1888 (published in the November 20, 1888 issue):

Superintendant [sic] Shaw asked me about him. . . . People familiar with the history of the man always talked of him as a brute, and as brutal in his actions. He was known as a thorough woman-hater and as a man who never associated with or mixed with women of any kind. It was claimed that he was educated as a surgeon in Canada and he was said to have been quite an expert in surgical operations. I have not heard his name mentioned in ten years.

In view of this, if Anderson truly had a significant investigation underway in an attempt to gain knowledge of Tumblety's North

American past, he would also have solicited Canadian authorities. In 1888, Canada—although a sovereign nation—was still part of the British Empire, therefore, Scotland Yard's interaction with law enforcement in Canada would have been different than in the United States. In the United States, there was no centralized federal law enforcement department overseeing state and city law enforcement and criminal conduct, so Scotland Yard would have had to contact city police directly, just as they did with Crowley and Campbell. In Canada, however, the federal government in Ottawa not only had a governmental tie with Scotland Yard it also had a more centralized legal system, maintaining jurisdiction over the control of criminal procedures throughout the country, including Canadian municipalities. Williams states:

> In the United States, individual states define criminal conduct; each state has its own catalogue or code of crimes, and its own rules of procedure to deal with them. . . . In Canada, the position was and is markedly different. The Ottawa government enjoys exclusive jurisdiction to define criminal conduct and procedures for dealing with it, applicable to all provinces.

If Scotland Yard was interested in contacting Canadian municipal police officials for information on Francis Tumblety, they still would have contacted them directly, as they did in the United States. Case in point, Scotland Yard was in direct cable communication with the Toronto Police Department, specific to the Barnett extradition; Barnett being wanted for fraud against the Central Bank of Toronto. Because Canada was nominally part of the British Empire, Scotland Yard likely had more influence over Canadian chiefs of police to not divulge private correspondence to the press.

Do we have evidence Scotland Yard contacted any chiefs of police in Canadian cities that Francis Tumblety had a history in? Note the cable news report published in the *Evening World*, December 21, 1888:

*ALL THE WAY FROM SCOTLAND YARD.*
*An English Detective Coming Here in Search of Jack the Ripper.*
*[SPECIAL TO THE WORLD.]*
*    MONTREAL, Dec. 20—Inspector Andrews, of Scotland Yard, arrived here to-day from Toronto and left to-night for*

*New York. He tried to evade newspaper men, but incautiously revealed his identity at the Central Office, where he had an interview with Chief of Police Hughes. He refused to answer any questions regarding his mission, but said there were twenty-three detectives, two clerks and one inspector employed on the Whitechapel murder cases, and that the police were without a jot of evidence upon which to arrest anybody.*

*'How many men have you working in America?'*

*'Half a dozen.' He replied; then, hesitating, continued: 'American detective agencies have offered to find the murderer on salaries and payment of expenses. But we can do that ourselves, you know.'*

*'Are you one of the half dozen?'*

*'No, my boy; don't say anything about that. I meant detective agencies.'*

*'But what are you here for?'*

*'I had rather not say, just at present, anyhow.'*

*Ten days ago Andrews brought Roland Gideon Israel Barnet, charged with helping wreck the Central Bank of Toronto, to this country from England, and since his arrival he has received orders from England which will keep him in America for some time. It was announced at Police Headquarters to-day that Andrews has a commission, in connection with two other Scotland Yard men, to find the murderer in America. His inaction for so long a time, and the fact that a man suspected of knowing considerable about the murders left England for this side three weeks ago, makes the London police believe Jack has left that country for this.*

*It is said among Irish Nationalists here that they have information that Andrews is remaining in America for the purpose of hunting up certain men and evidence to be used by the London Times in the Parnell case.*

The exact article was reported in the *St. Louis Republic* on December 22, 1888, with the exception of the title, which stated, *"AFTER JACK THE RIPPER." A Scotland Yard Detective Looking for Him in America*, and the following line, *"Special to The Republic."* Barrat discovered a similar article reported in the *Montreal Herald* on December 21, 1888, but in much less detail:

INSPECTOR Andrews of the Scotland Yard detective force, London, who brought over the celebrated Gideon Barnett, was in the city yesterday on his return to England. At the Central Station, which he visited yesterday morning he met several members of the press, and to their inquiries about the Whitechapel murders, said that so far the force was at sea, having no clue to work upon. They have arrested scores of suspected persons, but were forced to release them for want of sufficient evidence. The search is still kept up and will be until the culprit is captured. Twenty-three detectives, two clerks and an inspector are specially detailed for the Whitechapel affair, and they have received as many as 6,000 letters from police officers and others trying to give clues to the fiend.

One suggestion is that the information absent in the *Montreal Herald* article demonstrates that the *New York World* added unsubstantiated information in order to make the reader believe Andrews came to North America for the Ripper murders. Note the *World* subtitle, *An English Detective Coming Here in Search of Jack the Ripper*. The problem with this claim is that the *Republic's* title and subtitle also stated the same information connecting Andrews with the search for Jack the Ripper, although rephrased. The practice of daily newspapers in the late nineteenth century receiving news over the wire from contributing news organization was to change both the title and statement, "Special to the [name of their paper]". Point, the connection between Andrews and the search for Jack the Ripper came from the Montreal reporter who was face to face with the Montreal police. The *World* and the *Republic* did not receive their information from the *Montreal Herald* article. Since Andrews met up with multiple reporters, it makes sense that the two US daily newspaper organizations received their information from a different Montreal reporter. The information is the similar, because both reporters heard the same information from Central Office.

Interestingly, Andrews' December 20th interview with Police Chief Hughes occurred near the end of his return trip, just four days before he boarded a ship back to England. Because Andrews received his new orders two weeks before their meeting, this could not have been the reason for the interview. The article infers they discussed the Ripper case, specifically, Francis Tumblety, and for good reason. Tumblety arrived in Montreal in the latter half of 1857 and was promptly arrested for assisting a local prostitute named Philmeme Dumas to intentionally have a miscarriage.

Those who reject the claim that Andrews came to North America specific to the Whitechapel case must brush off two intriguing realities. First, English journalist and crime writer Guy Logan stated in 1928,

I know that one of Scotland Yard's best men, Inspector Andrews, was sent specially to America in December 1888, in search of the Whitechapel fiend on the strength of important information, the nature of which was never disclosed—Nothing, however, came of it, and the Inspector's mission was a failure.

Logan's statement thirty years later corroborates Andrews' Whitechapel mission in America. Logan phrased the sentence with, "*I know,*" impressing upon the reader a level of certainty as that of having a personal discussion with a Scotland Yard official "in the know." His statement, "*strength of important information, . . . never disclosed,*" infers receipt of inside information, as opposed to miraculously discovering an article reporting on Andrews in contemporary papers thirty years earlier. When Andrews was ever interviewed about his American mission involving the Ripper murders, he declined to answer, which supports Logan stating that the nature of which was never disclosed.

Some have argued that Logan got it wrong, because he stated Andrews was "searching" for the fiend and not "seeking information" on the fiend. The phrase, 'searching for the fiend' might just have been a general phrase by Logan's Scotland Yard source as to mean all facets of the Whitechapel investigation, including seeking information, or the source may not have been absolutely clear; either intentionally or unintentionally. Notice how the *Evening World* article also stated Andrews was coming to America in "*search of the Jack the Ripper*" or "*to find the murderer in America.*" In this case, the source is revealed - during an announcement at Headquarters. The last thing Andrews wanted the press to know was his focus being solely on Tumblety, so his name not being announced makes perfect sense. Even if Logan translated his sources properly and they meant a more literal connotation of search, it still fits. Recall, Anderson tasked Inspector Jarvis in the Cream case with a nearly identical North American mission as Andrews—discovering the background of a serial killer suspect; in his case, Neill Cream. Only after Anderson was satisfied with the results of Jarvis' completed mission did he "search" for Cream. If Anderson did receive satisfactory

information on Tumblety, convincing him he was the killer, his
later actions in the Jarvis/Cream case suggest he would have had
Andrews and company "search" for Tumblety and arrest him with
an extraditable offense. It may not have been a coincidence both
New York City and Scotland Yard detectives attempted to keep
their eye upon Tumblety in New York for a possible apprehension,
only to have him quickly skip town.

The second reality is Scotland Yard detective Walter Dew. In
his later memoirs, *I Caught Crippen* (1938), Chief Inspector Walter
Dew—a young detective on the East End at the time of the
murders—informs us that Andrews was indeed involved in the
Ripper case and involved extensively:

> *I knew Whitechapel pretty well by the time the first of the
> atrocious murders, afterwards attributed to Jack the Ripper,
> took place. And I remained there until his orgy of motiveless
> killing came to an end . . .*
>
> *The officers sent from Scotland Yard were Chief-Inspector
> Moore, Inspector Abberline and Inspector Andrews, assisted,
> of course, by a large number of officers of subordinate rank.
> In addition to them was Detective-Inspector Reid, the local
> chief, who worked under the direction of his colleagues from
> the Yard. Looking back to that period, and assisted in my
> judgment by the wideness of my own experience since, I am
> satisfied that no better or more efficient men could have been
> chosen. Chief-Inspector Moore was a huge figure of a man . . .
> Inspector Abberline was portly and gentle speaking. The type
> of police officer—and there have been many—who might
> easily have been mistaken for the manager of a bank or a
> solicitor . . . Inspector Andrews was a jovial, gentlemanly
> man, with a fine personality and a sound knowledge of his
> job.*
>
> *These three men did everything humanly possible to free
> Whitechapel of its Terror. They failed because they were up
> against a problem the like of which the world had never
> known, and I fervently hope, will never know again.*

It is well documented that both Abberline and Moore were
involved in the case in Whitechapel and the surrounding East End
districts, and at the same time, Andrews was not; or at best, very
little. With volumes of contemporary theories of Jack the Ripper
living outside of the East End, such as the Jekyll and Hyde theory
of an eminent physician from the West End transforming into a

medical maniac or even the fiend was an American, it is no surprise the murder investigation was not limited to just the East End. In view of this, Andrews' involvement was likely outside of the East End, and the only evidence connecting Andrews with the Ripper case has him across the Atlantic, which corroborates this.

Some suggest Walter Dew's memory failed him and Andrews was not involved, at all. Note what Dew stated about his memory: "One of my chief assets then—and, indeed, through the whole of my police career—was a splendid memory. I made notes, of course, sometimes lengthy ones as to what prisoners said on arrest, but it was rarely indeed that I made use of my notebook when giving evidence." Dew's recollection of details in his memoirs is quite impressive, which conflicts with the claim he had a failed memory even in his later years.

Curiously, Andrews was reported to have boarded a ship to England a full four days after his Montreal meeting with the chief of police. With at most a two day train ride to Halifax, what did he do for the other two days? Notice a clue in a local Halifax newspaper:

> *The Morning Herald (Halifax), March 22, 1889,*
> *The inspector returned home by way of Halifax, and as he stepped from the train at the deep water terminus and on board the steamer Oregon he was accosted by the reporter and questioned upon this delicate point. The inspector did not appear any too well pleased at the question, but allowed himself to be drawn into conversation when he admitted, as far as professional etiquette would allow, that such was his mission. But he would go no further . . .*

If true, Andrews arrived in Halifax on board a train, thus, he did not stay in Halifax. Where was he for two days or more? Some have suggested he stayed in Montreal from December 20 to December 24, the date he left Halifax for England. This creates an interesting possibility not only paralleling his activities in Toronto but also explaining an unusual statement by the Montreal reporter:

> *MONTREAL, Dec. 20—Inspector Andrews, of Scotland Yard, arrived here to-day from Toronto and left to-night for New York. [The Evening World, December 21, 1888]*

Interestingly, Montreal is only thirty miles north of New York! Being a resident of the State of New York for the last two decades and residing in other states prior to this, it was immediately apparent that many assume "New York" always means New York City, but this is simply not the case. The reporter did not state "New York City," but simply "New York." Regardless of the reason for Andrews' trip from Toronto south sixty miles to the US border at Niagara Falls around December 17, it was part of his Canadian agenda—collecting information from the mid- to western United States—so he continuing this agenda at the end of his trip on the east coast makes perfect sense. Montreal is the closest location for Andrews to cross the US border and retrieve information from Scotland Yard officials working out of the east coast of the US, especially, New York City. Montreal is due south of New York City. Note the Grand Trunk Railway map of 1885; altered to highlight possible train routes Andrews may have taken.

There were two train depots just on the US side of the Canadian/New York border, Rouse's Point and Mooer's Junction; either location being the logical stop Andrews would have met up with Scotland Yard officials if he met them at the border.

Andrews could even have travelled to Albany, New York; it being similar in distance to his short trip from Toronto to Niagara Falls and it being the halfway mark between Montreal and New York City. It would also have allowed any Scotland Yard official collecting information from Boston convenience to drop it off. Recall, Andrews did not show up to Halifax until the day of his departure, on December 24, 1888. A quick look at a map shows a simple and logical two day trip, which not only conforms to nineteenth century train routes and also places Andrews in three cities Francis Tumblety set up offices in—the first leg from Montreal to Albany, where he may have met up with Scotland Yard detectives to retrieve documents from New York City and Brooklyn, the next leg Albany to Boston, followed by a trip back across the Canadian border to St. John. Andrews' first leg was reported to be in the evening, which would have been to Albany on the evening of December 20.

Andrews arrived in Canada on the SS Sarnia on December 9, and this same transatlantic vessel was leaving for England on December 22. Even if Andrews was attempting to make the return transatlantic trip on the SS Sarnia, but could not make it due to inclement weather, Andrews traveling through New York would easily have been accomplished.

David Barrat went to the British Library and found a follow-up report to the December 21, 1888, World article in the December 31, 1888, issue of the Daily Telegraph. The report was a one paragraph excerpt (paragraph nine) in a large full page column article reporting on numerous "American" stories, titled, *AMERICANS "AT HOME."* While the *World* reported that Inspector Andrews left for New York, the *Daily Telegraph* reported he arrived:

> Inspector Andrews, of Scotland-yard, has arrived in New York, from Montreal. It is generally believed that he has received orders from England to commence his search in this city for the Whitechapel murderer. Mr. Andrews is reported to have said that there are half a dozen English detectives, two clerks, and one inspector employed in America in the same chase. Ten days ago Andrews brought hither from England Roland Gideon Israel Barnett, charged with helping to wreck the Central Bank, Toronto; and since his arrival he has received orders which will keep him in America for some time. The supposed inaction of the Whitechapel murderer for a considerable period, and the fact that a man suspect of knowing a good deal about this series of crimes left England for this side of the Atlantic three weeks ago, has produced the impression that 'Jack the Ripper' is in America. Irish Nationalists pretend that the inspector is hunting up certain evidence to be given before the Parnell Commission.

Researchers already knew about the follow-up story, reporting it published in the *Pall Mall Gazette* (Dec 31), and the *Eastern Morning News* (Jan 2, 1889), and in both cases, the articles stated the source was a correspondent from the *Daily Telegraph*. The assumption, though, was the *Daily Telegraph* correspondent was not giving a follow-up story to the one recorded in the *World* report, but was merely passing the same story—utilizing the liberty of rephrasing—onto his readers across the Atlantic. The correspondent certainly did repackage the Andrews story out of Montreal, as evidenced by nearly identical information, but the first sentence is different. It is a follow up to the story, reporting his arrival in New York. Reinforcing this firsthand account is who the correspondent was. Underneath the title of the *Daily Telegraph* article it states: "[FROM OUR NEW YORK CORRESPONDENT]." The New York correspondent wrote the statement as if he had knowledge of Inspector Andrews arriving in New York City from Montreal. There are two possibilities, the correspondent actually did have knowledge of Andrews' arrival "in this city" or he lied. Considering the first possibility, the *Daily Telegraph* correspondent was in the perfect position to gain firsthand knowledge of Andrews' arrival, being the New York correspondent operating out of New York City. Per the *World* report, the news cable was wired the evening of December 20, and being a newspaper reporter, he would have received the wire at the same time as the *World*, easily beating the train's arrival nearly fourteen hours later. This would have given him ample opportunity to report his arrival.

Considering the second possibility that the *Daily Telegraph* correspondent lied, maybe to give the impression of personal involvement, he not only repackaged the story, he altered it. Regardless, this unprofessional altering has no bearing upon the truthfulness of the original Montreal story of Andrews leaving for New York. It actually reinforces Andrews' mission to New York was upstate and not all the way to the city. The *Daily Telegraph* correspondent clearly believed the Montreal reporter meant New York City, but if he lied, we have no contemporary reports conflicting with a quick trip across the border. The *Daily Telegraph* story in the *Pall Mall Gazette* and *Eastern Morning News* would have given earlier researchers the misconception the Montreal reporter meant New York City.

Andrews sneaking off to New York solely to retrieve documents collected by other Scotland Yard officials stationed on the east coast is entirely consistent with his earlier action of traveling off to Niagara Falls from Toronto having that very agenda. This eliminates two assumptions used to argue against a New York visit. First, his New York excursion was to 'chase' Tumblety with intentions to extradite him back to England. Second, Andrews would have visited the New York City Police Department and had a high-profile interview with the chief inspector; virtually guaranteeing headlines in the paper. He avoided the press in Niagara Falls and he would have avoided the press in New York.

The *Evening World* reported Inspector Andrews' trip to New York began on December 20, 1888, likely arriving on the 21$^{st}$, so why were the British papers reporting this follow-up event a full ten days later on December 31? An argument mounted against the credibility of the British report is this gap, suggesting the *Daily Telegraph* reporter claimed to see him in New York around December 29 when we know Andrews boarded a ship in Halifax on December 24. There were two ways foreign correspondents sent stories to their home newspapers, the speedy telegraph and the slow mail sent on board a transatlantic cruise ship. Foreign correspondents had a limited budget and sending large non-time critical news through the mail saved money. Transatlantic cruises were about nine days, as evidenced by Francis Tumblety boarding the *Le Bretagne* on December 24, 1888, in France and arriving in New York on December 2, 1888. Notice this British report being nearly identical in time, meaning, the British papers home office received the Andrews report from their New York correspondent, via, ship mail. The *Daily Telegraph's* December 31 date is merely the date home office received the story or when they sent it over the wire, not when Andrews was seen in New York.

Note the *Daily Telegraph's* New York correspondent's opinion on the Andrews' mission not being that of the Whitechapel murders: "Irish Nationalists pretend that the inspector is hunting up certain evidence to be given before the Parnell Commission." Barret discovered the *Daily Telegraph* Andrews story was also picked up by the *Dundee Evening Telegraph* (Dec 31), the *Edinburgh Evening News* (Dec 31), the *Sheffield Daily Telegraph* (Jan 1), the *Lancaster Gazette* (Jan 2), the *Western Gazette* (Jan 4), the *Whitstable Times & Herne Bay Herald* (Jan 5), the *Manchester Courier* (Jan 5), the *Aberdeen People's Journal* (Jan 5), the *Taunton Courier* (Jan 9), and others. In each and every case, including from the *Eastern Morning News*, the word "pretend" was used. This is not a surprise response, since the *Daily Telegraph* was a major competitor to the *London Times*, a major player in the Parnell Conspiracy.

It can now be argued—supported by evidence—that the *World's* and *Daily Telegraph's* stories reporting on Andrews' Whitechapel mission have no blatant misinformation, therefore, the credibility of the Montreal reporters' fact finding skills are not an issue. A New York side trip not only explains where Andrews was for the two missing days just before he boarded his ship for his trip back to England the New York excursion also closely matches the duration of his Niagara Falls side trip.

If Scotland Yard did contact Canadian officials about Francis Tumblety, would they have contacted anyone else besides municipal police departments? Law enforcement organizational structure was, and is, different in Canada than in the United States, thus communication with Scotland Yard would correspondingly have been different. US cities were controlled by individual state regulations under the authority of city and state governments, while Canadian cities were like British cities (with the exception of London) and controlled by federal regulations under the authority of the federal government and a federal police force.

The federal law enforcement arm of the Ottawa Government for Eastern Canada was the Dominion Police Force. It was past practice and professional courtesy for the leadership of Scotland Yard to involve the Commissioner of the Dominion Police on issues involving international criminals, such as Francis Tumblety, and the commissioner in 1888 was Arthur Percy Sherwood. David Ricardo Williams states:

> *Senior officials of Scotland Yard considered Sherwood an equal. . . . In eastern Canada the Dominion Police Force was for many years a patron of Pinkerton's, beginning in the mid-1880s with A.P. Sherwood as commissioner. . . . It was during McMicken's de facto commissionership (1869) that he worked with Pinkerton's on the famous Reno case. . . . In 1882, A.P. Sherwood, later Lieutenant Colonel A.P. Sherwood and, still later, Brigadier General Sir Percy Sherwood, became superintendent of the Dominion Police and its acting head. Three years later he became commissioner, a position he held until his retirement in 1918.*
>
> *Sherwood had occasional dealing with Scotland Yard, officials of which looked upon him as an equal. Now and then a three-way investigation took place involving the Yard, the Dominion Police, and Pinkerton's; trans-Atlantic swindlers were the usual subject of such investigations. The three organizations formed a de facto club, three legs of a stool, none superior to the others. Sherwood wanted to keep it that way. . .*

Because Scotland Yard was soliciting information directly from municipal authorities, there is another reason why they would have solicited Sherwood. Prior to him being the Commissioner of the Dominion Police, he was the Chief of Police of Ottawa, another city Tumblety set up an office.

Another difference between the United States and Canada receiving communications from Scotland Yard was the level of governmental control of telegraph communications with private telegraph companies. Scotland Yard sending telegraphs to US city officials through private telegraph companies afforded little privacy, while the Canadian government mandated greater a level of control. According to the Historical Data on Radio Regulations and Spectrum Management in Canada, today's regulatory arm of communications in Canada, telegraph employees were required by federal law to sign an oath of secrecy pertinent to the contents of incoming messages:

On April 8, 1875, the Marine Telegraph Act placed the supervision of private underwater cable companies in the hands of the Department of Marine and Fisheries. It did not take long to decide that the privacy of communications was important, and on March 21, 1881, an Act was adopted putting the government in charge of administering an oath of secrecy to telegraph line employees, as well as penalties for divulging the content of messages, a first regarding the right to the privacy of communications.

The deputy minister running the Department of Marine at the time was a very prominent figure named Deputy Minister William Smith. Smith had become deputy minister upon its inception in 1867 under the first administration of the Dominion of Canada. He was educated in Scotland and appointed to British customs in Leith in 1840 at the age of 19. Two years later, he was transferred to St. John, New Brunswick, Canada, and eventually became the controller of customs and navigation and registrar of shipping. When a New Brunswick politician, Peter Mitchell, became Minister of the Department of Marine and Fisheries twenty five years later, he brought the well-experienced Smith with him to Ottawa. The Department of Marine and Fisheries became so successful because of Smith's efforts that successive administrations kept him on as deputy minister and even expanded his responsibilities. In 1888, the Minister of the Department of Marine and Fisheries was Sir Charles Hibbert Tupper, future Prime Minister. In 1889, Tupper responded to a question from a member of the House of Commons about keeping the aging Smith on as deputy minister (68 years old at the time) by saying he had no intentions of recommending Smith's superannuation. Smith was the senior deputy minister in the government. As a newly elected Member of Parliament, Tupper had no experience with Marine and Fisheries issues and counted upon Smith entirely.

In September/October 1888, Smith was on the west coast of the United States inspecting lighthouses and establishing news lights, as reported in *The Daily Morning Astorian* (Astoria, Oregon), on October 3, 1888:

*Lighting the Path of Commerce.*

*Hon. William Smith, the Canadian deputy minister of marine, was in Tacoma last evening on his return from a visit along our coast to San Diego. He came out from Ottawa to inspect the Canadian lighthouse service on this coast and to establish new lights. This morning he went to Victoria, and as soon as the weather permits will go down on the Cormorant to the mouth of the straits to. . . . The Dominion telegraph manager is now exploring a route for a telegraph from Vancouver to the mouth of the Straits of Fuca, to be operated in connection with the lighthouse service . . .*

His office was in the same suite as the Prime Minister's office in Centre Block on Parliament Hill and was in daily contact with the entire ministry cabinet. Not only was Smith responsible for the secrecy of telegraph communications, Smith was in charge of Canada's maritime law enforcement and defense. In modern terms, he was second in command of Canada's Coast Guard, which, by 1888, was operating the first major Canadian warship named *HMS Charybdis*. The following was in the *Evening Star*, September 4, 1888:

*The Coast Defenses of Canada.*
*CHIGAGO, Sept. 4—A special from Ottawa, Ont., says: One of the objects of the visit of Deputy Minister of Marine William Smith to the Pacific coast is to expedite the strengthening of the coast defenses of that province. It appears that the imperial government, in conjunction with that of Canada. . . . Her majesty's ship Caroline, now in Pacific water, has been ordered to San Juan, having on board Mr. Waton, hydrographer of the Royal navy . . . and the deputy minister of marine, will proceed to San Juan for a similar purpose . . .*

With Scotland Yard in a position to better control sensitive correspondences between them and Canadian law enforcement, especially with A.P. Sherwood and the Dominion Police Force, is there any evidence that Scotland Yard wired the Commissioner about Ripper suspect Francis Tumblety? We return to the Canadian Deputy Minister of Marine in 1888, William Smith, a man not only privy to private cable communications in Ottawa, he was in the same professional and social circles as Sherwood. The following is a private letter sent by him from Ottawa to a friend and former colleague in St. John:

*My dear Barber. . . . Do you recollect Dr. Tumblety who came to St. John about 1860 and who used to ride on a beautiful white horse with a long tail, and a couple of grey hounds following after him? Do you recollect how he used to canter along like a circus man? And do you recollect that it was asserted that he killed old Portmore, the Carpenter who built the extension to my house and fleeced me to a large extent? Do you recollect how he suddenly left St. John, circus horse, hounds and all, and afterwards turned up at different places in the States and Canada? He was considered by Dr. Bayard and others an adventurer and Quack Doctor. He is the man who was arrested in London three weeks ago as the Whitechapel murderer. He had been living in Birmingham and used to come up to London on Saturday nights. The police have always had their eyes on him every place he went and finally the Birmingham Police telegraphed to the London Police that he had left for London, and on his arrival he was nabbed accordingly. He must now be 58 or 60 years of age as he left St. John about 1860. He was a tall handsome man and a beautiful rider. When I was in Eastport in 1860 detained by a storm, I met him there and spent part of the day with him. He was very agreeable and intelligent. I do not think he could be the Whitechapel fiend. He now spells his name Twomblety. I believe his original name was Mike Sullivan.*

Some have argued Smith did not receive this information on Tumblety from Scotland Yard but merely read the many newspaper articles transmitted across the wire. Of particular interest is the following *New York World* article dated just before Smith's private letter to Barber:

*New York World, 27 November 1888*
*THEY KNEW DR. TWOMBLETY.*
*HE WAS AN 'ELECTRIC' DOCTOR AT ST. JOHN, N.B., BUT FLED SUDDENLY*

*Dr. Twomblety, the eccentric character under arrest in London in connection with the Whitechapel crimes, appeared in St. John, N.B. (New Brunswick) in 1860 and left there a fugitive from justice. He located in Boston, where he is well known as a mysterious person of questionable reputation. He has made money, but his curious method of spending it first brought him under the surveillance of the London police.*

*The mysterious Dr. Twomblety, the American arrested in London, Nov. 16, suspected of having had some connection* with the Whitechapel murders, an account of whose singular actions appeared in yesterday's World, seems to have figured extensively in Boston, where he is very well known. The same veil of mystery enveloped his life in that city as everywhere else.

The first appearance of Twomblety was in 1860 and 1861, when he cut a great figure at St. John, N.B. He claimed to be an electric physician of international reputation. He put up at the leading hotel of the city, and by his pretentious airs convinced the people that he was all he represented himself to be. He adopted the same system of personal advertisement he has followed up ever since, only in those early days he was given to extremes in dress. He would dash through the streets mounted on a superb white horse, followed by a troop of thoroughbred greyhounds, and arrayed in the most gorgeous style. Practice poured into him, he charged whatever fee he pleased and made money rapidly.

Presently it began to be whispered about that the "doctor" was a pretentious humbug and vulgar charlatan. The more respectable portion of the community dropped him. Just at this time one of his patients died, and under very peculiar circumstances. The man's name was Portmore, and as he was well known and had many friends, his death created a sensation. A request was made by the family for an autopsy, and when it was held it was found that Portmore's death was entirely due to the "doctor's" atrocious treatment. So gross was the malpractice that the case was at once given to the Coroner, and a jury was empanelled to more fully investigate.

There is a great deal of red tape about Coroners' juries in that part of the country, and by the time the jury had thoroughly sifted all the evidence and proved that the "doctor" was guilty of manslaughter, he had fled to Boston. For some unknown reason he was never pursued, and he was soon as conspicuous in Boston as he had been in St. John. There was the same white horse, the same collection of dogs, the same gorgeous dressing.

His St. John experience made him careful about the general practice of medicine, and he appeared in Boston as the inventor of a sure cure for pimples. He devoted his time entirely to ladies and did a rushing business. His trade increased to such an extent that he opened a branch office *in this city, and afterwards he worked Jersey City and Pittsburgh and many western cities, going as far as San Francisco.*

*He also made himself conspicuous in Canada, and his big form, set off by striking attire, is as familiar to Toronto and Montreal as it is to New York. In Canada he was very fond of exhibiting to newly made acquaintances a medal which purported to be the gift of his admirers when he left Canada to begin what he termed his 'crusade against the pimples which disfigured the faces of American women.' In his wanderings he did not forget the fashionable watering places, and at even so exclusive and aristocratic a spot as White Sulphur Springs he paraded himself, with all his offensive vulgarity of attire, to the great horror of the staid old Virginia aristocracy.*

*By some it is said that Twomblety is not the man's real name at all, but that he was known as Sullivan and lived in Nova Scotia up to 1864. There is evidently either a confusion of names or dates about this statement as there is conclusive proof that the 'doctor' was known as Twomblety in St. John two years before 1862, and as Twomblety he was quite well known in New York and Boston in 1864 and for many years afterwards. There appears to be no doubt that Twomblety in his myriad of movings did at one time live in Nova Scotia, where it is said he behaved in such a scandalous manner as to bring himself into great odium . . .*

*A few years ago the pimple banishing enterprise was moved to London, where the doctor for a time is said to have made money. It was his queer method of spending his money that attracted the Scotland Yard detectives to him, and after a slight investigation he was arrested, the idea being that if he were not the Whitechapel fiend, he is a dangerous character, and is not entitled to his liberty.*

In all probability, Smith read this particular newspaper article on Francis Tumblety before he sent his private letter, especially since local Ottawa newspapers paid for the *New York World's* news cable service. The *New York World* and the *Sun* were the only major news gathering organizations promoting Tumblety's name as "Twomblety," and the *World's* article contained much of what Smith wrote about, such as Tumblety's history in St. John, and it even mentions the name of "Sullivan."

Smith's comments about Tumblety traveling on a train from Birmingham to London on Saturday under the watchful eye of Scotland Yard, then being arrested upon his arrival, closely match an *Associated Press* article published in the *Ottawa Free Press* on November 19, 1888. Curiously, the article does not mention the name of the suspect. Smith either read the story, then connected the Birmingham suspect with Tumblety or he received the information from a Scotland Yard source, just as the London correspondent of the *Associated Press* did.

Assuming we accept much of what William Smith passed onto Barber in the letter came from him reading the paper, how could this be evidence that Scotland Yard contacted Ottawa about Ripper suspect Francis Tumblety? First, Smith had the perfect opportunity to have known about Scotland Yard wiring the Ottawa government. Sherwood and his boss, the Minister of Justice John Sparrow David Thompson, not only walked the same halls as Deputy Minister Smith; they also sat in many of the same ministry and advisory meetings. Smith had the opportunity and governmental authority to hear about Scotland Yard's request. According to Stewart Evans, the Smith letter to Barber was postmarked from Ottawa, which demonstrates Smith was working at Parliament Hill in late November 1888.

Interestingly, Minister of Justice John Sparrow David Thompson and Smith's boss, Minister of Marine and Fisheries Charles H. Tupper, were very close. Tupper joined Thompson's private law firm in 1881. Both being members of the ministry cabinet, their job was executive council, which meant giving advice to the Prime Minister. At the time of the Whitechapel murders in the fall and early winter of 1888, Thompson was working closely with Tupper, spearheading the Fisheries Negotiations between the British government, Canada, and the United States:

> Thompson's performance in 1887–88 at Washington during the fisheries negotiations between Canada and the United States made him more indispensable. Tupper was the main Canadian delegate, and technically Thompson was only a legal adviser; but Tupper was not a lawyer, just a knowledgeable, noisy politician, and he needed someone like Thompson who knew the legal side. Thompson's experience advising the Americans at the Halifax arbitration of 1877 made him especially valuable. Joseph Chamberlain, the senior plenipotentiary for the British-

Canadian side, was impressed, so much so that although Thompson was the youngest member of cabinet, he was awarded a KCMG in 1888 with the assent of two grateful governments. The treaty of 1888, so laboriously put together, was rejected by the American Senate. Both governments then fell back upon a usefully arranged modus vivendi . . .

Second, Sherwood and Smith were also likely in the same "Ottawan" social circles and may have discussed this intriguing news outside of any business conversations. Williams states:

They [Commissioner Sherwood and the Pinkertons] called upon each other for help in locating wanted persons, asked each other for personal favours, and often connected with visits by mutual friends to New York, Chicago, or Ottawa. Once Sherwood asked Robert Pinkerton to lay out the red carpet for a deputy minister and show him the sights of the metropolis, which Pinkerton gladly did. . . . Occasionally, Sherwood would personally go to New York to interview Pinkerton or his operatives.

This suggests that Sherwood considered deputy ministers from his country as social superiors; or at least social equals and would have been quite willing to socialize. Of all the deputy ministers, Smith's job was often out of the office, and he did indeed visit New York in the late 1880s. The following was in the *Sacramento Daily Record-Union*, November 8, 1887:

*Arrival of One of British Fishery Commissioners.*
*NEW YORK. November 7th.—The Cunard steamer Etruria, on which Chamberlain, Member of Parliament, was a passenger, arrived this morning. The revenue cutter Manhattan took the illustrious visitor from the Etruria and landed him at the barge office, where he was received by William Lane Booker, British Consul-General, and Hon. William Smith, Deputy Minister of Marine to Canada . . .*

Another of Deputy Minister's New York trips was recorded in the *New York Tribune*, on May 15, 1884: "PROMINENT ARRIVALS. St. Denis Hotel—William Smith, Deputy Minister of Marine, of Canada." Third, Sherwood had a reason to speak with Smith about Francis Tumblety. According to Williams, Sherwood had a subscription to the *New York World*, and would likely have known of Tumblety's legal problems in St. John. If Scotland Yard's request was for information on Tumblety, Sherwood would have been interested in what Smith had to say, since Smith worked in St. John at the time the papers reported Tumblety's troubles there. Smith certainly did recall Tumblety in St. John.

Deputy Minister Smith had the opportunity and even the legal authority to be apprised of any private cable communications between Scotland Yard and Ottawa about Ripper suspect Francis Tumblety, and there was even a reason for him to be approached . . . but is there evidence? The answer is yes; something revealed in his letter to Barber. Notice when Smith claimed Tumblety's initial arrest was: "He is the man who was arrested in London three weeks ago as the Whitechapel murderer." Since the letter is dated December 1, 1888, this would put the initial arrest on or about November 7, which is exactly when the November and December London Criminal Court Calendars stated Tumblety was initially taken into custody.

The reports are clear; Tumblety was first arrested on suspicion, and only later was he held on gross indecency, therefore, his arrest on suspicion was either on that day or earlier. A search through all of the available major daily newspaper articles in North America reveals a significant find. No one in the investigative newspaper reporting business knew the date when Francis Tumblety was initially arrested on suspicion. Note the specific date for this event given in the November 27, 1888, *New York World* article William Smith likely read from: "The mysterious Dr. Twomblety, the American arrested in London, Nov. 16, suspected of having had some connection with the Whitechapel murder . . ." This date refers to the court assigned warrant arrest on November 16, 1888, the day after the *New York World* London correspondent, Tracy Grieves, sent the original telegraph informing the world of a Dr. Kumblety from New York was arrested on suspicion. The court issued warrant for Tumblety's arrest was dated November 14, 1888, and Tumblety posted bail on November 16. Grieves did not know Tumblety was "placed into custody" on November 7, 1888.

The same ignorance of the date of Tumblety's initial arrest is seen with all of the daily newspaper organizations. Note the report from the *New York Times*:

*New York Times, November 19, 1888*
*THE SAME TUMBLETY*

*'His Arrest in London not His First Experience.'*
   *The Dr. Tumblety who was arrested in London a few days ago on suspicion of complicity in the Whitechapel murders, and who when proved innocent of that charge was held for trial in the Central Criminal Court under the special law covering the offenses disclosed in the late 'Modern Babylon' scandal, will be remembered by any number of Brooklynites and New-Yorkers as Dr. Blackburn, the Indian herb doctor . . .*

Most daily newspapers did not even attempt to place a date on the original arrest on suspicion, and merely state he was arrested first on suspicion then re-arrested on the gross indecency and indecent assault charge:

*Evening Star (Washington, D.C.), 19 November 1888*
*Arrested on Suspicion.*
DR. FRANCIS TUMBLETY THOUGHT TO BE CONCERNED IN THE WHITECHAPEL MURDERS.
   *Dr. Francis Tumblety, who, according to a cable dispatch, was arrested in London on suspicion of being concerned in the Whitechapel murders and held on another charge for trial under the special law passed after the 'Modern Babylon' exposures, is known in nearly every large city in this country. He has lived in Boston, New York, San Francisco, and in this city at different times during the last twenty-five years. During the war he was arrested here, either in mistake for Dr. Blackburn or on the charge of being his accomplice.*

Not only does Smith write a different, earlier date, the date matches the court calendar, while the papers got it wrong. If Smith received all of his information from this article, why did he not state the initial arrest as reported in the story—November 16?
   There was one report that stated Tumblety was initially arrested on suspicion around the first week of November or earlier, but this actually reinforces the claim that this news of came directly from Scotland Yard. Note the *Brooklyn Citizen* article mentioned earlier:

*Brooklyn Citizen, November 23, 1888, 'Is He The Ripper?'*
   *A Brooklynite Charged With the Whitechapel Murders Superintendent Campbell Asked by the London Police to*

*Hunt Up the Record of Francis Tumblety—Captain Eason Supplies the Information and It Is Interesting*

*Police Superintendent Campbell received a cable dispatch yesterday from Mr. Anderson, the deputy chief of the London Police, asking him to make some inquiries about Francis Tumblety, who is under arrest in England on the charge of indecent assault. Tumblety is referred to in the dispatch in the following manner: 'He says he is known to you, Chief, as Brooklyn's Beauty.'*

*Tumblety was arrested in London some weeks ago as the supposed Whitechapel murderer. Since his incarceration in prison he has boasted of how he had succeeded in baffling the police. He also claimed that he was a resident of Brooklyn, and this was what caused the Deputy Chief of Police to communicate with Superintendent Campbell. The superintendent gave the dispatch immediate attention, and through Captain Eason, of the Second Precinct, has learned all about Tumblety. He came to this city in 1863 from Sherbrook, Canada, where he said he had been a practicing physician. He opened a store on the southeast corner of Fulton and Nassau streets, and sold herb preparations. He did a tremendous business and deposited in the Brooklyn Savings Bank at least $100 a day. He was a very eccentric character, six feet high, dark complexion, large and long flowing mustache, and well built.*

Much of the news in this report came from Assistant Commissioner Anderson's private cable, and since all other newspaper organizations either omitted the approximate date of Tumblety's initial arrest or incorrectly reported at the time of his arrest from the warrant on November 16, the logical conclusion is Anderson reported the approximate date of the arrest on suspicion in his cable.

Did Smith see this newspaper article and equate the relatively vague "*some weeks ago*" to the precise statement of '*three weeks ago*' in his letter to Barber, even though the *New York World* article stated a specific November 16 date? Smith was not in Brooklyn, so he would have received this report over the wire from the *Associated Press*. The story did indeed get transmitted by the *Associated Press* across the continent, but it occurred later. The following is the same article in the *Associated Press* sections of the *Wahpeton Times* (North Dakota, George P. Garred, Publisher), dated Dec 6, 1888, and *New Ulm Weekly Review* (Minnesota, Brandt & Weddendorf, Publishers), dated Dec 5, 1888:

*Jack, the Ripper, Ubiquitous.*
 *Police Superintendent Campbell of Brooklyn received a cable dispatch from Mr. Anderson, the deputy chief of the London police, asking him to make some inquiries about Francis Tumblety, who is under arrest in England on the charge of indecent assault. Tumblety is referred to in the dispatch in the following manner: 'He says he is known to you, chief, as Brooklyn's beauty.' Tumblety was arrested in London some weeks ago as the supposed Whitechapel murderer . . .*

As evidenced by the consistent dates of the two identical articles, published in independent newspapers, the *Associated Press* transmitted the story across the repeater stations to local newspapers AFTER December 1, 1888; the date of Smith's letter to Barber. In view of this, William Smith did not see the *Associated Press* story when he wrote his letter.

 There is another anomaly in the Smith letter. Note the following sentence: "I believe his original name was Mike Sullivan." A search in all available newspaper articles reporting on Tumblety discussing this particular alias, from his battle with the chemical bank in early 1861 where the alias originated to the date of Smith's letter on December 1, 1888, never is the first name of "Mike" reported . . . with the exception of one out of Albany, New York:

*Albany Evening Journal, 28th November 1888,*
*A PRECIOUS VILLAIN.*
*An Old Albanian Arrested as the Whitechapel Murderer*
 *Dr. Francis Tumblety has been arrested in London, charged with the Whitechapel murders. Tumblety is an odd character, if there ever was one. His original name was Mike Sullivan. He has had a number of other names. He is an irishman, as his name indicates, and must be 50 years old at the present time.*
 *THE ZENITH OF HIS CAREER*
 *The period of his most eccentric and successful career was from 1856 to 1866, when he swindled scores of poor people and broke the hearts of unsuspecting girls in the United States and Canada. Sullivan got his name Tumblety*

*from a doctor in Rochester in whose service he was and whom it is believed he murdered. He flitted from Rochester to Buffalo, to Montreal, to St John's and other places, finally winding up in Albany in September of 1863.*

*MONTREAL HAD ENOUGH OF HIM*

*While he was here he was closely watched by Elisha Mack, then an Albany detective and still a resident of this city, who received this letter from the Montreal police—*

*'MONTREAL, Sept. 25th 1863—Dear Mr Mack: About four years ago Dr F. Tumblety was in this city and he had an office here. He professed to be an Indian herb doctor. He was looked upon by all the medical men of the city as a quack. Notwithstanding all this, he had an immense crowd of people going to him for advice and he made money here. He was arrested for abortion and went to jail. Then he employed a good lawyer who finally got him discharged. When he was here he cut a great swell. He drove two horses and a peculiar kind of buggy, and had a large Newfoundland dog following him to attract attention, which he succeeded in doing. He left here for New Brunswick and I never heard of him until about six months ago I had seen his name mentioned in a newspaper as a veterinary surgeon in some cavalry regiment of the Union army. —Eugene Flynn, Sub-Chief of Police.'*

*HIS NEW YORK CAMPAIGN*

*Tumblety's occupation, as shown by the letter, was that of an Indian herb doctor, and he worked on the herb idea with a cheek which paralyzed the people of both New York and Brooklyn, where a large part of his campaigning was done.*

*In 1861 he arrived in New York from Ireland, deposited $3700 in the Chemical bank, got drunk, signed checks and then tried to get the money back from the bank on the ground of forgery. He avoided a counter-suit neatly, but left New York for richer fields in more unsuspecting hamlets.*

*The National Police Gazette of April 13, 1861, thus describes the man who is supposed to be the author of the horrible crimes in London: 'He stands 5 feet 11 inches, with jet black hair, brow broad, flat and low. The eyebrows are thick, and heavy, partly concealing a pair of catish, cunning grey eyes, the lips, so much of them as are seen, are of the thick, voluptuous order, the moustache is of the Imperial,*

*Baby Furniss character, long and fanciful, with a twisting twirl at the ends.'*

*IN ALBANY AND BROOKLYN*

*When Tumblety was in Albany he started his establishment for herb cures in the Delavan House (a temperance hotel which eventually lost money, so the manager used a loophole in the lease to introduce liquor). He had the big Newfoundland dog still and he drove about with two piebald ponies. His career in Albany was not as satisfactory as he could wish and he soon packed off to Brooklyn, where he cut a great swell, and was known everywhere both in that city and on Manhattan island as the 'Nankeen swell.' There were very few young ladies in that vicinity who had not felt palpitations in their hearts at the sight of this audacious lady-killer. His Newfoundland dog ran against them in the street while the irresistible drove about with his valet and hostler at his side. The fun of the whole show was that Tumblety came out with a new coat and 'nankeens' every day, while the valet wore the clothes of the day before and the hostler those of the day before that. That was the end of the gradation . . .*

At least two other daily newspapers in the state of New York picked up the Albany story two days later, the *Syracuse Evening Herald* the *Buffalo Courier*. Since the "Sullivan" incident was published during his battle with the Chemical Bank court battle in 1861 after being in St. John (where Smith was) and the incident had nothing to do with that city, Smith merely recalling the first name from the old days is doubtful. A more probable scenario is he received the "Mike Sullivan" fact in November 1888 thanks to Albany detective Elisha Mack. If Smith knew this, chances are Inspector Andrews knew it, especially since it reported a possible murder by Tumblety. It also reported Tumblety having a history in Albany, New York. Andrews taking a trip to Albany, possibly asking the local newspaper reporter how they received this information, makes sense.

An appropriate follow up question would be, if Assistant Commissioner Anderson considered Francis Tumblety such a hot suspect just after the Kelly murder, then why did he never mention him later on in life, and was even convinced of a different suspect being Jack the Ripper? When the post-Kelly murders occurred—murders Scotland Yard was generally convinced were from the hands of Jack the Ripper—Francis Tumblety was safely in the United States, giving him an iron-clad alibi. Of course, today these murders are generally accepted as not being Ripper victims. Note the following article:

*Olean Democrat, 8 August 1889, From an article by E.H. Eaton entitled 'Oleanders in New York.'*

*I enjoyed a peculiar adventure the other morning. I had just finished my night's work, and was riding across the big bridge. I had barely secured a seat in the bridge car when a peculiar looking man entered. He was over six feet in height, his face was square and red, and his gigantic, wiry, black mustache was of such huge proportions and singular cut that it would have attracted attention anywhere. It attracted my attention at any rate and as its owner sat down beside me I immediately decided in my mind that he was Dr. Tumblety. . . . We parted at the Brooklyn end of the bridge. Shortly thereafter the last Whitechapel murder occurred in London, and as Tumblety was without doubt in Brooklyn at the time, he is evidently unjustly suspected of being 'Jack the Ripper.'*

Assistant Commissioner Anderson privately telegraphed two US chiefs of police in November 1888, requesting any and all information on American Francis Tumblety, a man they just arrested on suspicion, suggesting he was considered a significant suspect in the Whitechapel murder case. It logically follows he expanded the investigation to include North America in a quest to gain more information on this suspect; a common Scotland Yard practice in the late nineteenth century. If he did spearhead such a task, we should have evidence he contacted other US authorities in cities Tumblety had a history in, and the evidence indicates this. New York City's chief of police was in private contact with Scotland Yard prior to Tumblety's arrival, Scotland Yard detectives were waiting for Tumblety at the ship, then following him, and there are newspaper reports of British authorities conducting the same investigation in Cincinnati. It was also common practice for Scotland Yard to involve the Pinkerton Detective Agency in investigative matters of international criminals, and we see evidence they were in communication with each other about Tumblety. Scotland Yard Inspector Andrews came to Canada in December 1888, and one of the two reported reasons for his visit was to collected information on Tumblety. Newspaper reports have him coming to the United States at the

US/Canadian border in two locations; Niagara Falls at the beginning of his trip and New York at the end. Andrews stated to the effect that they did not need the assistance of American detective agencies, since they had Scotland Yard detectives in America to accomplish this very task. In Canada, we also see evidence of Anderson's investigation on Tumblety. Inspector Andrews had a personal meeting with the Montreal chief of police about the doctor; mirroring Anderson's cable requests in the US. There is also evidence Scotland Yard contacted the Ottawan government—as expected—and in communication with their usual point of contact; the Commissioner of the Dominion Police Force, Arthur Percy Sherwood. Sherwood likely discussed the investigation with the Deputy Minister of Marine, William Smith, not only because they walked the same halls on Parliament Hill and were in the same professional and social circles, but also because Sherwood would have wanted to speak with him. Smith had firsthand knowledge of Tumblety's manslaughter charge in St. John. The most convincing evidence that Smith was privy to the private correspondence was the letter he sent to his friend in St. John on December 1, 1888. He passed on information that no one other than English authorities knew, when Tumblety was initially arrested; on or just prior to November 7, 1888. The newspapers assumed his initial arrest was his second arrest on a warrant on November 16, 1888. This pattern of evidence points to one conclusion; Assistant Commissioner Anderson invested Scotland Yard resources in November and December 1888 for a clandestine investigation on Ripper suspect Francis Tumblety.

# BIBLIOGRAPHY

Aeragon, *The US Civil War, the First Modern War,* 2009. available at
   http://www.aeragon.com/03/.

*Annie Chapman aka Dark Annie, Annie Siffey, Sievey or Sivvey,*
   Casebook: Jack the Ripper (Stephen Ryder & Johnno), 2009 –
   2013, available at
   http://www.casebook.org/victims/chapman.html.

Appleton, T.E., *History of the Canadian Coast Guard and Marine
   Services, Canadian Coast Guard,* Government of Canada, 2013.

Barnett, R., Lost wax: medicine and spectacle in Enlightenment
   London. *The Lancet,* Volume 372, Issue 9636, Pages 366-367,
   August 2, 2008.

Barrat, D., *The Third Man* (May 2015), Orsam Books, available at
   http://www.orsam.co.uk/xthethirdmanx.htm.

Bates, A.W., *"Indecent and Demoralising Representations": Public
   Anatomy Museums in Mid-Victorian England, Medical History,*
   V. 52 (1): 1-22, Jan 1, 2008.

———, *Dr Kahn's Museum: Obscene Anatomy in Victorian London,
   Journal of the Royal Society of Medicine,* V. 99 (12): 618-624,
   December 2006.

Beatty-Kingston, William, *A Journalist's Jottings,* London:
   Chapman and Hall, 1890.

Begg, P., Fido, M., & Skinner, K., *The Jack the Ripper A – Z,*
   Headline Book Publishing PLC, 1996.

Blondheim, M., *News Over the Wires,* Harvard College, 1994.

Bolt, C., *The Women's Movements in the United States and Britain
   from the 1790s to the 1920s,* University of Massachusetts
   Press, 1993.

Burn, G., *Somebody's Husband, Somebody's Son,* Faber & Faber,
   2004.

*Capitalism by Gaslight*: The Shadow Economies of 19th-Century
   America, *Selling Sex* (2012), Library Company of Philadelphia,
   available at
   http://www.librarycompany.org/shadoweconomy/section4_10
   .htm.

Casebook: Jack the Ripper, available at www.casebook.org,
   Stephen P. Ryder & Johnno, 1996-2013, Thomas Schachner.

Cazeau, T., *A Brief Account of the Thirteenth New York State Volunteer Regiment 1861 – 1863*, Commander, Captain Henry Lomb Camp, S.O.V., Rochester, NY, available at Central Library of Rochester and Monroe County, Historic Monographs Collection.

Central Criminal Court Calendars, London, England, November and December 1888.

Chauncey, G, *The Bowery as Haven and Spectacle* in *The Columbia Reader on Lesbians and Gay Men in Media, Society, and Politics,* 1999.

Chetcuti, J., Knocking on Pall Mall's Door, *Ripperologist 87,* January 2008.

Chetcuti, Lieutenant Sullivan, *The New Independent Review* (Issue 2), pp. 2-9, January 2012.

Cook, A., *M:MI5's First Spymaster,* History Press, 2011.

Coram, J., *Doing 'Write' by Annie – A Closer Look at Annie Chapman's Murder, Ripperologist* No. 73, November 2006.

Crawford T.C., *English Life,* Frank F. Lovell & Company (Princeton University), 1889.

Cumming, C., *Devil's Game: The Civil War Intrigues of Charles A. Dunham.* Univ. of Illinois, 2004.

Currie, A.W., Historica Canada Foundation, *Grand Trunk Railway of Canada*, available at http://www.thecanadianencyclopedia.ca/en/article/grand-trunk-railway-of-canada/

Curtis, L Perry, *Jack the Ripper and the London Press*, Yale University Press, 2001.

Dannes, J., *Hermetic Order of the Golden Dawn* (Jan 2009), Washington and Lee University, 'Magic, Science, and Religion', available at http://home.wlu.edu/~lubint/touchstone/GoldenDawn-Dannes.htm

Eckert, W.C., The Ripper Project: Modern Science Solving Mysteries of History, *American Journal of Forensic Medicine and Pathology*, 10(2), 164-171, 1989.

Ellis, H., *Sexual Inversion,* F. A. Davis Company, 1897.

Evans, S.M., *Born for Liberty A History of Women in America,* Simon & Schuster Inc., New York, 1997.

Evans, S. and Gainey, P., *Jack the Ripper: First American serial Killer,* Kodansha International, 1998.

Evans, S. and Rumblelow, D., *Jack the Ripper, Scotland Yard Investigates,* Sutton Publishing, 2006.

Federal Bureau of Investigation, U.S. Department of Justice, *Serial Murder Multi-Disciplinary Perspectives for Investigators*, Behavioral Analysis Unit National Center for the Analysis of Violent Crime, 2005.

Ford, P., and Howell, M., *The True History of the Elephant Man: The Definitive Account of the Tragic and Extraordinary Life of Joseph Carey Merrick*, Skyhorse Publishing, Inc, 2010.

FTL Design, *The Atlantic Cable*, 2014. available at http://atlantic-cable.com/.

Gilbert, R. A., *the masonic career of A. E. Waite*, Grand Lodge of British Columbia and Yukon, available at http://freemasonry.bcy.ca/aqc/waite/waite.html.

Hawley, M., Charles A. Dunham: for the Better Good, *The New Independent Review* (Issue 2), pp. 10-17, January 2012.

Hawley, M., Charles A. Dunham Part II: Tumblety's Anatomical Collection Reconsidered, *The New Independent Review*, Issue 3, April 2012.

Hibbert, Charles, Dictionary of Canadian Biography, University of Toronto, available at http://www.biographi.ca/en/bio/tupper_charles_hibbert_15E.html.

History Learning Site, *The Great Famine of 1845*, available at http://www.historylearningsite.co.uk/ireland_great_famine_of_1845.htm.

Hobson, F., *Mencken: A Life*, Random House, Inc., 1994.

Hoolihan, *An Annotated Catalogue of the Edward C. Atwater Collection of American Popular Medicine and Health Reform. Volume III, Supplement: A-Z*, 2008.

*Irish Wedding Rings*, Wedding Bands, 2015, available at http://www.weddingbands.org/irish-wedding-rings/ .

JTRForums, available at www.jtrforums.com, Howard & Nina Brown, 2000 – 2005.

John Sparrow, David, Dictionary of Canadian Biography, University of Toronto, available at http://www.biographi.ca/en/bio/thompson_john_sparrow_david_12E.html .

Johnson, A., *The Blackwell Dictionary of Sociology: A User's Guide to Sociological Language*, Wiley, 2000.

Jones, G., Dictionary of Canadian Biography, University of Toronto, Volume XII (1890 – 1900).

KPI Productions, *Jack the Ripper, Mystery Quest*, Season 1, Episode 8, November 11, 2009.

Lander, K.E., A Brief Account of the Use of Wax Models in the Study of Medicine, *Journal of the History of Medicine and Allied Sciences*, Volume XXV, Issue 1, 1970.

Lindgren, C. E., *The Rose Cross in America 1800-1909* (Chapter three of The Rose Cross (1996)), available at http://users.panola.com/lindgren/rosecross-2.html.

———, *Randolph, Paschal Beverly* (Jan 2000), American National Biography, ACLS and Oxford.

Littlechild Letter, dtd September 23, 1913. Sent privately to George R. Sims.

Logan, Guy, *Masters of Crime*, S. Paul, 1928.

Macintyre, B., *The Napoleon of Crime: The Life and Times of Adam Worth, Master Thief*, Crown Publishing Co.,1997.

*McBride's Magazine*, The Foreign Correspondent. Volume 51. 1893.

McEnnis, John T., *The Clan-Na-Gael and the Murder of Dr. Cronin*. San Francisco: G. P. Woodward, 1889, origin: *Chicago Tribune*, June 30, 1889.

*Missouri Association of Public Administrators,* Founded March 11, 1981, available at http://www.mapainfo.org/mapa2/index.cfm.

National Park Service, U.S. Department of the Interior, The Civil War: Union New York Volunteers, 13th Regiment, New York Infantry (2016), available at http://www.nps.gov/civilwar/search-battle-units-detail.htm?battleUnitCode=UNY0013RI.

O'Brian, J., *President Lincoln in Civil War Washington* (2014), available at http://www.lincolninwashington.com/.

Palmer, R., Inspector Andrews Revisited, *The Casebook Examiner*, Issues 1, 2, & 4, April, June, & October 2010.

Pascoe, C. E., *Our Actors and Actresses: The Dramatic List*, 'Fanny Sterling' (p. 319), Benjamin Blom, Inc., Bronx, NY, and London, 1880, Reissued 1969.

Pilbeam, P., Madame Tussaud and the Business of Wax: Marketing to the Middle Classes (University of London), *The Emergence of Marketing*, Routledge, 2003.

Prescott, A., *Brother Irving: Sir Henry Irving and Freemasonry* (Dec 2003), Director at the Centre for Research into Freemasonry, University of Sheffield, available at http://www.theirvingsociety.org.uk/brother_irving.htm.

Riordan, T., *Prince of Quacks: The Notorious Life of Dr. Francis Tumblety, charlatan and Jack the Ripper suspect*. McFarland & Co., 2009.

Rumbelow, Donald, *The Complete Jack the Ripper*, Virgin Books Limited, 1988.

Sappol, "Morbid curiosity": The Decline and Fall of the Popular Anatomical Museum. *Common-Place, A Cabinet of Curiosities*, Volume 4, Number 2, January 2004.

Smith, William, Dictionary of Canadian Biography, University of Toronto, available at http://www.biographi.ca/en/bio/smith_william_1821_97_12E .html.

Storey, N., *The Dracula Secrets: Jack the Ripper and the Darkest Sources of Bram Stoker*, The History Press, 2012.

Strand, Ginger, *Killer on the Road: Violence and the American Interstate*, University of Texas Press, 2012.

*The Fraternitas Rosae* Crucis Fraternity, 'General Ethan Allen Hitchcock', available at http://www.soul.org/E%20A%20Hitchcock.html.

*The Practice of Banking*, Effingham Wilson, Royal Exchange, London, Volume 2, June 1883, page 526, (John Hutchison).

Tumblety, F., *A Few Passages in the Life of Dr. Francis Tumblety, The Indian Herb Doctor*, 1866. Russells' American Steam Printing House, New York, NY.

———, *A Narrative of Dr. Tumblety: how he was Kidnapped during the American War, His Incarceration and Discharge, A Veritable Reign of Terror* (1872), Russells' American Steam Printing House, New York, NY.

Turvey, B., *Criminal Profiling: An Introduction to Behavioral Evidence Analysis*, Academic Press, 2012.

*Urology Today*, 'History of Urology', AUA 2006, available at http://www.urotoday.com/287/conference_reports/history_of _urology/2024/.

Western Union Telegraph Company, *Postal Telegraph Pamphlets*, 1868.

Wetsch, E., *Yorkshire Ripper*, available at www.crimezzz.net, 2005.

Williams, David Ricardo, *Call in Pinkerton's: American Detectives at Work for Canada*, Canadian Heritage, 1998.

Williams, M., *Round London*, Charles Dickens and Evans, Crystal Palace Press, 1892.

# INDEX

# ABOUT THE AUTHOR

Michael Hawley holds a master's degree in invertebrate paleontology and secondary science education from the State University of New York, College of Buffalo, and a bachelor's degree in geology and geophysics from Michigan State University. He has published ten research articles in *Ripperologist, Whitechapel Society Journal,* and *Casebook Examiner.* He is the author of *Curse of the Bayou Beast* (fiction, 2015), *Jack's Lantern* (fiction, 2014), *The Ripper's Hellbroth* (fiction, 2013), and *Searching for Truth with a Broken Flashlight* (nonfiction, 2010). He has been involved in genealogical research since 1992, which ultimately led to his interest in Ripperology research. He is a commander and naval aviator in the U.S. Navy (retired), and is currently enjoying a career as a secondary earth science and chemistry teacher at Tonawanda City High School. He resides with his wife and six children in Greater Buffalo, New York.

Printed in Great Britain
by Amazon